"A great read, Dye and Garman's book allows leaders to take an honest and reflective approach to evaluating their own behaviors and experiences. In turn, it gives them the opportunity to confidently build on strengths and explore new ways of improving their performance. Worth the time!"

Michael H. Covert, FACHE, president and CEO, CHI St. Luke's Health System, and senior vice president, Catholic Health Initiatives

"I learned firsthand from Carson Dye how important it is for a leader in healthcare to possess certain behaviors and competencies. How leadership competencies can work for you or against you . . . and lead to success or failure. How do you choose the right path? By reading *Exceptional Leadership: 16 Critical Competencies for Healthcare Executives.*"

Randy Schimmoeller, senior vice president of operations, ProMedica Continuum Services

"Dye and Garman continue their reputation for giving us an understandable foundation on which to build our professional leadership competencies. *Exceptional Leadership: 16 Critical Competencies for Healthcare Executives* is designed for healthcare leaders at all levels of an organization and all stages of a career. This book is most effective when one competency is read per week, considered, matched to the self-reflective questions, then applied during the ensuing week. That plan alone will improve healthcare across our nation."

David Rubenstein, FACHE; Major General, US Army (retired); past chairman, American College of Healthcare Executives; clinical associate professor of health administration, Texas State University

"Too often, healthcare executives continually search for the leadership 'magic bullet' rather than concentrating on mastering the fundamentals. *Exceptional Leadership* is a vitally important resource that allows a clear understanding of the most critical leadership competencies for early careerists as well as seasoned professionals."

Kathleen R. Krusie, FACHE, CEO, St. Joseph Regional Health Center

# EXCEPTIONAL LEADERSHIP

SECOND EDITION

# EXCEPTIONAL LEADERSHIP

## 16 CRITICAL COMPETENCIES
### FOR HEALTHCARE EXECUTIVES

## CARSON F. DYE | ANDREW N. GARMAN

ACHE Management Series

Your board, staff, or clients may also benefit from this book's insight. For more information on quantity discounts, contact the Health Administration Press Marketing Manager at (312) 424-9470.

Library of Congress Cataloging-in-Publication Data

Dye, Carson F.
  Exceptional leadership : 16 critical competencies for healthcare executives / Carson F. Dye, Andrew N. Garman. — Second edition.
      pages cm
   Includes index.
   ISBN 978-1-56793-673-5 (alk. paper)
   1. Health services administration. 2. Medical care—Quality control. 3. Leadership. I. Garman, Andrew N. II. Title.
   RA971.D49 2015
   362.1068—dc23
                              2014012646

The paper used in this publication meets the minimum requirements of American National Standard for Information Sciences—Permanence of Paper for Printed Library Materials, ANSI Z39.48-1984. ∞ ™

Acquisitions editor: Janet Davis; Project manager: Amy Carlton; Cover designer: Mark Oberkrom; Layout: Cepheus Edmondson

Found an error or a typo? We want to know! Please e-mail it to hapbooks@ache.org, and put "Book Error" in the subject line.

For photocopying and copyright information, please contact Copyright Clearance Center at www.copyright.com or at (978) 750-8400.

Health Administration Press
A division of the Foundation of the American
   College of Healthcare Executives
One North Franklin Street, Suite 1700
Chicago, IL 60606-3529
(312) 424-2800

For exceptional leaders—those who push down their own egos and pull up the people around them

*Carson F. Dye*


For the practitioner faculty of the Health Systems Management department at Rush University in Chicago, who lead by example every day in developing the next generation of healthcare executives. Some of the finest teachers and mentors in the world walk quietly among their ranks.

*Andrew N. Garman*

# Table of Contents

## Part I:   Well-Cultivated Self-Awareness—The First Cornerstone

## Part II:   Compelling Vision—The Second Cornerstone

## Part III:   A Real Way With People—The Third Cornerstone

## Part IV:   Masterful Execution—The Fourth Cornerstone

**Part V: Putting the Competencies to Work**

# *Foreword*

THE DEBATE PERSISTS on whether leaders are born or made. Thankfully, the Dye–Garman competency model does not require us to know the answer. Rather, we can take leaders from where they are—with core strengths and ability—and seek to move them to extraordinary, using the best-practice tools outlined in the book to assess and improve critical success skills.

In the updated version of the extremely popular and highly regarded *Exceptional Leadership: 16 Critical Competencies for Healthcare Executives,* authors Carson Dye and Andrew Garman present a relevant perspective on today's leadership imperative. The second edition maintains its ability to provide a proven competency model to develop the individual leader while adding six new chapters that provide the broader context for leadership competencies in our changing industry.

The case study framing the chapter vignettes provides a great guide and practical way to explore each competency. This allows context for the challenges we, as leaders, face in the ever-changing healthcare landscape.

The need for extraordinary, even courageous leaders is at an all-time high. Having an updated perspective to guide further development of leaders is helpful. The Dye–Garman model suggests that although the 16 competencies have not changed, reviewing them in the context of today's landscape is imperative. I was extremely impressed with the focus of the six new chapters. They show the full balance required for good leaders to evolve into exceptional leaders. Coaching, mentoring, and feedback are among the new areas of focus that are critical to success, in my experience. I particularly enjoyed the focus on the physician leader and the pivotal role this key stakeholder will play in the evolution and reform of healthcare.

As Gandhi said, we must be the change we want to see in the world. In *Exceptional Leadership: 16 Critical Competencies for Healthcare Executives,* Dye and Garman provide us with a current and focused competency model that will allow us to be the best leaders we can be and to be the change we want to see.

*Denise Brooks-Williams, FACHE*
*President and Chief Executive Officer*
*Henry Ford Wyandotte Hospital*

# *Foreword*

MASSIVE CHANGES ARE facing the healthcare field, and we need more leaders who are uncommonly better than average. The stakes are high when it comes to delivering the best care to our patients and the best prevention to our communities. We must have people in positions of power who are exceptional in their leadership ability. The word *exceptional* captures the theme of this book clearly.

What Carson Dye and Andy Garman have given us is not only knowledge about leadership—of which there are more detailed academic tomes on the subject—but rather a more practical application of leadership knowledge to competencies (skills and behaviors) that can be learned and measured. This application is important in the academic context because we have moved to competency-based curricula in our health administration programs and we also must measure and evaluate those competencies. One way to do that is by applying the Dye–Garman model to real-life situations. The case study that sets the stage for application of the model throughout the book is useful in the classroom (real-time and virtual), and it builds critical thinking and judgment skills. The additional minicases and discussion points at the end of the chapters also give faculty supplementary material that will enhance real-world learning.

The foundation of the Four Cornerstones of exceptional leadership is having a healthy self-concept. Dye and Garman point out that regardless of a person's natural or learned ability to lead, the competencies are difficult to develop and fine-tune unless the person has a realistic and comfortable view of self. In academia, this may be called emotional and social intelligence, or the "right stuff." Are all the raw materials on board so that the best education will hone the knowledge and skills to be exceptional? As leaders in the academy, we must take a lesson from this self-concept foundation and apply it to our student admissions policies and interview questions. To have the right stuff from which to develop leaders is necessary for lift off. As academic leaders, we share in the task of ensuring that the future leaders in healthcare be individuals who can mature into exceptional leaders.

What can be done to describe healthcare leaders as *exceptional*? Carson Dye and Andy Garman have taken the lessons they learned from the field and distilled the themes into 16 competencies that rest upon a foundation of a healthy self-concept. Written for both healthcare executives and students of healthcare management and leadership, this book sets out to help individuals at all stages of their careers understand where gaps may exist in individual competencies and how to develop themselves to close those gaps. This book is a road map for the way to exceptional leadership and a must-read for today's healthcare leader—from the classroom to the management conference room to the boardroom.

*Kenneth R. White, PhD, A/GACNP-BC, FACHE, FAAN*
*University of Virginia Medical Center Professor of Nursing*
*Associate Dean for Strategic Partnerships and Innovation at*
*the School of Nursing*

# *Preface*

THERE ARE GOOD leaders, then there are *exceptional leaders*.

We wrote this sentence for our first edition back in 2006. Looking back now and considering how much change has occurred in healthcare leadership development since then is incredible, especially as it relates to the use of competencies. When we wrote the first edition, leadership competencies were not systematically used in many healthcare organizations; today, most organizations use competencies in at least some manner. The dialogue and work around gaining a better understanding of leadership has flourished, and organizations have become more sophisticated in their approach to leadership development. Although the industry still has plenty of room for improvement, we are excited by how far we have come. We are particularly energized by the extent to which the broader concept of strategic talent management has gained traction, with leadership competencies serving as an organizing framework. The most sophisticated of these high-performance work systems touch practically every aspect of management practices, including selection, promotion, development, and performance evaluation. They serve to develop a common behavioral language for clearly discussing performance needs. And they make a difference in organizational performance—quality, patient safety, employee engagement, financial results, and community impact.

For most of us, identifying an exceptional leader is easier than explaining what makes that person exceptional. The answer to "What makes a leader exceptional?" is simple: competencies. Because the term *competencies* is explored in the Introduction, we present a basic definition here. Leadership competencies are a set of professional and personal skills, knowledge, values, and traits that guide a leader's performance, behavior, interaction, and decisions.

Any leadership book will tell you *how* to make a leader exceptional. This book offers that and an added advantage: it tells you *what* makes a leader exceptional. We define these competencies and fully discuss what they entail.

In 2006, we assembled the 16 competencies for three reasons:

1. Many good leaders in healthcare truly want to be great leaders, and they want it for the right reason—to make a genuine difference to the patients and communities they serve.

2. Most healthcare leaders do not have a wealth of mentors, do not continually attend many leadership programs, or are not presented with skill-development opportunities on a proverbial silver platter.
3. In this period often marked by the war for talent, leaders must be better equipped to assess the skills and competencies of other leaders, especially those they are hiring.

At the writing of this second edition, the entire health ecosystem is in the throes of the greatest changes it has seen in more than 50 years. Some leaders are lamenting the challenges faced, but others are excited at the greatest opportunities in their careers to meaningfully engage in remaking the entire healthcare system. Also, as we reflect on the original reasons for our selection of the 16 competencies, we find that those reasons continue to guide our opinions.

The 16 competencies we chose to include in our model were selected because (a) they are the ones most consistently identified by search committees as distinguishing exceptional leaders from simply good leaders; (b) they are most associated with other highly regarded competency sets that we have reviewed; and (c) they drive the most effective leadership success that we have observed. Although their applications may have changed over the years, the competencies themselves have not. They remain the most in-demand competencies in healthcare—the markers of exceptional leadership.

## WHY ANOTHER BOOK ON LEADERSHIP?

We asked this question in 2006 when we wrote the first edition; the question remains relevant today. Since 2006, many more books have been written to add to the vast library of leadership literature. Yet many of them continue to fall into what Hogan and Kaiser (2005, 171) call the "troubadour" literature, or those books that seem to fill the business sections of airport bookstores. We agree with their statement that, "Despite its popularity, the troubadour tradition is a vast collection of opinions with very little supporting evidence; it is entertaining but unreliable." We chose not to list titles but know our readers will appreciate the point of view.

### Healthcare Leadership Is Different

Many leadership issues are the same regardless of industry, but healthcare presents many unique challenges. The relationships, life-and-death nature of the work, emotional demands, and financial challenges in this industry are different from those in other fields. Because of these unique qualities, the healthcare field requires its leaders to have a distinctive approach as well, so the competencies in this book give leaders this edge.

## Healthcare Is in Desperate Need of Great Leaders

As the healthcare industry dives headfirst into the vast changes brought about by value-based reimbursement, population health management, cost and capacity pressures, and the impending changes from personalized medicine and consumer-driven care, the greatest challenges of the next decade in healthcare could well be the development of leaders equipped to navigate the system changes these opportunities and challenges will bring. All of these challenges will continue in this high-stakes environment, where disruptive innovations can change the course of a healthcare organization's future in a heartbeat.

## The Science of Leadership Continues to Evolve

Although great strides have been made in the past decade in the science of leadership assessment and development, extracting solid information from the scientific literature remains difficult, and the relative value of service vendors is equally difficult to evaluate. Bookstores are filled with books on leadership, but most of these books reflect the perspective of a single successful leader, author, or firm, and many of these books are merely anecdotal and subjective observations not rooted in scientific research.

In this book, we inform the areas of leadership performance that need critical attention with the most current research available in these areas. In this way, we provide the most advanced thinking on how to develop in these competencies.

## Not All Leadership Competencies Are Equally Important

At the time of the first edition of this book, leadership competencies were much less widely used within the healthcare sector. Since that time, many more consulting firms, healthcare organizations, and professional associations have created their own sets of leadership competencies. If every competency in every one of these models were compiled, they would quickly add up into the hundreds.

In our experience, long lists of competencies are not helpful in planning for development. They are even less helpful when used as a way to rank candidates for leadership positions.

For this reason, we focus on just the 16 competencies that seem to make the biggest difference between good leadership and great leadership. If your goal is to be an exceptional leader, these are the competencies you need to master.

## Having a Leadership Competency Model Does Not Guarantee Success

Another concern with competency models is the weight that has been placed on them. We certainly believe that having and using an effective model is critical to an organization's journey toward enhancing organizational performance through leadership. While the organizations that use competencies are admirable, some organizations believe that implementing leadership competency models will solve leadership problems. This simply is not the case. Ulrich, Zenger, and Smallwood, (1999, 27) wrote about the "search for a 'holy grail' of leadership attributes" and how adopting one does not necessarily mean that leadership issues are resolved. William Linesch (2014), a human resources executive, stated, "Leadership competency models can be great assets to a talent management program, but organizations need to be careful not to allow them to become another bureaucratic burden on managers." The Exceptional Leadership Competency Model is presented in this book as a focused and workable tool but in no way do we propose that it is the end-all, be-all tool of leadership.

## Leadership Development Is *Your* Responsibility

Exceptional leaders take responsibility for their own development. They do not wait for their superiors to guide them or for their organizations to sponsor events. If you want to be an exceptionally effective leader, it is up to you to learn your development needs and to find your own ways to improve.

# WHAT CAN BE GAINED FROM READING THIS BOOK?

Our goal is to present the competencies that mark an exceptional leader. Throughout the book we offer tools to help good leaders develop their own capacity, that of their direct reports, and even that of their organization.

## A Deeper Understanding of Leadership

By reading and reflecting on each of the 16 competencies, you will derive additional insight into leadership and a better understanding of the key qualities that drive highly effective leadership.

## Guidance in Coaching and Developing Skills

This book provides practical suggestions for developing leadership skills that can immediately be implemented. You can use this book to plan your own development or to help others in planning their development. Executive coaches may use the material to help guide and shape the behavior of those they are coaching. Executives may find the discussion helpful in counseling and advising direct reports about their leadership behavior.

## Guidelines in Assessing Executive Candidates

This book serves as an excellent guide in assessing candidates for executive leadership positions. The 16 competencies can be used as a benchmark to develop interview questions and to evaluate leadership capability.

## Counsel on Avoiding Derailment

No one sets out to purposely derail his career. Still, career derailments often happen. Skill deficits in any of these areas can stall or even disrupt a leadership career. Understanding your own development needs can help you prevent derailing your own career.

## A Foundation for Customized Leadership Competency Models

Because the competencies in this book focus on exceptional leadership, you may find them to be a useful springboard to develop competency models of your own.

## A Practical Foundation for Teaching Leadership

The material in this book lends itself to use in academic instruction—for example, as a complement to theory-based texts. Competencies can be used as stand-alone topics, and the vignettes at the beginning of each chapter can serve as discussion starters. The self-assessment and development suggestions also lend themselves well to career-development planning assignments. Additionally, this book can serve as the foundation for peer-led leadership-development meetings in practice settings.

## INSTRUCTOR RESOURCES

For instructors who use this book as part of a leadership or management course, excellent instructor resources are available. The book's contents are built around a major case study (St. Nicholas Health System) that is followed throughout the book. This case study is complex enough to give instructors many avenues of use. Sprinkled throughout the book are many questions that can be used during classroom discussion. In addition, each chapter in the book's first four parts has short case studies at their ends: answer guides are available in the book's instructor resources. Also available in the instructor resources is an extensive set of PowerPoints and additional discussion questions and answer guides. If this book is adopted for use in a course, the resources can be requested by e-mailing hapbooks@ache.org.

*Carson F. Dye*
*Andrew N. Garman*

## REFERENCES

Hogan, R., and R. B. Kaiser. 2005. "What We Know About Leadership." *Review of General Psychology* 9 (2): 169–80.

Linesch, W. 2014. Senior vice president human resources and organizational effectiveness, Premier Health, personal conversation with author, February 13.

Ulrich, D., J. Zenger, and N. Smallwood. 1999. *Results-Based Leadership.* Boston: Harvard Business School Press.

# Acknowledgments

So many people deserve mention for their role in this book. It is truly the culmination of many years of interactions in the living laboratory of leadership. My executive search career gives me almost daily interaction with exceptional leaders, and I am so privileged to have worked with so many great organizations. I hope the lack of a long litany of names from clients, candidates, and working peers does not cause concern; there are simply too many to name.

Let me begin with special recognition for Andy Garman. This is our third book collaboration, and I truly appreciate his ability to stay grounded, to bring an appropriate academic eye and mind to our work, and to focus on what counts. This second edition has been a challenging endeavor for him because it hit him in the midst of significant work demands, but he met the challenge. Thanks, Andy—I think our team approach produces an incredibly solid product. I also thank you for your rigor in your work and your eye for detail.

I would also like to single out Richard Metheny, my colleague at Witt/Kieffer, who used the first edition of this book to build the foundation that has turned the 16 competencies into a solid and unmatched set of leadership assessment measures. Certainly the ability to accurately assess leadership is one of the most important skills to ensure that organizations have the top leadership possible. The Dye–Garman model has gone a long way to provide this, and Richard was helpful is seeing its value.

As more of my work—and avocation as well—morphs into the physician leadership realm, there are many physician leaders to thank. Several of them helped in a direct way with the new physician leadership chapter: Akram Boutros, MD; Frank Byrne, MD; John Byrnes, MD; Kathleen Forbes, MD; Lee Hammerling, MD; David James, MD, CEO; Greg Taylor, MD; and Ginger Williams, MD. I also continue to be indebted to Jacque Sokolov, MD, my coauthor on *Developing Physician Leaders for Successful Clinical Integration* (Health Administration Press 2013). I recognize as well Mark Peters, MD; Scott Ransom, DO; and Liz Ransom, MD. A number of Healthcare Roundtable physician leaders have also given me thoughts and ideas, and I thank them—Michael Ivy, MD; Mark J. Hauser, MD; Mark Valliere, MD; Ken Marshall, MD; Robert C. Peltier, MD; Raymond DeCorte, MD; Heather N. Lorenzo, MD; Ray King, MD; Michael Schultz, MD;

John Kosanovich, MD; Jim Schell, MD; Paul Hintze, MD; Nancy J. Downs, MD; Joseph Mazzola, DO; Robert Coates, MD; Steven Cox, MD; Herbert A. Schumm, MD; Buster Mobley, MD; John Paris, MD; Bob Gill, MD; and Tom McGann, MD. Special thanks as well to Ken Cohn, MD, my friend and excellent physician healer.

The book has been the anchor for an online program at the American College of Healthcare Executives since its first publication, and I want to thank the many participants who provided suggestions that helped frame the second edition.

My respect and appreciation for the staff of Health Administration Press deepens each year. Janet Davis is a superb colleague and always helpful in guidance and cheer. Amy Carlton is truly an exceptional editor; her work goes past standard editing as she paints far better pictures than an author could ever imagine. The rest of the staff at HAP serve behind the scenes and readers rarely see them, but it is so clear to me that our field is blessed to have this publisher serving us.

My daughter Emily Dye is always great help with models and graphs and the visual "things." She has taken many of my ideas and made them shout with visual clarity. Also, my daughter Liesl continues to provide great input. I am also deeply appreciative of the rest of my family.

*—Carson Dye*

THE REQUEST TO revisit this book came at a point in my career when carving out time for focused work had become almost impossible. Were it not for Carson's tenacious yet cheerful insistence that the time had come for us to update this work, this revision would probably never have taken place. Thank you, Carson, for making this happen. Of course, we would not have had cause to revisit the book at all were it not for the many people who had told us how practical and useful they found the first edition to be. To everyone who took the time to express this to us, thank you for your encouragement to continue this work. I next need to thank my wife, Deborah, and our children, Emily and Tyler, who continue to provide more support and tolerance than I probably deserve. Thanks also to my parents and grandparents for instilling a strong familial culture of critical thought and a respect and appreciation for the scientific method, especially in areas commonly regarded as too "soft" and "squishy" to be meaningfully subjected to rigorous scientific inquiry.

A special thanks to the role-model leaders who I have had the privilege of meeting and working with in my roles with Rush University and the National Center for Healthcare Leadership (NCHL). Rush's Health Systems Management department is blessed with an unusually strong core faculty team, under the outstanding leadership of Peter Butler and Tricia Johnson, including Diane Howard, Shital Shah,

Frank Phillips, Jeff Canar, and Chien-Ching Li, and rounded out by our equally outstanding program administrator Matt Stern and administrative assistant Angela Freeman. NCHL is similarly blessed with an incredible core team, led by Joyce Anne Wainio and including Cassia Carter, Cara Gallagher, and Marie Rowland as well as our Michigan colleagues Christy Lemak and Kyle Grazier. My work with NCHL has also introduced me to many outstanding healthcare leaders, including our incredibly dedicated current board: Peter Butler, Joe Cabral, Pat Connolly, Kathy McDonagh, Tim Rice, Bob Riney, Amir Rubin, Dr. Bruce Seigel, Jeffrey Selberg, Irene Thompson, and, of course, Gail Warden. This role has also given me the privilege to hear the inspiring stories of our recent leadership award winners and the organizations they represent, including Michael Dowling, Peggy O'Kane, Mitch Katz, John Bluford, Glen Steele, and Nancy Schlichting. For as busy as these dual responsibilities keep me, I feel very privileged every day to be able to work with such amazing leaders.

Thanks to the American College of Healthcare Executives for championing healthcare management as a profession, with its own unique competencies, values, responsibilities, and contributions to pursuing a high-value learning health system. Another special thanks to the many leaders who have willingly contributed their time and expertise to the leadership research projects we have pursued over the years.

This revision benefited tremendously from the editorial guidance of Janet Davis, Amy Carlton, and their colleagues at Health Administration Press. Thank you very much once again for all your help, support, and patience.

—*Andy Garman*

# Introduction

WE CAN ALL think of people who seem to have been born to lead. Every organization almost always has at least a couple such leaders. They stand out because they give the impression that they can make things happen and that they are going to succeed at anything. We often assume the success of these leaders long before their performance results come in.

Many other leaders become exceptional over time, through perseverance and attention to their own development. They identify their strengths and development needs, find opportunities to gain the experience they need, and seek out mentors who can help them make the most of these crucible experiences.

For both groups—the "born" and the "made"—the path to exceptional leadership is crossed faster with a good roadmap. A good competency model (see Exhibit 1) will provide just such a roadmap.

---

**Exhibit 1  What Is a Competency?**

Many definitions of competency exist, but David McClelland (1973) is widely regarded as providing the original and most authoritative definition. At the time of his writing, intelligence and skills tests were the main tools used to make selection decisions. McClelland's work was an attempt to move beyond a narrow, skills-focused definition of success to examine broader, underlying characteristics of individuals that could be used to predict success.

In brief, competencies are a broad collection of knowledge, skills, abilities, and characteristics. They include values (such as ethics and integrity), cognitive skills (such as thinking and problem solving), interpersonal skills (such as communicating and listening), embracing diversity (such as tolerance and respect), and change management (such as strategic planning and risk taking).

As deeper-level constructs, competencies are not something learned from a day-long training workshop or a class. They are more accurately described as slow improvements over time as a result of mindful practice, feedback, and more practice.

---

One of the more significant reasons that competencies work so well is that they are so practical. Dye (2010) wrote that leadership competencies are "one of the only theories of leadership that actually offers the chance to 'see' leadership. For example, the trait theory of leadership states that a leader is an effective communicator; the competency theory provides specific behavioral examples of what effective communication is." This is one of the reasons that many organizations have adopted their use.

Those in the position of selecting leaders can also benefit from learning about competencies. It will help them in their assessments of candidates and in their hiring decisions. A hiring mistake at the senior level is disastrous for any organization, and a better understanding of exactly what comprises highly effective leadership will minimize this risk.

## EXCEPTIONAL LEADERSHIP COMPETENCY MODEL

We organized the first edition of this book around 16 leadership competencies. These are the competencies we have found to be most frequently associated with exceptional leadership in healthcare. We arrived at this list through the following steps:

1. We examined the competency lists prepared by boards and executives for use in their executive searches.
2. We pared this list down to those competencies that reliably differentiated the leaders perceived to be the highest-performing—those who made the short lists and who usually got hired.
3. We surveyed eight seasoned search consultants (with more than 100 collective years of search experience) who work exclusively in healthcare. We asked each of them the following questions:
   – What are the most important competencies your clients request when looking for new executives?
   – Consider the three best executives you have ever placed in your search careers. Exactly what leadership competencies did these leaders have that set them apart from the others?

We retained the competencies submitted by multiple search consultants.

4. We also posed similar questions regarding leadership competencies to healthcare chief executive officers (CEOs) and executive coaches.

5. To refine our conceptualizations of these 16 competencies, we compared and contrasted them with reviews of the academic leadership literature and competency lists of well-known consulting firms.

Our end goal was to develop a competency model focused enough to help aspiring exceptional leaders zero in on their greatest development opportunities and rich enough to be revisited many times in the years to come.

After almost nine years of use, examination, and application, the 16 competencies have stood the test of time. To reverify the accuracy and the application of the competency model for this second edition, we:

◆ talked to several CEOs and other senior healthcare leaders, human resource executives, and leadership development executives about their use and acceptance of the competencies in the model;
◆ reviewed the use of our competency model with organizations, executive search, and consulting firms; and
◆ considered the many comments of support for the 16 competencies we have received over these years from individual readers.

Since the publication of the first edition of the book in 2006, this competency model has appeared in many places and forms. It has served as the foundation for several leadership development programs, some sponsored by the American College of Healthcare Executives, and some sponsored by other associations and individual healthcare organizations. The authors have received communications from many individuals who said the book deepened their personal understanding of leadership and improved their leadership skills. A number of colleges and universities have adopted the book as a text for leadership classes and other related courses. Consulting and executive search firms have used the model to evaluate leadership as well as to assess candidates for leadership positions. Outplacement firms have used the book to help counsel their clients. The model has been used in several settings for physician leadership assessment and development. The competencies have been used in many situations as an underpinning for developing behavioral interview questions in selection situations. Input from many of these individuals has been positive in regard to the effectiveness, relevance, and application of this leadership competency model. One review summarized the thoughts of many others: "The book is concise and very clearly structured, making it a quick and enjoyable read for executives in just about any industry." Another review praised "the way the charts that were highlighted explained the good as well as the bad points for each point that was being explained in that chapter."

The use of leadership competency models has also been shown to be a hallmark of excellent companies in many industries. A comprehensive study of numerous organizations done by Hewitt (Gandossy et al. 2007) showed that those companies with better financial performance were likely to use competencies as the basis for succession management, external hiring, and inside promotions.

One of the driving motivations for the authors to develop the exceptional leadership competency model in the first edition was their concern that most competency models had lists of competencies that were far too long to be useful. At that time, two of the commercially available competency models from consulting firms had competencies numbering 68 and 128. The authors felt that those lists were unmanageable and, in some cases, the specific competencies redundant. Interestingly, since the publication of the first book, most competency models have *shortened* their lists, which has made them more usable. *Talent management* has also become a buzz phrase in all industries, and most of these programs are built on a competency model foundation. A 2011 study by RBL Group of firms such as IBM, General Mills, Procter & Gamble, PepsiCo, and Eli Lilly concluded, "Top companies have a defined competency model that describes a unified theory of what leaders at their organization should know, be, and do. And they use their competency models in all phases of talent and leadership development." To be functional, competency models have to be concise enough to be usable and targeted enough to have meaning.

## AN OVERVIEW OF THE FOUR CORNERSTONES AND THE 16 COMPETENCIES

We have organized the 16 competencies into four traits, which we call the *cornerstones* of exceptional leadership:

> Cornerstone 1: Well-Cultivated Self-Awareness
>
> Cornerstone 2: Compelling Vision
>
> Cornerstone 3: A Real Way With People
>
> Cornerstone 4: Masterful Execution

These cornerstones anchor our leadership model and place them upon a foundation of a healthy self-concept, which is discussed later in this introduction. Exhibit 2 illustrates this foundation model.

**Exhibit 2  The Four Cornerstones and Healthy Self-Concept Foundation**

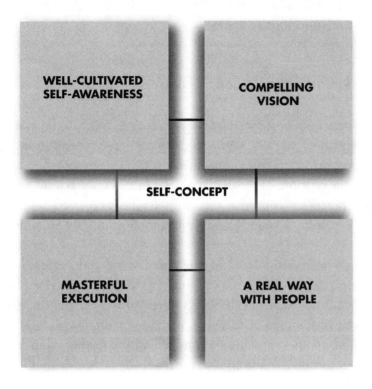

## Cornerstone 1: Well-Cultivated Self-Awareness

*Self-awareness* means understanding yourself as a leader—in particular, your strengths, limitations, hot buttons, and blind spots. Developing self-awareness requires leaders to intellectually and emotionally process on two levels. First, leaders must develop the ability to collect accurate, high-quality feedback from the work environment. Second, leaders must contemplate with an open mind what that feedback means to them and to their performance as a leader.

While these processes sound deceptively simple, in reality they are far from it. We all receive some feedback from the environment, and we all accept it with some open-mindedness. The magnitude of both this environment and our capacity for being open-minded makes the difference between good leadership and exceptional leadership. Exceptional leaders make sure their environment is rich in feedback (see Chapter 20 for suggestions on how to develop a feedback-rich environment) and internalize the feedback they receive.

High performance in the area of self-awareness also involves mastery of two competencies: Leading With Conviction and Using Emotional Intelligence. You can think of personal conviction as the driving force that guides you in serving a larger purpose; emotional intelligence, in contrast, involves the management of that purpose in the relationships you forge.

## Cornerstone 2: Compelling Vision

Of the four cornerstones, a compelling *vision* tends to be both the most visible and the most closely associated with senior leadership roles. At the senior level, if leaders hit their ceilings before reaching their career goals, it is usually because they have not mastered one or more of the competencies in this cornerstone.

Three competencies comprise this cornerstone associated with exceptional leadership: Developing Vision, Communicating Vision, and Earning Trust And Loyalty.

Developing vision is the heart of this cornerstone and begins this section of the book. Vision can be defined as the capacity to create effective plans for your organization's future, based on a clear understanding of trends, uncertainties, risks, and rewards. Defined in this way, we can separate creation of vision from the process of building awareness and understanding of the vision (i.e., communicating vision) as well as gaining support from the "unconverted" (i.e., earning trust and loyalty).

## Cornerstone 3: A Real Way With People

This cornerstone relates to implementation—making things happen through people and through process.

*Interpersonal relations* are a central part of the leader's role, and most leaders who have been around awhile already have a reasonably well-developed set of interpersonal skills. At a minimum, most leaders recognize that you can catch more flies with honey than with vinegar, that people care about more than just their paycheck, and that interpersonal conflicts rarely go away on their own. That said, our experience leads us to conclude that (1) outstanding leaders typically have outstanding interpersonal skills, and (2) most leaders have at least some room for growth in the area of interpersonal relations.

The interpersonal domain can be meaningfully split into five competencies: Listening Like You Mean It, Giving Great Feedback, Mentoring, Developing High-Performing Teams, and Energizing Staff.

In each case, our focus is on how to refine an already strong skill set to the level of outstanding performance. We begin this section with a chapter on listening, which in many ways is the central unifying characteristic of this cornerstone. In describing what makes an executive effective, Peter Drucker (2004) identified eight practices and just one rule: "Listen first, speak last."

### Cornerstone 4: Masterful Execution

The final cornerstone turns to an examination of *execution*—where the rubber meets the road in getting activities assigned to strategies, decisions made, tasks accomplished, and agendas moved forward.

Leaders are ultimately judged in terms of what they get done. Regardless of the leadership competencies they exhibit, the true measure of their impact is the success they bring to their organizations.

Although success in execution is strongly affected by the quality of a leader's working relationships, it is also affected by the approaches the leader uses. The six competencies that most distinguish the highest performing leaders in this domain are Generating Informal Power, Building True Consensus, Mindful Decision Making, Driving Results, Stimulating Creativity, and Cultivating Adaptability. We examine each of these in turn.

The model is portrayed graphically in Exhibit 3 where the 16 competencies are shown in each of their cornerstones.

## HOW IS THIS BOOK STRUCTURED?

The book has five parts. The first four introduce each of the 16 competencies in the leadership competency model. For individuals wishing to enhance their leadership performance, these four parts provide for a very introspective look at the specific competencies and give personalized counsel in each. The fifth part is more macro in scope and looks at the competency model within the context of the organization.

The book opens with the introduction of the St. Nicholas Health System Case Study. The case is intended to provide a context in which to place the leadership competencies. It provides a context for the vignettes that open each chapter and can be used to help tie all of the concepts together. However, each of the chapters can also stand alone; they can be read without the benefit of the introductory case, and in any sequence the reader chooses.

**Exhibit 3  Exceptional Leadership Competency Model**

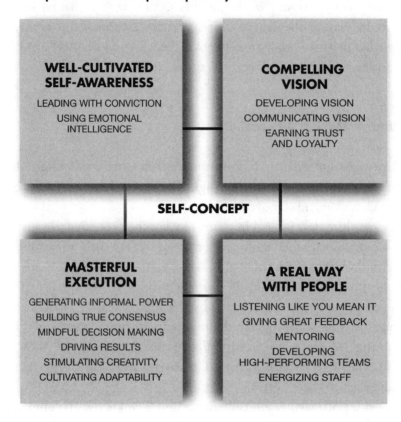

Each chapter is organized around the following sections:

- *Opening vignette.* This section provides an example of the type of situation in which leaders can shine if they demonstrate a mastery of the competency.
- *Definition of the competency.* This section explains what the competency is and why it is so important.
- *When highly effective leaders demonstrate the competency.* Here we describe, in specific details, what extraordinary leadership looks like when the competency is mastered.
- *When the competency is not all it could be.* Here we describe the common skill deficits that prevent good leaders from being great leaders in this competency.
- *Misuse and overuse: how the competency can work against you.* Sometimes leaders get into trouble because they overdo it. Here we describe what problems can arise for overdoing or misusing a given competency.

- *Finding role models.* One of the very best ways to learn new skills is to find a master to help you. In this section, we tell you where you are most likely to find people who have mastered the competency.
- *Additional opportunities for personal development.* Not all leadership development is equally effective. Here we provide options for developing a competency area, focusing on what has been shown to work best and what our colleagues and clients tell us have been most helpful to them.
- *Consider This.* These brief sections provide additional opportunities for reflection and study for each competency and are provided at the end of each competency chapter.

The final part, Putting the Competencies to Work, provides practical tools for using the competency model to drive improved leadership performance. Chapter 17, A Systems Approach to Leadership Development, summarizes the evidence base supporting high-performance leadership development systems. Chapter 18, Leadership Coaches and Coaching Programs, provides insight into the world of executive coaching and gives specific tips on how to select, use, and best benefit from coaching. Chapter 19, Mentors: Finding and Engaging for Maximum Impact, presents ways to best benefit from the use of mentors. Chapter 20, Developing a Feedback-Rich Working Environment, describes how to upgrade one's workplace and work culture to maximize its learning value. Chapter 21, Physician Development and Competencies, addresses the rapidly evolving world of physician leadership and presents special circumstances that surround the movement into leadership by physicians. Finally, Chapter 22, Final Questions About the Exceptional Leadership Model, discusses how different competency models can be "mapped" or compared to one another, and explores some of the questions about leadership competency models that arose from readers of the first edition. The first 16 chapters look at leadership from the perspective of what an individual does as a leader and are well suited for individual growth as well as coaching and leadership development within a larger organizational context. The final six chapters, all new since the first edition, address many of the broader and more contemporary issues that surround the practice of using leadership competency models.

## Appendixes

In the appendixes, we have assembled a wealth of additional tools to help you along the path of personal development.

Appendix A provides a set of self-reflection questions, which can help you prioritize your development by assessing your strengths and development needs. Appendix B provides a framework for structuring, implementing, and monitoring your leadership self-development plan. Appendix C provides behavioral interview questions that can be used in interviewing and assessing candidates for leadership positions.

## SELF-CONCEPT: THE FOUNDATION

As with real cornerstones, the four cornerstones of exceptional leadership must rest on a firm foundation. In the case of leadership, this foundation is a healthy self-concept.

### The Critical Importance of Self-Concept

To be an exceptional leader and to perform at a superior level, it is essential that you have a healthy *self-concept*. Having a healthy self-concept means you agree with each of the following:

- You are satisfied with your place in the world and feel that you have a purpose in life.
- You feel a sense of control over your life and destiny.
- You are confident in your ability to achieve what you set out to do.
- You have a positive self-image.
- You feel comfortable with how you relate to others.

More simply, self-concept is your own understanding of and comfort level about yourself. Some people may refer to self-concept as self-esteem, or self-confidence, or self-value. Regardless of the terminology, the message is the same: If you are content and happy with who you are and what you have accomplished, you are comfortable with others as well and are fully accepting of their achievements and contributions, regardless of whether those contributions may be deemed to be of higher value than yours.

We are disappointed in the lack of attention that this subject receives. Most leadership development courses and their content material focus principally on behaviors and competencies. The reality is that without a healthy self-concept, the other leadership competencies at best will feel unnatural and at worst will never be mastered.

In the words of one well-known CEO, "I can usually tell more about leaders and their potential through learning how they perceive themselves than in any other way." Leaders with a positive self-concept do not have to tear down others to bring themselves up. They rarely yell, scream, or curse, and they do not feel the need to play political games for their own gain. Their value systems engender a positive regard for others because they first have a high, but appropriate, regard for themselves.

We consider positive self-concept a prerequisite for exceptional leadership because it influences every aspect of a leader's effectiveness. Self-concept makes its most visible difference in the way leaders handle success and failure and work with others.

### Successes and Failures

Although highly effective leaders are driven to achieve, they are in control of that drive. They enjoy their accomplishments and take pride in them. Failures and setbacks may bother them but do not tear them apart.

Leaders with a poor self-concept view accomplishments as simple milestones—expected points of passage on the way to other landmarks. They rarely see the value of praise given to their organization or community. These leaders are often said to be out to prove something.

A similar phenomenon occurs with failures. Leaders with high self-regard view their failures in a balanced fashion—sure, there is pain in failing, but there is also the opportunity to learn from mistakes. Failures will not cause great leaders to retreat from daring decisions in the future; instead, they will continue to move boldly but do so in a better-informed manner. Leaders with low self-regard do not see failures in the same way. They blame failures on others and on bad luck, and they seldom learn from such mistakes.

### Working with Others

The more accepting leaders are of themselves, the better they are at accepting others. A leader's capacity to accept others creates a climate of psychological safety in the workplace. A safe climate allows people to better receive and use constructive feedback because they will not be distracted by feelings of personal vulnerability. Conversely, if people feel that their job is at risk, they are far more likely to act defensively, with self-preservation as their primary goal and the good of the team or organization as a secondary consideration.

A healthy self-concept also lends itself to encouraging and embracing diversity in the workplace. We have found that those who have a solid self-concept are more tolerant and accepting of people who have different backgrounds and beliefs. One of the hallmarks of exceptional leadership is the willingness and ability to assemble teams made up of diverse individuals. These leaders know that having such a team is a great advantage. Today's great leaders must continually incorporate diversity initiatives into their strategies; a strong self-concept makes doing this much easier.

Make no mistake: leaders can go far *without* a healthy self-concept. We have observed several leaders who possess a low sense of self-worth but still reach top positions in healthcare. They may even be successful throughout their entire careers. In fact, some are driven overachievers, and others are absolute perfectionists or are compulsively controlling. However, these leaders' achievements typically come at the expense of others. They use tactics such as fear, intimidation, and political manipulation that can tear at the fabric of an otherwise positive organizational culture. Their direct reports are unlikely to reach their full potential, and there are limits on how far people will follow these kinds of leaders.

We are clearly not alone in this perspective. A stream of research has been emerging that links self-regard to effectiveness. Several studies have found significant connections between self-concept (termed "core self-evaluations" in academia) and both job performance and job satisfaction (Judge and Bono 2000; Wu and Griffen 2011). Perhaps even more telling is that self-concept may also determine how much mentoring leaders receive during their career (Hezlett 2003), how effectively leaders can hear and use feedback on their performance (Bono and Colbert 2005), how well they do in training programs (Stanhope, Pond, and Surface 2012), and how capable leaders are to recognize and pursue strategic opportunities on behalf of their organizations (Hiller and Hambrick 2005).

## What to Do If Your Self-Concept Needs Strengthening

If you do not see this foundation in yourself, we recommend that you make building your self-concept a top priority. That may well mean putting this book aside for a while, or at least not beginning with these competencies as your primary focus. A positive self-concept is not something you can get from a book. However, we can suggest some useful first steps.

### Consider How You Feel About Yourself

Are you satisfied with your life? Do you enjoy who you are, or do you have a nagging sense of regret? What about your career? Do you feel good about your achievements, or bad about the opportunities you may have missed out on? When you accomplish something, can you take pride in it, or do you view every achievement as nothing more than a means toward some greater end? When you fail at something, can you accept the lessons learned, or do you just curse yourself for trying in the first place? When someone else fails you, are you able to see their side, or do you find yourself quickly turning against them? If you were to learn that this day was your last, would you feel you had spent your life well?

The greater your personal discomfort with yourself, the more room you have to grow in the area of self-concept, and the more likely it is that this development should be your first priority.

### Ask Those Closest to You for Their Candid Feedback

Consult a spouse, significant other, family member, or spiritual confidante to seek their opinion of your self-concept. Listen to them with an open mind, and try to take what they say at face value. Often the people who know us well know us better than we know ourselves. Remember also that perceptions are frequently more important than reality.

### Build on Your Positive Qualities

Build a focus on your positive physical, mental, and emotional qualities. What are you good at? What do you do well? What do you like about yourself? Use these positive concepts to counterbalance the aspects you feel less positive about. Enumerate your accomplishments. Celebrate achievements. Congratulate yourself on things you do well.

### Seek to Understand Your "Dark" Side

Having a healthy self-concept does not mean that you have no sore spots or hot buttons. But it does mean that you know your vulnerabilities so that you can prevent them from undermining you. Understanding your "dark" side requires the discipline to face your vulnerabilities, to examine how they have interfered with your effectiveness in the past, and to learn how to spot the warning signals and what to do when you see them.

### Enlist Some Help

Unlike the competencies in this book, self-concept may *not* work as well as a self-development project. Professional assistance from a coach, spiritual counselor, therapist, or other professional with specialized training can make a big difference in the speed of your progress.

## A FINAL WORD

With a mastery of these competencies, you will have the capacity to be an effective leader; however, you should expect the process to take considerable time and effort (see Exhibit 4). To master these leadership competencies, you will need to invest time to reflect on how you practice each competency. You may also need to develop

**Exhibit 4  Is a Competent Leader an Effective Leader?**

Not necessarily. Competence is most accurately described as the *capacity* to perform. To translate competency into *actual* performance requires both motivation and opportunity. Putting in the time and energy required for success requires motivation; we all face barriers to success, but exceptional leaders overcome these barriers more often. Opportunity relates to the environment in which leadership takes place; some environments are conducive to successful leadership, while others are not. We have seen exceptional leaders enter organizations and then leave because the environments were not set up to allow them to be successful.

That said, our experience tells us you do get what you give. If you put in the time and effort, you can become a more successful leader. In the process, your ability to help others and your organization will expand along with your influence. In short, it is time well spent.

---

and maintain reliable and accurate feedback mechanisms in your workplace. You will also need to master the ability to maintain your ground during times of substantial turbulence.

We wish you the best on your self-development and your career, and we hope you find this book to be a helpful guide along the way.


## REFERENCES

Bono, J. E., and A. E. Colbert. 2005. "Understanding Responses to Multi-Source Feedback: The Role of Core Self-Evaluations." *Personnel Psychology* 58: 171–203.

Drucker, P. F. 2004. "What Makes an Effective Executive?" *Harvard Business Review* 82 (6): 58–63.

Dye, C. 2010. *Leadership in Healthcare: Essential Values and Skills,* 2nd ed. Chicago: Health Administration Press.

Gandossy, R., M. Salob, S. Greenslade, J. Younger, and R. Guarnieri. 2007. "The Top Companies for Leaders 2007." Hewitt & Associates in partnership with *Fortune* and the RBL group. Lincolnshire, IL: Hewitt & Associates.

Hezlett, S. A. 2003. "Who Receives Mentoring? A Meta-Analysis of Employee Demographic, Career History, and Individual Differences Correlates." Unpublished doctoral dissertation, University of Minnesota, Minneapolis.

Hiller, N. J., and D. C. Hambrick. 2005. "Conceptualizing Executive Hubris: The Role of (Hyper-) Core Self-Evaluations in Strategic Decision-Making." *Strategic Management Journal* 26: 297–319.

Judge, T. A., and J. E. Bono. 2000. "Relationship of Core Self-Evaluation Traits—Self-Esteem, Generalized Self-Efficacy, Locus of Control, and Emotional Stability—with Job Satisfaction and Job Performance: A Meta-Analysis." *Journal of Applied Psychology* 86 (1): 80–92.

McClelland, D. C. 1973. "Testing for Competence Rather Than 'Intelligence.'" *American Psychologist* 28 (1): 1–14.

The RBL Group. 2011. "Top Companies for Leaders." http://rblip. s3.amazonaws.com/Articles/top-companies-2011-research%20report.pdf.

Stanhope, D. S., S. B. Pond III, and E. A. Surface. 2012. "Core Self-Evaluations and Training Effectiveness: Prediction Through Motivational Intervening Mechanisms." *Journal of Applied Psychology* 98 (5): 820–31.

Wu, C.-H., and M. A. Griffen. 2011. "Longitudinal Relationships Between Core Self-Evaluations and Job Satisfaction." *Journal of Applied Psychology* 97 (2): 331–42.

# St. Nicholas Health System Case Study

THE FOLLOWING CASE study will be used throughout the book to introduce many specific aspects of competencies. This opening portion gives you substantive background on the organization and its leadership team. Please note that the case is fictional, and any resemblance to actual events or locales or persons, living or dead, is entirely coincidental.

## INTRODUCTION

St. Nicholas Health System is a leading integrated health delivery system composed of the following entities:

- 525-bed St. Nicholas Medical Center
- 225-bed Suburban Western Health Center
- 185-bed Suburban East Health Center
- Three small rural hospitals, all at least an hour drive away
- The St. Nicholas Medical Group, with 230 employed physicians and 60 advanced practitioners
- St. Nicholas Health Plan, with almost 500,000 covered lives
- St. Nicholas Ambulatory Care Company (set up in the past year, and includes home care and visiting nurse services, two free-standing emergency departments [EDs], three urgent care centers, two health centers, multiple outpatient clinic locations, two durable medical equipment companies, several ambulatory pharmacies, and a hospice program)

St. Nicholas operates within the city of Barkley, population 3.5 million, representing a highly competitive healthcare market.

# ORGANIZATIONAL STRUCTURE

Headed by CEO Elizabeth Parris, the executive leadership group for the health system is detailed in Exhibit 1.

The entire Executive Leadership Group (ELG) has a scheduled meeting every other week on Tuesdays from 7:30 to 11:30 a.m. A preset agenda is developed, and Parris chairs the meeting (John Vardez chairs in her absence). Agenda items have historically been 80 percent tactical operations and 20 percent strategic. The agenda items are covered first (with Parris's report always first on the agenda) and then, if time allows, the group moves around the table allowing each individual time to discuss any items that are not on the agenda. Some of the group members have tactfully remarked to one another that the meeting is primarily "show and tell," and that missing it is not a big deal.

Among the many types of dynamics inside the group is the fact that following every Tuesday meeting, many of the group members spend additional time splintering off into different sub-groups to discuss other issues. Two of these groups in particular have become very closely knit, and will often go to lunch together as well as get together outside of work with their significant others. One of these groups includes CFO Sam Stoman, senior VP of business development Dave Damron, and executive director of the PCP practice Dr. Bob Borman. The other group includes COO John Vardez, senior VP of medical affairs Dr. Howard James, and VP of legal services Terry Tolls.

Although the Suburban West and East hospitals are critical to the success of the system and are both quite profitable, their administrators (Mary Moses and Wayne Walters, respectively) have not felt as much a part of the executive group. They have great autonomy in running their shops, and their primary responsibilities are internal operations. They have a high degree of contact with Dr. Borman regarding some of the physicians who are employed by his network. In addition, the three rural hospitals run by Duhal Malinka have little to do with the system. Their geographic distances have allowed them great autonomy. Although there has been some discussion of putting the two suburban hospitals under the direction of Malinka, Vardez has been quietly vying to have them report to him directly because of their closer ties to the downtown medical center.

Much of the work at St. Nicholas is accomplished through interactions between executives and their direct reports. Parris is a hands-off leader who takes most of her counsel from Dr. James, Stoman, and Damron.

Parris meets with each of her direct reports once every two weeks. She sees Dr. James much more frequently and stops in to see Stoman every day or so in his office. Although she rarely lunches, she will go to a long lunch every week or so with Damron.

**Exhibit 1 Organizational Chart for St. Nicholas Senior Leadership**

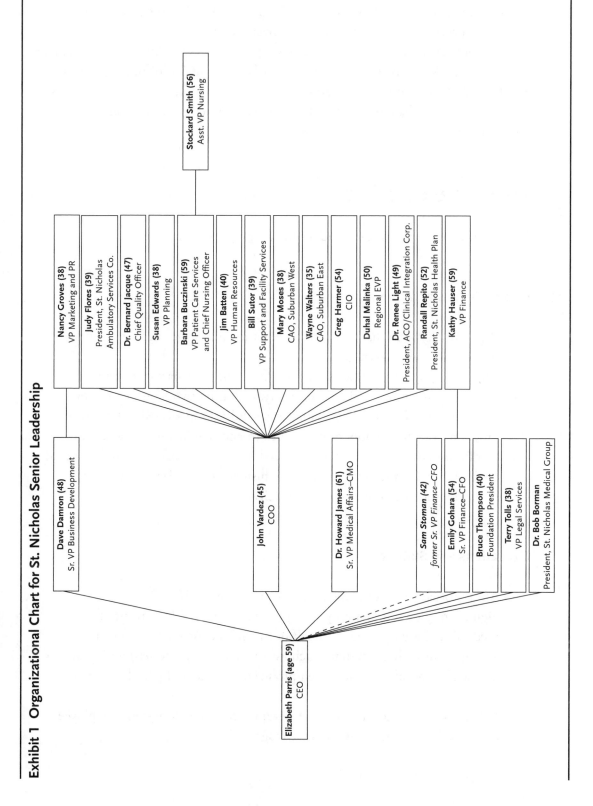

The entire executive leadership group has been employed at St. Nicholas for at least three years. Parris has been at St. Nicholas for eight years, the last three as CEO. The previous CEO had been in the position for 20 years.

Some of the executives—such as VP of support services Bill Sutor, VP of finance Kathy Hauser, VP of planning Susan Edwards, assistant VP of nursing Stockard Smith, and VP of patient care services Barbara Buczinski—have been with St. Nicholas for more than 20 years and have never worked for any other healthcare organization.

## STRATEGIC CONTEXT

St. Nicholas's current context includes the following trends:

### Demographics and Community

◆ Population growth that is tracking the national average, and diversifying at about the national average
◆ An elderly population that is growing faster than the national average
◆ A thriving urban university community, including two Commission on Accreditation of Healthcare Management Education–accredited master's programs, one in a school of public health and one in a business school
◆ Significant city and state deficits, caused in part by pension-related financial obligations (city and state) as well as a history of privatization decisions driven by short-term financial needs (city)

### Operations and Staffing

◆ An up-to-date electronic medical record system (EMR)
◆ Significant growth in employed physicians (currently 75 percent of medical staff is employed, and half of the independents have some type of arrangement with the system, such as comanagement models) with plans to increase the number of employed physicians substantially in the next two years
◆ Relatively low turnover across the system, with many long-term employees, as well as less union activity than average.

## Business

◆ A two-year trend of 5 to 7 percent declines in inpatient admissions
◆ Twenty percent growth in year-over-year ED visits (including the free-standing EDs)
◆ Significant growth in ambulatory encounters

## Strategic

◆ Involvement of the St. Nicholas Health Plan in the health insurance exchanges and the development of a clinical integration corporation
◆ Emphasis on the development of their patient-centered medical homes
◆ Pursuing expanded use of data analytics and the transparency of this data between health plans, providers, and employers
◆ Considering a tiered and narrow network to offer to several local large employers
◆ Beginning involvement in some multi-payer collaboratives
◆ Pursuing growth in the post-acute market
◆ Competitors have already formed accountable care organizations (ACOs)

The Barkley market is now composed mostly of three large systems, and all three are in the ACO business. St. Nicholas's inpatient strength currently lies in heart, vascular, and orthopedics. The system had strength in cancer services but lost its main physician group to one of its competitors. Of note is the fact that St. Nicholas is the only system in the Barkley area to have its own health plan and experience with Medicare Advantage plans and Medicaid managed care.

Following a recent update of their strategic plan, St. Nicholas's major current strategic initiatives include:

◆ Bundled payment programs in heart and orthopedics with four large employers
◆ Physician-led clinical integration corporation
◆ Value-based payment program trial
◆ Population health initiatives and ACO development
◆ Care coordination project, including emphasis on reduction in readmissions and building stronger ties to nonacute care lines of business
◆ Targeted quality improvement programs

- Joining a statewide collaborative to be primary providers in state Medicaid
- Introduction of physician leadership dyadic models
- Growing physician employment by 25 percent; employed physicians will represent 90 percent of the medical staff
- Major work transformation projects in nursing and other clinical areas
- LEAN projects in all inpatient facilities

## TEAM DYNAMICS

As our case opens, CEO Elizabeth Parris has recently announced to the Executive Leadership Group that the senior VP of finance, Sam Stoman, has accepted a position as senior VP and CFO for HealthAmerica, a $5 billion health system in the Southeast. Stoman had responsibility for managed care contracting during his tenure as senior VP of finance and CFO. Senior VP of business development Dave Damron has discussed his desire to take over the managed care area now that Stoman is leaving. Separately, VP of finance Kathy Hauser met with Parris to express her interest in the CFO job.

Following an exhaustive search, an external candidate, Emily Gohara, was appointed the new senior VP and CFO. Although Gohara was chosen, two other external candidates were close "seconds"; Hauser was eliminated from consideration in the first round of interviews. Although not openly discussed among the Executive Leadership Group, many preferred the other external candidates to Gohara. Some believed that the main reason she got the final offer was that she worked for a CEO who once served as Parris's mentor. A number of the senior executives expressed concern that the interview process was solely based upon chemistry and personality. VP of human resources Jim Batten had suggested to Parris that they use a leadership competency model in the selection process but had not been able to get one integrated into the decision making in time.

Parris's decision to hire Gohara was driven in part by a belief that the team had become stale and needed to start thinking differently about St. Nicholas's future. She anticipated resistance to Gohara's hiring, but now recognized that the decision was straining the sense of collaboration the group had enjoyed in recent years. In discussing the team's new dynamics with Jim, they decided the timing was right to begin the more robust approach to team and leadership development they had been talking about for years.

# INDIVIDUAL STYLES AND APPROACHES IN THE SENIOR TEAM

Several weeks after Gohara started as CFO, Batten presented a comprehensive proposal to the senior team to begin integrating leadership competencies as well as a greater focus on individual work styles into St. Nicholas's talent management program. Batten gave the following remarks to the group:

> I am proposing today what will become the backbone of our entire talent management program. We have had many parts of this in the past but they have not been linked nor have they been strategically tied to our business objectives. To get there, we'll need our talent management decisions to be driven by a specific set of organizational competencies, and for specific competencies tied to positions. A competency model is simply a description of successful behavior for a leader. Agreeing on a competency model gives us a shared language by which to talk about performance and how to improve it. The competency model I am advocating reflects contemporary leadership thinking and provides easy-to-grasp behavioral descriptors. This should help us more clearly and reliably define boundaries for success, enhance our understanding and assessment of leadership, and ultimately help reduce the risk of making a hiring or promotion mistake.
>
> In addition to competencies, our team will work better together if we invest the time to understand our individual work styles. This was the goal of the style inventory I asked you to complete in advance of our meeting today. In your packets you each have the results of the survey you took, as well as the results from the rest of the team.

Batten then walked the group through a description of each of the four styles for the style inventory, which are summarized below:

|      |                               |    |
| ---- | ----------------------------- | -- |
| I.   | Command and Control           | CC |
| II.  | Influence and People-oriented | IP |
| III. | Research Thinker              | RT |
| IV.  | Loyalty and Cooperation       | LC |

**Command and Control (CC):** A more direct style in terms of interactions with others; more of a driver and at times, demanding; goal orientation and results are hallmarks of this style, with some risk of too little attention to individual interests and needs of others.

**Influence and People-Oriented (IP):** A friendly and outgoing style, very people-focused; gets things done through the quality of relationships they are able to cultivate; some risk of being viewed as soft or easy to persuade.

**Research Thinker (RT):** An analytical, meticulous, and controlled style; attentive to detail; tends to be highly organized; some risk of spending too much time "in the weeds" or having difficulty communicating with people less knowledgeable about a given area.

**Loyalty and Reliability (LR):** A style focused on sincerity and stability; loyal to the organization and its mission as well as trusted colleagues; values traditions; some risk of having too little focus on the need for evolution and change.

Equipped with this work style information, as well as an understanding that St. Nicholas would be adopting a leadership competency model, the senior team began to reflect on recent experiences from which they might be able to learn through the use of these new tools.

**A Look at the St. Nicholas Senior Management Group and Their Work Styles**

| Executive | Title | Work Style |
|---|---|---|
| Elizabeth Parris | CEO | RT |
| Dr. Howard James | Senior VP, Medical Affairs | LR |
| John Vardez | COO | CC |
| Sam Stoman | Former Senior VP, Finance | CC |
| Emily Gohara | New Senior VP, Finance | RT |
| Kathy Hauser | VP, Finance | CC |
| Dave Damron | Senior VP, Business Development | CC |
| Susan Edwards | VP, Planning | RT |
| Nancy Groves | VP, Marketing and Public Relations | IP |
| Dr. Bernard Jacque | Chief Quality Officer | RT |
| Barbara Buczinski | VP, Patient Care Services | LR |
| Stockard Smith | Assistant VP, Nursing | IP |
| Jim Batten | VP, Human Resources | RT |
| Bruce Thompson | Foundation President | IP |
| Terry Tolls | VP, Legal Services | RT |
| Bill Sutor | VP, Support and Facility Services | LR |
| Mary Moses | Administrator, Suburban West | LR |
| Wayne Walters | Administrator, Suburban East | IP |
| Judy Flores | President, St. Nicholas Ambulatory Services | IP |
| Dr. Bob Borman | President, St. Nicholas Medical Group | CC |
| Greg Harmer | CIO | RT |
| Duhal Malinka | Regional Executive VP | RT |
| Dr. Renee Light | President, ACO/Clinical Integration Corp. | CC |
| Randall Repito | President, St. Nicholas Health Plan | RT |

# Part I

# WELL-CULTIVATED
# SELF-AWARENESS—
# THE FIRST CORNERSTONE

THE FIRST CORNERSTONE, a Well-Cultivated Self-Awareness, is the foundation of all leadership competencies. Knowing yourself and behaving in an authentic manner are critical to consistently ethical leadership. One CEO once commented, "Self-awareness means that you have a good understanding of what you have and what you don't have." Of the 16 competencies, the two that comprise this cornerstone—Leading With Conviction and Using Emotional Intelligence—are the most inwardly focused. The word *insight* comes to mind when contemplating the skill sets described in this section. Socrates has been given credit for saying "know thyself," which is a good theme to consider when studying these competencies.

> In my experience, the best leaders I have worked with really know themselves—their strengths and weaknesses—and they are always seeking feedback about how they are perceived. You know that old saying, "know thyself"? I think it is a mark of a great leader.
>
> *Health System CEO*

## CHAPTER ONE

# Competency 1: Leading With Conviction

Six months ago, Elizabeth Parris woke suddenly at 2:45 a.m., thinking again about the search for the health system's new executive vice president and chief operating officer (COO). As president of an organization that had grown too big for its management structure, Parris was eager to bring someone on to take over many of the operating responsibilities so she could focus some much-needed attention on strategy and board relations. The organization faced many detailed operational and tactical issues, and these had been taking up far too much of Parris's energies for several years. Adding an executive VP/COO would allow drill-down focus on these types of issues, giving Parris the time she needed for the more externally-facing roles she increasingly needed to take.

The health system was far along in the search process and had narrowed the field to two candidates: John Vardez and Lisa French. Parris had involved her executive team members in the interview process and wanted to allow them significant input. She believed Vardez was the right person for the job. Although he had not been in a similar position previously, he had a variety of experiences that gave him strong operations and turnaround exposure. A creative thinker, Vardez had experiences that included many different types of complex organizations, and in every case he had parlayed them into a clear sense of urgency and personal commitment to excellence. Moreover, he had been able to achieve impressive results with a variety of approaches. Parris knew Vardez would do whatever was necessary to make the organization run as efficiently as possible. This was evident in his accomplishments and was confirmed by his references.

The only problem? No one on Parris's executive team favored Vardez.

*(continued)*

(continued from previous page)

In Vardez's interviews with the executives, he made it clear he saw his role in terms of results. Although he said he intended to deal with people fairly, he was definitely not afraid to let people go if he thought doing so would serve the organization's needs. Across the board, the executives felt threatened by Vardez.

When it became clear Parris was favoring Vardez, staff reacted by rallying around French. Unlike Vardez, French already had been in this role in another system. She also had more years of work experience. During her onsite interview, she had done a far better job of establishing rapport with the team—everything from learning about their career goals to finding out about their history with the organization. She expressed accolades for the work the group had done and tremendous optimism about what could be accomplished in the future. But French had her own limitations. She lacked Vardez's sense of urgency, her approaches tended to involve incremental changes rather than transformational ones, and she would be slow to change management if needed. The level of results she achieved reflected this—acceptable but not particularly stellar. In short, Parris thought that French would probably do fine in the role, but Vardez could clearly do better.

Parris's entire leadership team was against her on this one. A number of them had made veiled threats about leaving if Vardez was hired. One had insinuated Parris was being sexist in her decision. All were waiting for her to make an announcement that morning.

IN THIS VIGNETTE, we find Elizabeth Parris grappling with a tough decision involving, among other elements, competing values. The setting, a middle-of-the-night awakening, is one during which internal conflicts are often most apparent. The distractions and intrusions of the workday are there only as memories, which allows the real internal struggles to come forward.

## WHAT IS LEADING WITH CONVICTION, AND WHY IS IT IMPORTANT?

Leading With Conviction is the competency closest to the core of the leadership role. The highest-performing leaders we have encountered all are strongly driven by their personal convictions. These convictions suggest to them how the world should be. They conceptualize their leadership role as moving an organization from its current world to its ideal world. Personal conviction is closely linked to vision, another important leadership competency (discussed in Chapter 3).

> **Leading With Conviction** means you know and are in touch with your values and beliefs, are not afraid to take a lonely or unpopular stance if necessary, are comfortable in tough situations, can be relied on to remain consistent even in tense circumstances, are clear about where you stand, and will face difficult challenges with poise and self-assurance.

For exceptional leaders, strong personal conviction is derived from various sources, including religious beliefs, deeply held connections to community, and a fundamental sense of morality—that is, what is right and wrong. All of these values are often, though not always, instilled at an early age by important caregivers and role models. More than merely a compass, personal conviction provides leaders with the strength to carry on when they may feel they are the only person behind a cause or a goal. Perhaps most important, the strength of personal convictions helps highly effective leaders deal with the inevitable setbacks and professional disappointments that come with the role.

## WHEN HIGHLY EFFECTIVE LEADERS LEAD WITH CONVICTION

Everyone has some sense of personal conviction or some unifying set of principles by which he lives. Decision making of any kind would not be possible in its absence— without a standard or metric by which to judge options, one option would never prevail over another one. Exceptional leaders, however, more consistently incorporate their personal conviction into their decisions. Several qualities of these leaders are as follows.

### Demonstrating Conviction

Highly effective leaders with strong personal conviction demonstrate their moral and ethical principles through the work they do. They know their values and beliefs and are comfortable discussing them. Their peers and direct reports, if asked, would describe these leaders with phrases such as "highly principled," "standing for what they believe in," and "walking their talk."

### Keeping Conviction in Check

While these highly effective leaders hold powerful convictions, they are also able to keep them appropriately in check. In addition, although they feel their convictions throughout their work, they are simultaneously able to recognize their convictions as personal and not universal. They are willing to blend the views and convictions of others into their decisions. They recognize their beliefs as "right for me" but not right in the absolute sense. While they may take delight in sharing their views, they are not overzealous missionaries out to convert their direct reports and peers. They view others' efforts to find their own individual larger purposes as virtuous in their own right, seeing this process as more important than the conclusions that are drawn.

### Keeping Ethics in Mind

Highly effective leaders are well known for having high integrity and ethics. They understand the ethical dimension to most decisions, and they are not afraid to ensure ethical considerations are addressed before a decision is implemented.

## WHEN LEADING WITH CONVICTION IS NOT ALL IT COULD BE

Less effective leaders do not use their conviction to its fullest potential. As a source of guiding light, conviction may occasionally serve as a flashlight when a beacon is needed. It may affect thinking but fail to guide decision making. It may steer leaders in a virtuous direction at first but will ultimately lose out to outside pressures. Following are some common reasons that Leading With Conviction falls short.

### Conflicted Convictions

Although leadership roles inevitably involve compromise, leaders who lack strong personal conviction may find that the course their organization is following frequently shifts direction. They may agree to one direction in a physician meeting and then reverse the direction when under pressure from board members. Other times, they may sacrifice individual goals for the good of the team, and the team for the good of the organization. They may hold social goals at arm's length when the hospital has a fiscal crisis and use the argument "no margin, no mission." The sheer pace of decisions and trade-offs in a leadership role can leave a leader little time for reflection and integration to the point where she begins to lose her sense of identity and becomes uncertain about her own beliefs.

## Lacking Conviction

Some leaders cope with their personal compromises through avoidance. They tell themselves their ideals are not so important, or they avoid thinking about these ideals entirely. For others, the conviction may not have been strong to begin with. As they progress in their careers, these leaders do little to cultivate their beliefs, assuming their life is easier that way.

In well-run organizations, leaders can be focused on personal beliefs and still make substantial organizational contributions. Well-designed incentives and careful monitoring can keep personal beliefs well enough in line that organizational goals are not sacrificed. However, such leaders do not perform to their full potential. Their direct reports view their relationships as transactional and have little incentive to work past the point of expected accomplishment.

## Disconnection Between Conviction and Work

Other leaders have strong personal convictions but choose not to allow these convictions to be expressed in their work roles, or they fail to see the opportunities to support their convictions through their work. We have seen many such leaders—all talented individuals—halt themselves at midlevel roles, gradually diminishing their focus on work while increasing their commitment to outside activities. They may champion great social causes, such as starting and running volunteer organizations, while at work they contribute at a reasonable but not superior level.

Even more troubling are leaders who simply give up on thinking they can make a difference in their organizational roles. In this category, we find leaders who are experiencing executive burnout—those who may have had admirable but unrealistic ideas about what they could achieve in their senior roles but who find they are unable to recalibrate their expectations and fully engage in the considerable good they *can* accomplish. They have truly "retired on the job."

## Overfocusing on Personal Goals

A final area where personal conviction can be detrimental involves allowing personal goals to become the *raison d'être*. In this type of environment, staff have little desire to help each other, and leaders view their position primarily as a vehicle for personal achievement. Leaders who allow this to occur find that organizational goals are ignored and that leadership teams have members who play harmful games of politics and act selfishly.

---

**When Living by Personal Conviction Is Not All It Could Be**

The following are often the reasons that personal conviction is not as strong as it could be:

- Conflicted convictions
  - Leaders are uncertain about their own beliefs.
  - The organization's course frequently switches direction.
  - Individual beliefs are too often sacrificed for the good of the team.
- Lacking conviction
  - Leaders either ignore or do not cultivate personal convictions.
  - Direct reports view their relationships with the leader as transactional.
- Disconnection between conviction and work
  - Leaders fail to see opportunities to support their personal convictions in their work.
  - Leaders focus too much on nonwork outlets and too little on work.
- Overfocus on personal goals
  - Staff lack a desire to help others.
  - Leaders view their position primarily as a vehicle for personal achievement.

---

# MISUSE AND OVERUSE: HOW LEADING WITH CONVICTION CAN WORK AGAINST YOU

Although strong convictions can drive leaders and their teams to deliver breakthrough performance, they can also have a serious downside when relied on too heavily, leading to one or more of the following patterns.

### Overvaluing One's Own Perspective

This can occur if leaders genuinely believe their views are the only correct ones. This pattern is often associated with fervent religious beliefs; however, in reality, such an orientation generally says more about the individuals than the religion they claim to support. In extreme cases, these leaders may regularly make statements such as

"I answer only to God" as a means of invoking moral one-upmanship rather than engaging meaningfully in the face of conflict.

More frequently, these less effective leaders may say things such as "This is a matter only the board and I would fully understand." Such an inflexible orientation tends to directly interfere with the leader's ability to build and sustain effective working relationships. Regardless of their other talents, such leaders typically find themselves unable to scale many rungs on the corporate ladder. Leaders who place such a high value on their own points of view also often shut off creative input from their team members.

## Failing to Own One's Perspectives

A more subtle but related challenge stems from the nature of the leadership role as a position of implied authority. Leaders can fall into the trap of viewing their personal convictions as correct by virtue of their leadership role—"I'm right because I'm the boss." Such an orientation, while perhaps not overtly hostile to others' perspectives, nonetheless fails to acknowledge and affirm others' views as valid. Leaders who follow this pattern also run the risk of creating a team of "yes people" and stifling team creativity. Groups led by such leaders rarely venture outside the box and almost never engage in innovative problem solving. In the end, valuable opportunities to develop understanding and trust through the experiences of work may be lost at the expense of higher performance.

## Being Overly Moralistic

Moral thinking and judgments become dangerous the moment they enter the interpersonal realm. Internally, statements about what one "should" or "must" do may speak of personal conviction, but externally, they may come across as moral one-upmanship, chastising, and holier-than-thou.

Leaders who are tough on themselves often struggle to avoid being just as tough on their direct reports, their peers, or, even worse, their superiors. People in general have a low tolerance for being considered morally inferior. Leaders do not get to make the mistake of being overly moralistic many times before it comes back to haunt them.

So why would a leader make this mistake, not once, but repeatedly? Because convictions can create blind spots. When a decision is proposed or an action is taken that runs against what the leader stands for, he can be thrown into a moral outrage that prevents him from seeing the appropriate considerations of interpersonal judgment. The leader then does not think about consequences, reactions, or impressions. Instead, he is consumed by indignation. He will react defensively and out of concern, but the tone will come across as a sermon or a lecture.

**Misuse and Overuse: How Leading With Conviction Can Work Against You**

Overuse of personal conviction yields the following symptoms:

- Overvaluing one's own perspective
  - Leaders view their beliefs as the only correct ones.
  - Leaders are unwilling to consider other perspectives, or even to allow others to state their opinions.
- Failing to own one's perspectives
  - Leaders consider themselves to be right by virtue of their position.
  - Teams are composed of "yes people" who do not challenge the leader or think creatively.
- Being overly moralistic
  - Conviction comes across as a sermon rather than a point of view.
  - Nonsupporters of the leader's view are cast as morally inferior.

## HOW TO BETTER LIVE BY PERSONAL CONVICTION

### Finding Role Models

As with all of the competencies discussed in this book, you can take two approaches to finding good mentors who will help you live by your personal convictions. The first is to look for people with a strong reputation in this area. Think about the following questions or pose them to well-connected colleagues:

- Do you know anyone who really lives by her principles?
- If you had a moral dilemma at work and wanted to talk to a mentor about it, who is the first person you would want to call?
- Who is the best person at supporting his or her convictions without coming across like a preacher in a pulpit?

The second approach is to look for people whose occupation requires them to master this competency to succeed. Faith-based organizations are an excellent place to find people with a strong sense of leading with their convictions. Alternatively, persons of the cloth who have become effective leaders in secular organizations likely have struggled with balancing their roles and identities and, as such, can be good role models. Leaders of organizations that have strong social purposes (e.g., indigent clinics, American Red Cross, American Cancer Society) may also be good mentors.

## Additional Opportunities for Personal Development

Strength in personal conviction comes from having a better understanding of yourself and your principles. Participation in organizations that foster a deeper understanding and allegiance with the greater good (e.g., social service organizations, religious groups, other mission-driven associations) can be useful in helping you gain a better understanding of what is most important to you. Another helpful exercise is to conduct a personal inventory of your convictions; Carson Dye's (2010) book, *Leadership in Healthcare: Essential Values and Skills* provides an approach to use. However, if you need to focus your efforts on a particular deficiency, suggestions for improvement in specific areas are listed below.

### Reconnect with Yourself

If you are having problems keeping in touch with your personal convictions, we recommend giving some thought to your "origin story"—the reasons you chose healthcare as a profession in the first place. You might even consider digging up the essay you wrote for admission to graduate school, or think back to the first healthcare leadership role you took. Spending the time to reconnect with what first brought you into healthcare can help you become a personally stronger, more authentic leader to others.

Find time to think reflectively about your work. You might try scheduling this time at the end of the day, the end of the week, or on an as-needed basis, depending on the challenges you face. Regardless of the frequency, time to reflect, alone or with a trusted colleague or loved one, can help you remain in touch with your personal convictions.

### Broaden Your Horizons

A powerful way to gain a sense of your personal conviction is to spend time in a context that is foreign to you. When we look into the histories of breakthrough leaders, we notice that many have lived, at some point in their lives, within a culture different from their own. This experience can help leaders cultivate a far richer understanding of themselves because it enables them to come into regular contact with their own convictions.

Travel is a great way to broaden one's perspective; however, if this is not a realistic option for you, consider reaching out to individuals or groups who hold different worldviews. If you can think of a group you "just can't understand," they are probably an ideal choice. A good exercise involves placing yourself in situations where your only goal is to be more open to others' opinions—for example, by visiting another religion's place of worship or the rally of a competing political party. Learn to recognize within yourself when you begin to close down to the opinions of others or to react with hostility. Chapter 6, "Listening Like You Mean It," provides additional useful guidelines on improving your receptivity to others' ideas.

If you need to become more open-minded about other opinions and perspectives, take it upon yourself to proactively challenge your own perspectives in settings other than the workplace, where it is safer to do so. Have dialogues with people who hold very different views from your own, and challenge yourself to summarize their perspectives aloud before jumping in with rebuttals. Make it a point to find opportunities to give others' perspectives center stage once in a while. You might also work on catching yourself when you want to say, "Do it because I said so." If you do say this, challenge yourself to come up with a clearer rationale for the course of action.

### Focus Less on Your Personal Goals

If others describe you as focusing too much on your own goals, we recommend you take this feedback seriously. You may be creating a counterproductive work climate—no one will go the extra mile for leaders they see as just out for themselves. Start by taking an honest look at your motives. What do you hope your achievements will do for you? What will be "enough," and what does "enough" look like? Leaders who are able to confront these questions can start themselves down the road toward a healthier and more rewarding sense of personal conviction.

## SUMMARY

Given the central role Leading with Conviction plays in exceptional leadership, mastering it is worth your time. Doing so requires work on self-awareness as well as becoming mindful of how you turn your personal convictions into leadership actions.

---

### Consider This

VP of human resources Jim Batten was having a discussion with Bill Sutor, VP of support and facility services, about self-awareness. Sutor argued that having too much conviction made a leader a tyrant. Sutor reminded Batten

*(continued)*

---

*(continued from previous page)*

of the Jonestown phenomenon and said that he thought leaders who pushed too hard were no better than Jim Jones. Batten argued that this viewpoint was extreme. Sutor asked Batten what controls could be put into place by an organization to ensure that this would not happen.

- How would you answer Sutor?
- What controls do you feel can be put into place to ensure that a single leader's personal conviction cannot lead an organization astray?
- Practically all organizations have chief compliance officers. Should one of the roles of this position be to oversee the directives given by leadership that might not be congruent with the values of the organization?

## Consider This

Some organizations have codes of ethics. The American College of Healthcare Executives' *Code of Ethics* can be found at www.ache.org/abt_ache/code.cfm.

- How can these codes help curb abuse in the area of personal conviction?
- How might these ethical guides get more traction and become more meaningful in the day-to-day life of an organization?

## REFERENCE

Dye, C. 2010. *Leadership in Healthcare: Essential Values and Skills,* 2nd ed. Chicago: Health Administration Press.

## CHAPTER TWO

# Competency 2: Using Emotional Intelligence

Two members of the senior team at St. Nicholas Health System had the following conversation.

"Our new CFO, Emily Gohara, definitely knows how to read people and has a real way with them. She always manages herself with poise. She is so different from Kathy Hauser. Kathy was on Sam Stoman's team, and she got away with a lot of bad behavior. Kathy thinks she is a master motivator, but everyone is afraid of her. Her outbursts have gotten worse since she was turned down for the CFO job. Who knew she could be such a hothead? She doesn't care about anyone but herself. I know she is smart and has done some great things for our health system, but she is just too wrapped up in herself."

"We had a similar situation several years ago when Dave Damron was passed over for promotion. I think he should have gotten the promotion then, but he hung in there and took it well. We all thought he would leave after being passed over, but he stayed, became an even stronger contributor and was very supportive of his new boss. He really showed great poise. I am sure that it was one of the major reasons that Liz Parris moved him up as soon as the job became vacant again. And he is getting great results. I think he has been a real asset for us lately. Now if only Kathy Hauser would be a little more grown-up about things."

A year after this conversation took place, Gohara and Parris asked Hauser to leave the health system because she had not been able to fit within the new changes in the finance team.

THIS VIGNETTE DESCRIBES a script we frequently see in leadership roles: Drive and skills are enough to earn a promotion but not enough to keep it. Long-term effectiveness depends on the quality of the leader's working relationships, which are in turn a function of the leader's capacity to understand and work effectively with emotions—of others as well as themselves.

## WHAT IS EMOTIONAL INTELLIGENCE, AND WHY IS IT IMPORTANT?

*Emotional intelligence* is a construct that unifies a slate of interpersonal skills. Although the concept of emotional intelligence has its roots in academia, its popularity as a management model began with author Daniel Goleman (1995). Some suggest emotional intelligence simply means having interpersonal skills. Although interpersonal skills are an important part of emotional intelligence, they are a subset of the broader concept. Understanding and working with other people's emotions while understanding and managing your own emotional responses requires emotional intelligence. In addition to being able to read others, the most effective leaders have a deeper understanding of their own emotions.

**Using Emotional Intelligence** means you recognize personal strengths and weaknesses; see the links between feelings and behaviors; manage impulsive feelings and distressing emotions; are attentive to emotional cues; show sensitivity and respect for others; challenge bias and intolerance; collaborate and share; communicate openly; and can handle conflict, difficult people, and tense situations effectively. A person's emotional intelligence is sometimes referred to as his emotional intelligence quotient, or EQ.

## WHEN HIGHLY EFFECTIVE LEADERS USE EMOTIONAL INTELLIGENCE

Leaders regularly find themselves in circumstances where emotions run hot. An emotional charge can be a productive energy source, and emotional intelligence can spell the difference between putting this energy to good use and watching it burn out of control. Exceptional leaders learn to manage these emotional charges in themselves and others, so that the energy is channeled most productively. They do so through developing greater self-awareness as well as through a more attuned sensitivity toward the emotional responses of others. Some of the ways in which emotional intelligence needs to guide leadership decision making are described in the following balancing acts.

## Acting with Self-Interest Versus Acting with Selfless Interest

A fundamental polarity in leadership involves the balance between self-interest (what you do to serve your own needs) and selfless interest (what you do to serve the needs of others or the needs of the organization). Balance means both sets of needs are adequately served. If too much emphasis is placed on the selfish side, your influence in the organization may erode or fail to develop in the first place. If too much emphasis is placed on the selfless side, the responsibilities of your role will erode your familial relationships, health, and well-being.

Most leaders have vulnerabilities, or blind spots, on either side of the balance. On the selfish side, we have the temptations associated with leadership roles. As you reach higher levels, your ability to influence the resources you receive, even your own salary, expands, and the line between purposeful influence and influence for its own sake becomes difficult to see. Others, such as your direct reports, will feel greater pressure to curry your favor and to convince you that everything is going great (regardless of how things are really going). The selfish temptation is to lose your objectivity and begin believing your own press releases.

However, danger lurks on the selfless side, too. As your influence and resources increase with higher-level positions, you will be approached with greater frequency to contribute to causes of all types. You will have expanded opportunities to do good on behalf of your organization and to support pet causes, which may or may not align with your organization's goals. A soft spot can quickly become an Achilles' heel.

This is where cultivating self-awareness comes in. Effective leaders use their self-awareness to identify and overcome their blind spots, enabling them to keep an objective, optimal balance.

## Engaging Others Versus Maintaining Distance

Being "one of the gang" is difficult for the CEO or other leader. Leaders must master a healthy balance between engaging the people they work with and maintaining a distance from them.

An imbalance on either side of this continuum diminishes the leader's effectiveness. If too much distance exists, coworkers will find it difficult to trust you. A lack of engagement with direct reports can create an emotionally cold environment that people do not look forward to coming to and are eager to leave at the end of the day. Without getting occasional messages of approval, some direct reports will suspect the worst and assume the distance is a signal of personal vulnerability.

For all the danger inherent in failing to engage with coworkers, being overengaging can be even more dangerous. For some leaders, work relationships serve emotional needs that are above and beyond the accomplishment of work-related goals. If leaders find they need regular approval from the people they work with, they may be too quick to give in to requests from direct reports or, alternatively, may shamelessly gratify their bosses. Another common pattern is possessiveness around working relationships, in which leaders not only fail to facilitate but actively block the development of social networks that do not pass through them. These leaders may also hold too tightly onto "their" talent, which can impair the career development of their direct reports and will make these leaders appear less collaborative.

Exceptional leaders exhibit enough engagement that relationships of trust, familiarity, and comfort can evolve. On the other hand, these leaders keep enough distance that they can pursue with some objectivity the kinds of candid feedback, appraisals, and personnel changes that may be in the best interests of the organization's goals.

## Trusting in Self Versus Trusting in Others

Trust forms another polarity requiring careful balance. Leaders who are too trusting will overdelegate responsibilities, handing them to others and putting them entirely out of their mind. If the work does not get done or does not get done properly, they will be quick to pass along blame and will have trouble recognizing their own failure to provide supportive check-ins and other monitoring.

On the flipside are leaders who place too much trust in themselves and not enough in others. This is the more common pattern of suboptimal performance, perhaps in part because it tends to get leaders in less immediate trouble than the former pattern. Leaders who do not learn to place adequate trust in others will either fail to delegate, creating a growth-stifling work environment in which no high-potential employee will stay for long, or underdelegate, giving tasks to others but then checking in so frequently and with such force that the tasks require twice the work that they should.

Highly effective leaders achieve an optimal balance of trust by delegating important aspects of work to others while continuing to monitor that work in ways that are respectful and nonintrusive.

# WHEN POSSESSING EMOTIONAL INTELLIGENCE IS NOT ALL IT COULD BE

Less effective leaders do not use the full extent of their emotional intelligence. Ways in which they fall short of accomplishing this competency involve the following.

## Lacking Concern for Others

At times, leaders may lack an appropriate level of concern for others. They may get so wrapped up in working toward the organizational mission that they fail to recognize the individual needs of others around them. At other times, leaders may simply be so self-absorbed that they fundamentally have no respect for others.

## Needing Approval

Some leaders are overly concerned with how they are perceived by others. Their need for approval prevents their personal conviction from driving their principles and actions. A common example is found in CEOs who are confident and self-assured until they get in front of their boards, where they will quickly back down if challenged. Other common examples include leaders who are so concerned with others' approval that they are unwilling to make tough decisions that might offend some of their team members. These leaders are sometimes described as "country-club managers."

## Being Volatile

Leaders who are passionate about their jobs will occasionally be upset—maybe very upset—by the decisions or actions of others that frustrate their goals. Strength in leadership comes not from stifling these emotions but rather from controlling them. Leaders are described as volatile if others cannot predict what will set them off or if their emotions seem to control them.

### Mistrusting Others

Highly effective leaders who have a strong grasp of emotional intelligence are willing to trust others. They delegate often and regularly and help others develop. They share both responsibility and accountability. It is rarely said of them that they have to check everything before anything is done. Leaders should work hard to communicate the big picture and learn how to empower others.

---

**When Possessing Emotional Intelligence Is Not All It Could Be**

When emotional intelligence is not as strong as it could be, a leader may be described in the following ways:

- Lacking concern for others
  - Individual needs of others are not recognized.
  - Self-absorption prevents the leader from recognizing and respecting others' views.
- Needing approval
  - Action is driven by approval-seeking rather than personal conviction.
- Being volatile
  - Emotions are in control of the leader rather than the leader being in control of his emotions.
  - Staff feel they cannot predict what will set off their leader on any given day.
- Mistrusting others
  - Everything has to go through the leader before anything can get done.
  - Work is not delegated, and staff are not empowered.

---

## MISUSE AND OVERUSE: HOW POSSESSING EMOTIONAL INTELLIGENCE CAN WORK AGAINST YOU

Can you be too emotionally intelligent? Perhaps not. However, emotional intelligence definitely can be misapplied and at the expense of higher performance in the following ways.

### Getting By on One's Good Graces

Emotional intelligence tends to be highly prized in senior leadership roles; all else being equal, leaders with higher EQs (emotional intelligence quotient) will be more favored for promotion or, in the case of downsizing, more likely to be retained.

We all share a bias to want to work with colleagues who are agreeable, and no one knows how to be agreeable better than a high-EQ leader.

Conversely, high-EQ leaders may also be particularly adept at convincing others to overlook their underperformance. High-EQ leaders can be less effective in other areas and will suffer fewer confrontations about it. They tend to have political networks that are far stronger than those of their peers and can tap them for support whenever poor performance becomes a concern. Some leaders have held on to senior roles for long periods through little more than their good graces and social ties.

## Overextending the Emotional Role

Some leaders with high EQs enjoy the emotional aspects of their work to the point that they may actually foster a volatile work environment. For these leaders, the patterns of creating an emotional crisis and then working through and repairing relationships provide greater familiarity and comfort than a more stable environment. However, needlessly volatile environments unnecessarily draw attention away from the pursuit of organizational goals.

For some leaders, serving as on-call negotiators or interpersonal problem solvers can be gratifying roles. These leaders may be reluctant to let others work challenges out for themselves or, in the case of direct reports, work with them to develop their own emotional intelligence.

## Avoiding Noninterpersonal Aspects of Work

Some high-EQ leaders focus too much time on the interpersonal aspects of their roles. These parts of their roles are where they get the most positive feedback, but they may not be adding the most value. For example, more time than necessary may be taken up maintaining work ties (e.g., somehow always finding the time to attend every social event, no matter how far-flung) or processing interpersonal exchanges that may not need the level of scrutiny they receive, when the time would be better spent addressing other critical elements of the leader's role (e.g., budgeting, planning).

### Misuse and Overuse: How Possessing Emotional Intelligence Can Work Against You

If a person overuses this competency, the following problems can result:

*(continued)*

*(continued from previous page)*

- Getting by on one's good graces
  - Formidable social networks prevent performance problems from being addressed.
  - Underperformance is often overlooked and rarely confronted.
- Overextending the emotional role
  - Contribution as a facilitator, negotiator, or interpersonal problem solver becomes oversubscribed.
  - Direct reports are not encouraged to work through their own challenges or develop their own emotional intelligence.
- Avoiding noninterpersonal aspects of work
  - Social aspects of the role are overemphasized.
  - The less people-focused, more mundane but still critical aspects of the role are neglected.

## HOW TO ENHANCE EMOTIONAL INTELLIGENCE

### Finding Role Models

High-EQ leaders tend to be found in the greatest numbers in human resources, pastoral care, counseling, and social service roles. In these roles a higher EQ is a more central requirement for effectiveness, opportunities to develop and hone these skills are more frequent, and the skill set is tested more routinely. Whatever the challenges you face in your working environment, chances are people in these types of roles have seen it and worse. (A caveat: Not *all* such individuals have a high EQ; the notes about overuse earlier in the chapter also apply to individuals in these groups. Be sure a potential mentor has a reputation as both an effective leader and having a high EQ.)

### Additional Opportunities for Personal Development

Although many books, seminars, and courses cover this topic, the best way to improve your EQ is to improve the quality of the feedback you receive about yourself and your relationships. The opposite of self-awareness is blind spots, and we all have them to some degree. The only way to uncover these blind spots is to receive feedback about them and to be willing to internalize what that feedback means.

You can improve the quality of the feedback you receive in a variety of ways:

- Develop more structured ways of getting feedback (e.g., use 360-degree programs, ask subordinates to provide input to third parties about how they feel about you).
- Improve your ability to hear feedback (e.g., work with a facilitator or a coach).
- Create a climate more conducive to feedback (e.g., conduct staff training or build feedback reviews into the ongoing work that you do).

Chapter 20, "Developing a Feedback-Rich Environment" provides additional suggestions on how to hard-wire some of these activities into your workplace. Another suggestion that has been used in the literature on this topic for some time is the Johari Window (see Exhibit 2.1), which is discussed in some detail in *Leadership in Healthcare: Essential Values and Skills* (Dye 2010). This concept helps leaders better identify blind spots and develop ways to address them. For the more ambitious reader, the writings of Daniel Goleman (1995, 2000, 2005, 2011b) provide highly accessible and practical summaries of the broad research base on which emotional intelligence concepts are based.

The Johari Window, which was named after the first names of its inventors, Joseph Luft and Harry Ingham from Westinghouse, describes the process of human

**Exhibit 2.1 Johari Window**

|  | Known to Self | Not Known to Self |
|---|---|---|
| **Known to Others** | OPEN | BLIND |
| **Not Known to Others** | HIDDEN | UNKNOWN |

interaction. A four-paned "window" divides awareness into four quadrants: open, hidden, blind, and unknown. The lines dividing the four panes can move as awareness changes. The four quadrants represent the following:

◆ The *open* section represents things that you know about yourself and that others know about you. The knowledge that this window represents includes facts, feelings, wants, needs, and desires. As you continue to get to know people, the sections move to place more information into the open window.
◆ The *blind* section represents things that others know about you but that you are unaware of. Blind spots can affect the level of trust between individuals; the challenge here is to get this information out in the open.
◆ The *hidden* section represents things that you know about yourself but that others do not know. With higher EQ comes a more refined understanding of what you should keep hidden and what you should disclose to build trust with others.
◆ The *unknown* section represents things that neither you nor others know about you. Growing in this area is the most sensitive but often the most helpful for higher-level leadership growth.

## SUMMARY

Leaders' effectiveness depends heavily on their ability to get things done through their relationships with others. Most of the challenges healthcare leaders face involve the need to influence people they have little to no formal authority over. Doing so effectively requires a solid understanding of others' needs and desires, as well as an ongoing monitoring of where they are emotionally with respect to a given task or initiative. Doing so exceptionally requires an even deeper understanding of others and oneself, so that this emotional intelligence can be put to its best use.

---

### Consider This

Emotional intelligence seems to relate to self-awareness. Daniel Goleman (2005, 43) defined the term *self-awareness* as "having a deep understanding of one's emotions, as well as one's strengths and limitations and one's values and motives."

• What are some of the specific organizational mechanisms and tools that can enhance the ability of leaders to gain greater self-awareness?

---

## Consider This

VP of patient care services Barbara Buczinski returned from a national nursing executive meeting where she attended a workshop on the "bright side" and "dark side" aspects of leadership. Some references that she brought back to St. Nicholas included:

Hogan, R., and R. Kaiser. 2005. "What We Know About Leadership." *Review of General Psychology* 9 (2): 169–80.

Judge, T. A., R. F. Piccolo, and T. Kosalka. 2009. "The Bright and Dark Sides of Leader Traits: A Review and Theoretical Extension of the Leader Trait Paradigm." *The Leadership Quarterly* 20 (6): 855–75.

Resnick, C. J., D. S. Whitman, S. M. Weingarden, and N. J. Hiller. 2009. "The Bright-Side and the Dark-Side of CEO Personality: Examining Core Self-Evaluations, Narcissism, Transformational Leadership, and Strategic Influence." *Journal of Applied Psychology* 94 (6): 1365–81.

Simmons, B. 2010. "Five Evidence-Based Outcomes of Both the Bright-Side and Dark-Side of a Leader's Personality." Published August 29. http://ldrlb.co/2010/08/five-evidence-based-outcomes-of-both-the-bright-side-and-the-dark-side-of-a-leader%E2%80%99s-personality/.

Research the topic of bright side/dark side leadership and provide a review of how this theory impacts emotional intelligence.

## REFERENCES

Dye, C. 2010. *Leadership in Healthcare: Essential Values and Skills,* 2nd ed. Chicago: Health Administration Press.

Goleman, D. 2011a. *The Brain and Emotional Intelligence: New Insights.* Florence, MA: More Than Sound.

———. 2011b. *Leadership: The Power of Emotional Intelligence.* Florence, MA: More Than Sound.

———. 2005. *Emotional Intelligence: Why It Can Matter More Than IQ.* New York: Bantam Books.

———. 2004. *Primal Leadership: Learning to Lead with Emotional Intelligence.* Cambridge, MA: Harvard Business Review Press.

———. 2000. *Working with Emotional Intelligence.* New York: Bantam Books.

————. 1995. *Emotional Intelligence: Why It Can Matter More Than IQ.* New York: Bantam Books.

Salovey, P., and J. Mayer. 1990. "Emotional Intelligence." *Imagination, Cognition, and Personality* 9: 185–211.

Segal, J. 2008. *The Language of Emotional Intelligence: The Five Essential Tools for Building Powerful and Effective Relationships.* New York: McGraw-Hill.

# Part II

# COMPELLING VISION—THE SECOND CORNERSTONE

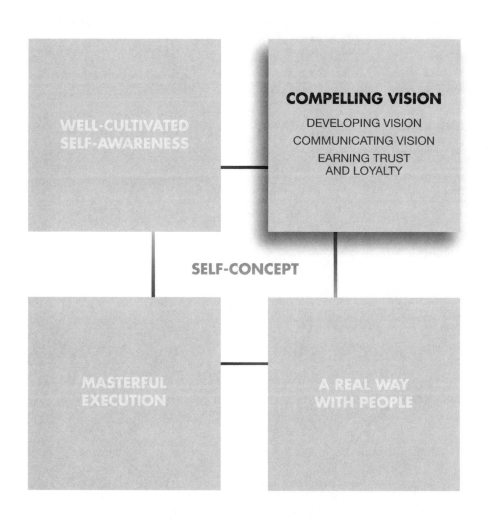

THE SECOND CORNERSTONE, Compelling Vision, involves the competencies that do the most to convince others that they should follow a particular leader. Built on the foundation of self-awareness and emotional intelligence, the Compelling Vision competencies—Developing Vision, Communicating Vision, and Earning Trust And Loyalty—are deployed to create a picture of the future that captivates others' hopes and aspirations, enough so that people will not only want to see this future realized, but will want to personally support its pursuit through their own efforts.

"Vision without action is a daydream. Action without vision is a nightmare."

*Japanese proverb*

## CHAPTER THREE

# Competency 3: Developing Vision

**Crisis.** Elizabeth Parris, CEO of St. Nicholas Health System, lay awake Wednesday night, still thinking through her board meeting earlier that day. Over the past several years she had maintained good relations with her board; lately, however, the issues that the organization faced had become far more complex, and her board was having problems accepting the ambiguous future. St. Nicholas had suffered several key setbacks, most of them centered around the main hospital in downtown Barkley. A historic building, the main hospital cost more and more to keep up to code every year. The inner city itself was in the throes of a major economic downturn, and competing with the other systems in Barkley was getting harder and harder. Physicians had the run of the place; decisions about healthcare capital equipment were driven almost entirely by efforts to recruit and retain physicians. Most of the employed physicians were at the main medical center, and those physician practices were losing substantial amounts of money. Every day it seemed like Parris's attention was being divided into smaller and smaller chunks. She was being pulled into operations challenges, and strategy was falling by the wayside. Parris was increasingly concerned that the board was overfocusing on St. Nicholas's major medical center, leaving little time for considerations of the system as a whole, including the pressing need to prepare in earnest for value-based reimbursement and population health management.

**Complacency.** At the same time, Suburban West Hospital (SWH) was experiencing great financial success. Located in the most rapidly growing area of greater Barkley, SWH seemed destined for success. SWH's CEO, Mary

*(continued)*

29

(continued from previous page)

Moses, had made this solid community hospital even more efficient during her tenure. Profitability was strong, turnover was low, staff were highly satisfied, and physicians were loyal and high quality.

Moses got her results by concentrating almost exclusively on the inpatient side of SWH's business. While her inpatient focus continued, the likelihood of its continuing success was waning. SWH had little competition in its western geography, and Moses was constantly pushing for support to increase the number of beds in her hospital. Between this focus and Parris's attention being pulled toward the main hospital, the trend toward outpatient and non-acute care was not getting the attention it needed, a reality that would eventually catch up with them both.

THESE TWO SCENARIOS both offer opportunities for a leader to develop and articulate a compelling vision, although both present formidable challenges to doing so. Parris's situation is perhaps more familiar in healthcare these days: waves of dramatic changes so numerous that they become difficult to keep track of, let alone address. Her challenge is to draw people's attention away from the crises they individually face long enough to allow them to see a collective vision—a beacon of hope showing what the organization could aspirationally become in the future. She also needs to get her board and others to focus on the unique changes occurring in the industry, changes that are foreign to the traditional acute care enterprise that so many have grown up in.

The suburban hospital, in contrast, may at first glance seem to be on autopilot. But while chaos is a more readily apparent barrier to higher performance, complacency can be just as bad, if not more so. How do you motivate a group that is comfortable with the way things are to take their organization even further?

## WHAT IS VISION, AND WHY IS IT IMPORTANT?

In our experience, *vision* is one of the most sought after competencies at the top levels of leadership. Vision can be defined most straightforwardly as the capacity to create effective plans for your organization's future based on a clear understanding of trends, uncertainties, risks, and rewards. Some might call it the art of developing strategy. Highly effective leaders who have strength of vision will position their organizations to take advantage of the trends they discern. For example, in healthcare, visionary leaders may see new clinical and technological advances long before they are prevalent and may commit their organizations to adopt them as they become available. They may see opportunities to get physicians more committed to their organizations by linking these physicians through more cutting-edge practices. We contrast this with the "chasing the trends" herd mentality; exceptional leaders have the capacity to identify the trends that make sense strategically and to adopt them early, before others copy them.

> **Developing Vision** means that you see the future clearly, anticipate large-scale and local changes that will affect the organization and its environment, are able to project the organization into the future and envision multiple potential scenarios or outcomes, have a broad way of looking at trends, and are able to design competitive strategies and plans based on future possibilities.

Organizations that have visionary leaders tend to be more successful. They are usually the first to market with new ideas and approaches to care; as a result, they often have better profitability, which allows them to attract higher-quality physicians and, ultimately, better serve their communities.

## WHEN HIGHLY EFFECTIVE LEADERS ARE VISIONARY

Although visioning is best thought of as an ongoing process, it has a definable sequence. The quality of vision relies on a solid awareness and understanding of broad trends and their implications. From these, a vision slowly takes shape, tempered (but not stifled) by the critical thinking of the key people needed to pursue it and communicated to those needed to implement it. Highly effective leaders use necessary skills to accomplish each of these elements of the visioning process.

### Maintaining an Awareness of Trends

Many, perhaps most, senior leaders have mastered the ability to track important trends in healthcare. If we go into any leader's office, chances are we will see copies of publications such as *Modern Healthcare, Healthcare Executive*, and possibly several trade journals more specific to their functional areas. We may even hear about news updates from the various health administration listservs. These are good resources for keeping track of trends within healthcare, but none gives a complete picture of the major trends happening outside the industry that will affect healthcare. These publications also tend to be "preprocessed"—the conclusions have already been drawn for the reader.

Exceptional leaders are broad thinkers who dig deeper to better understand the emerging trends, even outside of healthcare. If asked what they are reading from outside the healthcare industry, good leaders may cite the occasional business publication. Visionary leaders, on the other hand, are more likely to cite multiple sources with compelling, though perhaps indirect, associations with their leadership and industry roles, such as biographies of successful leaders throughout history, analyses of broad economic trends (such as the effects of energy policy on productivity), books on urban planning and development, articles on sustainable communities, or analyses of the rise and fall of ancient societies.

For exceptional leaders, this pattern extends far beyond what they read. Imagine for a moment that you wanted to learn more about how nanotechnology may affect health services delivery in the future. If you were a typical leader, you might scour the healthcare trade journals to examine the implications others are drawing about likely outcomes. Or you might go further and scan non-healthcare periodicals, such as *The Economist*, *The New Scientist*, or *Wired*. But if you were a truly visionary leader who sought to move your organization to the frontier, you could go as far as developing contacts and links well outside the field. Many scholars maintain lists of individuals who have requested updates on what is coming out of their labs. These lists contain other scholars but also industry members who simply want to stay informed about trends that could affect their businesses. They may even reach out to venture capitalists who are on the forefront of developing innovations, to keep tabs on where the funds are flowing.

## Understanding Risks, Rewards, and Uncertainties

Analyses to support strategic decision making represent something of a paradox. On the one hand, a fact-based analysis is essential to sound judgment, offering leaders their only hope to develop at least a minimally objective understanding of what the future holds. However, decisions always involve an emotional as well as a rational element; risk and uncertainty are always interpreted subjectively as well as objectively. Regardless of how well reasoned a course of action sounds, resistance will stem from the unfamiliarity the direction represents. People would prefer to believe that change is unnecessary; an exceptional leader's vision is strong enough to allow their trust in that leader to overcome this tendency.

## Communicating Vision

If the process is worked through effectively, the vision becomes the logical conclusion—the clear answer to the question raised by the analysis. There may be anxiety about how to get there, but there should be clarity about the appropriateness of the vision for the organization.

We discuss more about turning the vision into words and words into actions in Chapter 4. For now, we will leave it at the following key distinction: A good vision describes how the *organization* will be a better place because of the work of its people, but a breakthrough vision describes how the *world* will be a better place because of the work of the organization.

## WHEN DEVELOPING VISION IS NOT ALL IT COULD BE

We mentioned that strategic vision is one of the most important qualities boards look for in their senior hires. This competency, more so than the others in this Cornerstone, tends to be the rare bird. In other words, there are far more senior leaders with excellent trust building skills, outstanding communication skills, or both than there are strategic visionaries.

Part of the shortfall may be cognitive in nature; some elements of the visioning competency are difficult to develop. However, less effective leaders may also make the following mistakes.

### Focusing Too Much on Tactical Operations

Many executives work long and hard hours day after day but seem to have no long-term impact on their organizations or communities. They become so mired in the tactical, routine matters that they do not have the time to develop and evaluate long-term strategies.

Leaders who lack vision are often relegated to putting out daily fires. One well-known CEO said, "The best leaders are those who have the ability to transcend the day-to-day and see out into the future. Those are the leaders who are going to shape needed change in our field." In some management circles, this ability is called being proactive rather than reactive.

For some leaders, promotion into a role that allows for broader and more long-range influence provides a welcome opportunity to think strategically. For others, however, the opportunity is either not taken or is not taken far enough. Sometimes the reason is discomfort or the feeling that reaching out is too much like sticking one's neck out. For other leaders, the capacity to think strategically has yet to be developed.

Other leaders have the capacity to develop strategic vision, but hold themselves back because of the comfort of their operation's focus, their lack of experience with the visioning process, or both. Healthcare tends to provide many opportunities to focus on day-to-day challenges if leaders decide to do so at the expense of building and communicating a compelling vision.

Those leaders who do manage to focus some time and energy on thinking about the future run the risk that their vision will remain nothing more than a set of ideas that are discussed from time to time during social conversation or perhaps just once in a true operational context. In other words, the vision may be presented but not meaningfully hardwired into operational meetings.

### Restricting Focus to Healthcare

Another way in which vision can fall short is if leaders focus their sights strictly on the business of their health systems. Within health administration, already a high-involvement profession, there is a tendency to become cloistered. The risk here is of losing sight of how healthcare is affected by broader trends, as well as how healthcare can affect well-being above and beyond the service lines the hospital counts on for revenue.

### Relying on External Counsel

The sheer complexity of health administration creates a need for help in putting all the pieces together. Information digests, consultants, and other sources can be immensely helpful here, as long as leaders maintain a healthy skepticism. Questioning takes time, focus, and energy—it is tempting to let it fall by the wayside (analytic help is what you are paying for in the first place, right?).

A similar pattern we see frequently is following the leader, where a health system or group of health systems are known for being early adopters of promising trends and thus become the de facto leaders for the broader industry. Some psychological safety exists in deferring judgment to well-regarded, well-run health systems, and sometimes, perhaps often, the strategy works. But it is rare for a leader to be viewed as exceptional if their primary approach involves relying on other organizations to make sense of the future for them.

### Undervaluing Divergent Perspectives

Vision can also fall short if it is too tightly ascribed to a single leader—something that happens when leaders fail to engage their teams in honing, evolving, and challenging their organizational visions. For leaders who possess adequate power, peers and direct reports will go along with a vision they do not believe in simply to stay on the leader's good side. If they are not encouraged to discuss their concerns or ideas about the future, the energy they bring to the effort will be borrowed energy, which is soon depleted and in need of a refill.

We can extend this example to other situations in which leaders resist challenges to their visions or resist the visioning process entirely. Some leaders view the visioning process as frivolous; they pride themselves on their abilities to address problems in the moment or on chasing opportunities in whatever form they may take. The approach may provide them the greatest comfort, but it will not get the level of commitment from their needed collaborators that a shared vision will deliver. Jim Collins (2001) makes this point in distinguishing "foxes" from "hedgehogs" in his seminal book *Good to Great*. In this book, the hedgehogs take a complex world and simplify it, while the foxes are scattered and try out many different strategies at the same time. Collins's more recent book, *Great by Choice* (Collins and Hansen 2011), expands on these concepts by describing leadership roles in creating the future they wish to see.

---

### When Being Visionary Is Not All It Could Be

When vision is lacking, it can look like any of the following:

- Focusing too much on tactical operations
  - Control of day-to-day fires takes precedence over long-range planning.
  - Long-term perspectives are not structured into regular operations.
- Restricting focus to healthcare
  - Social and professional networks and information sources reside almost entirely within the healthcare industry.
  - Too little intellectual curiosity exists about broader trends or changes.
- Relying on external counsel
  - The analytic work of others is too heavily relied on, and conclusions are not questioned.
  - The organization follows whatever the other health systems are doing, with inadequate analysis as to whether it is appropriate.
- Undervaluing divergent perspectives
  - Staff go along with a vision simply because they want to stay on the leader's good side.
  - Concerns and ideas about the future are not discussed.

# MISUSE AND OVERUSE: HOW BEING VISIONARY CAN WORK AGAINST YOU

Without a doubt, leaders can focus too much on vision to the detriment of their organizations. When these downsides appear, they are often attributable to either an imbalance somewhere within the visioning process or overzealousness about visioning in and of itself.

## Balancing Poorly Between Planning and Operations

Leaders can become so engaged with the visioning process that the day-to-day management of the enterprise is ignored. A proper balance between long-term strategic focus and short-term tactics must be maintained. Problems often occur when leaders place too much emphasis on business development, strategic planning, and cutting deals. In the excitement of pushing new and exciting initiatives forward, operations may receive diminished focus, and the executives running operations may feel like second-class citizens. The imbalance can create a host of implementation problems as well. Planning executives may not develop the understanding of operations necessary to forge realistic plans. Conversely, operations executives may not have the influence they should on the strategic planning process, resulting in less buy-in and engagement with its implementation.

## Focusing Too Much on the Process of Planning

Another symptom of overzealous planning is a fondness for process over outcome. Leaders with this pattern are overly eager to try out a variety of strategic planning approaches to "see where it takes us." Moving through the planning process becomes the end in itself. This results in an inordinate amount of time moving through elaborate strategic planning retreats and a multitude of thick reports full of objectives, most of which are never achieved.

Another type of overzealous focus shows up in the use of data. Healthcare has more data sets available for analysis than almost any other industry; managers can be tempted to believe more is more to the point that analyses are pursued far beyond the point of diminishing returns. Executive teams can quickly fall into the bad habit of allowing analysis to unnecessarily slow down the execution of new initiatives or the implementation of needed changes.

## Underemphasizing Implementation

To paraphrase Thomas Edison, genius involves one part inspiration and 99 parts perspiration. Indeed, some leaders are so effective in crafting truly compelling visions that they overemphasize the vision itself at the expense of its implementation. Little attention may be paid to how the vision will be translated into specific plans. Worse, new visions may be created before they are needed and before the old visions have either proved obsolete or have been given a reasonable chance to take hold. In these cases, colleagues in the hospital may quickly develop an attitude of "let's just wait this one out," and trust on both sides will suffer in the process. (See Chapter 4, "Communicating Vision," and Chapter 14, "Driving Results," for more ideas about improving your implementation focus.)

---

**Misuse and Overuse: How Developing Vision Can Work Against You**

If a person overuses this competency, the following problems can result:

- Balancing poorly between operations and planning
  - Business development and strategic planning executives are elevated above the key operations people.
  - Day-to-day operations do not get the attention they need.
- Focusing too much on the planning process
  - Technique is valued over substance.
  - Data are collected far beyond the point of diminishing returns.
  - Execution is unnecessarily slowed down.
- Underemphasizing implementation
  - New plans are created too frequently, and old plans are abandoned with inadequate (or inadequately communicated) rationales.
  - Colleagues develop attitudes of "waiting it out."

---

## HOW TO IMPROVE VISIONING

### Finding Role Models

If you are not in a C-level position, you may find useful guidance from senior leaders as well as from leaders within the business development and marketing departments of your organization. At higher levels, however, identifying good mentors for vision can be challenging, and you may need to look outside your own organization to find them. In thinking about who might have real strength in this area, ask yourself the following questions:

+ Where are the innovations happening in healthcare right now?
+ Where are the success stories?
+ Where has a health system been taken from good to great?

You may need to develop relationships with consultants who are well traveled and well versed on new trends and ideas. Ongoing networking with healthcare peers outside your market can also be helpful.


## Additional Opportunities for Personal Development

An effective way to become more visionary is to expand your horizons beyond healthcare. Make sure you have opportunities for the outside world to reach you. Be mindful of the continuous tendency for healthcare to creep into the social engagements you keep and the books on your nightstand; set aside some time and focus specifically on nonhealthcare issues. Allocate time to interact with leaders from other industries. Finally, be certain that ample time is spent involved in community activities.

To hone your intuitions about how sector trends evolve, we recommend the writings of Clayton Christensen and colleagues. Disruptive innovation theory, in particular, can be very helpful to understanding the natural lifecycle of business models, and the process by which they tend to be disrupted. The seminal work in this area is *The Innovator's Dilemma* (Christensen 2013); three books covering healthcare-specific disruptive trends are: *The Innovator's Prescription* (Christensen, Grossman, and Hwang 2009), *The Creative Destruction of Medicine* (Topol 2012), and *The Future of Healthcare: Global Trends Worth Watching* (Garman, Johnson, and Royer 2011).

In terms of conceptualizing strategic options, the classic text is Michael Porter's (1998) *Competitive Strategy: Techniques for Analyzing Industries and Competitors*. If your education included a course in strategy, chances are either this text was assigned or the text that you did use quoted liberally from it. Porter's conceptual models will be familiar to almost anyone with a degree in business or administration; make reading this one a top priority.

For the actual process of developing a vision, we recommend *Visionary Leadership* by Burt Nanus (1992). It is a very readable guide to what a vision statement needs to do and how it needs to be created to accomplish its goals. Although the examples used in Nanus's book are becoming dated, the methods are not. Finally, for a healthcare-specific look at strategy development, we recommend *Healthcare Strategy: In Pursuit of Competitive Advantage* by Roice Luke, Stephen Walston, and Patrick Plummer (2004).

## SUMMARY

The capacity to develop vision, both individually and collaboratively, is a hallmark of exceptional leadership. It is also a set of skills that can be honed over time by learning useful frameworks, such as disruptive innovation theory, as well as applying them to key trends to examine the impact they may have. Most importantly, it also involves identifying your own unique perspective, which may be built with the help of others but is not completely dependent on them.

---

### Consider This

Sam Stoman, Dr. Bob Borman, and Dave Damron were at the Stomans' house one Saturday night when Dr. Borman stated, "You two know that St. Nicholas is just not going to go anywhere because we have no vision and no strategy. We just do not have any clear direction. We are trying to do everything and there is no logical foundation. And moreover, we do not have anyone at the senior table who can really craft a forward-looking vision."

Stoman countered by stating, "I just don't agree. That's all we do—deal with vision and strategy. If we don't spend more time on managing day-to-day operations in this new healthcare world, we are not going to continue to come out on top. Everyone knows that if you do operations right, you will thrive in the marketplace."

This is the traditional "operations versus strategy" argument that organizational leaders often get into. This balancing challenge can become a contest in which leaders who have roles that are more operational (such as the chief nursing officer or the chief operating officer) are pitted against those who are in jobs that are more strategic (such as the chief planning officer or business development officer).

- One of the major ways in which organizations balance the management of day-to-day operations with longer-range strategic issues is to segment their meetings. For example, a senior team may meet every Tuesday and focus exclusively on tactics and immediate problems and issues and then meet once per month to discuss and plan longer-range strategy.

*(continued)*

---

(continued from previous page)

What are other approaches that might help to keep an appropriate balance between the two?

- There are several keys to becoming a more strategic thinker. They include ensuring that you have an anticipatory sense of what is happening in the future, being able to interpret those trends, and getting others to see the changes that need to be made to prepare for that different future. If you are burdened by constant day-to-day operations challenges, what are some ways in which you can more fully develop this strategic side?

## Consider This

After a lengthy debate on strategy (which was going nowhere) in the recent St. Nicholas senior team meeting, Susan Edwards, VP of planning, made the following points:

"Colleagues, Michael Porter is the guru of strategy planning and visioning. He clearly states that to maintain a competitive advantage, an organization must either provide a cost benefit or differentiate their services—or possibly both. May I suggest that here at St. Nicholas, we are doing neither. We are the high-cost provider in the area, and while we do have some good quality indicators, we are not really providing any services that are unique."

As would be expected, this comment started a verbal brawl.

- Ponder carefully this brief case example. Did Edwards do the right thing by introducing a discussion around the *process* of strategy and visioning?
- If she wanted to take a more data-driven approach concerning St. Nicholas's cost- and market-differentiation position, what might that have looked like? How might the outcome have differed?

## REFERENCES

Christensen, C. 2013. *The Innovator's Dilemma: When New Technologies Cause Great Firms to Fail.* Cambridge, MA: Harvard Business Review Press.

Christensen, C., J. Grossman, and J. Hwang. 2009. *The Innovator's Prescription: A Disruptive Solution for Health Care.* New York: McGraw-Hill.

Collins, J. 2001. *Good to Great: Why Some Companies Make the Leap…And Others Don't.* New York: Harper Business.

Collins, J., and M. Hansen. 2011. *Great by Choice: Uncertainty, Chaos, and Luck—Why Some Thrive Despite Them All.* New York: Harper Business.

Garman, A., T. Johnson, and T. Royer. 2011. *The Future of Healthcare: Global Trends Worth Watching.* Chicago: Health Administration Press.

Luke, R., S. Walston, and P. Plummer. 2004. *Healthcare Strategy: In Pursuit of Competitive Advantage.* Chicago: Health Administration Press.

Nanus, B. 1992. *Visionary Leadership.* San Francisco: Jossey-Bass.

Porter, M. 1998. *Competitive Strategy: Techniques for Analyzing Industries and Competitors.* New York: Free Press.

Topol, E. 2012. *The Creative Destruction of Medicine: How the Digital Revolution Will Create Better Health Care.* New York: Basic Books.

## CHAPTER FOUR

# Competency 4: Communicating Vision

Elizabeth Parris was ecstatic. A year after facing many difficult issues with her board and several months after hiring her new executive vice president and chief operating officer, John Vardez, she had successfully led the development of Vision 2025, the organization's long-range strategic plan. Vision 2025 incorporated a $300 million rebuilding and renovation program, the creation of a more distinct ambulatory business unit, and a comprehensive approach to population health management that was coordinated through their health plan. It also included an agreement to partner with two other health systems in two other large cities to create a collaborative, allowing access to a far greater population base than just Barkley, as well as several new horizontal integration initiatives that could truly create the "health system of the future." This latter part of Vision 2025 was the most challenging to describe. While the financial challenges to fund this project were enormous, an even greater challenge in Parris's mind was the essential requirement that the entire physician and employee community understand what this collaborative meant and be totally engaged in the change initiative.

Parris had discussed this challenge with her executive coach, who encouraged her to keep focused on linking changes to a systematic communications strategy. She began her weekend with the goal of developing a set of outlines that would captivate the physicians and employees when she started her town hall meetings next month.

THIS VIGNETTE SPEAKS to the heart of successfully implementing vision. Leaders must engage various stakeholders to help them understand the rationale for change; leaders must, in essence, create a compelling call to action. To illustrate this point, consider this statement based on Greek history: When Pericles spoke, people said, "How well he speaks." But when Demosthenes spoke, they said, "Let us march."

In the previous chapter, we discussed what it means to develop vision. Developing and using vision as an instrument of organizational change requires effective communication of that vision—turning a set of strategic and often complex concepts into a compelling story of where the organization is, where it will go, and how it is going to get there.

We call this competency *Communicating Vision* for several reasons. First, we want to distinguish it from the more general concept of communication, which can be almost as broad as leadership itself. In this chapter, we specifically address how highly effective leaders communicate vision, and how they create an environment where staff and physicians feel compelled to move with them toward that vision.

## WHAT IS COMMUNICATING VISION, AND WHY IS IT IMPORTANT?

*Communicating Vision* throughout any change process is essential to its success. At the same time, it is also incredibly challenging to effectively pull off. Most leaders routinely underestimate the amount of communication necessary to drive change efforts; as a result, many employees inevitably feel lost and confused by the change process, which can make them cling even more closely to their old but familiar habits.

> **Communicating Vision** means that you distill complex strategies into a compelling call to action, inspire and help others see a core reason for the organization to change, talk beyond the day-to-day tactical matters that face the organization, show confidence and optimism about the future state of the organization, and engage others to join in.

Effective leaders not only communicate about day-to-day issues but also about vision. In his book *Leading Change*, noted scholar John Kotter (2012) describes the level of vision-related communication in comparison to total workplace communication during a change effort. In his estimation, vision-related communication tends to comprise only about one-half of 1 percent of the communication people receive about their work. With this much competition, communication had *better* be captivating!

Spending time communicating future vision also helps ensure that everyone is on the same page. It aids in collaboration and enhances the coordination of work effort.

## WHEN HIGHLY EFFECTIVE LEADERS COMMUNICATE VISION

Although there are as many communication styles as there are communicators, several qualities make any communication style stronger. Keep these in mind, and your communication will begin to reflect them.

### Communicating Clearly

Discussing clarity in vision communication may appear trite—after all, who would argue *against* communication clarity? However, in reality, few among us are as clear as we could be, as frequently as we could be, though most of us would like to think otherwise.

We can compare Communicating Vision to marketing. Think about the marketing slogans that you have found most memorable. What did they have in common? Chances are they were straightforward, novel, even catchy—and without a single vague or unnecessary word. If they were really good, they stuck in your mind—you could not help but think of them. These same structural elements can be usefully applied to vision communication. You want these ideas to be compelling and to stick in people's minds.

### Communicating Widely

Effective leaders ensure that everyone who will be responsible for moving the vision forward hear it. They also use a wide variety of communication methods to describe vision so that the message fully permeates. This skill separates exceptional leaders from their well-intentioned but less-effective counterparts. Because communication can be labor intensive, shortcuts become tempting—placing a message in a corporate newsletter and considering the communication process finished, for example. This may make sense if all staff are required to read the newsletter *and* if the expectation is effectively monitored, but it is hard to justify otherwise.

Highly effective leaders will take the communication process even further. Beyond simply ensuring the message is heard, they will ensure that the message is *discussed*. For example, they might instruct managers to explicitly incorporate a discussion of the vision into their next staff meeting and then report back on what was discussed. Such cascading communication structures can go a long way in making sure key messages are reliably received.

## WHEN COMMUNICATING VISION IS NOT ALL IT COULD BE

When communication falls short of captivating, often one or more of the following may be the reason.

### Lacking Clarity, Focus, or Information

Clarity can suffer because of a number of problems. The communication may lack clarity because the vision itself lacks clarity. Alternatively, the communication may lack focus; it may contain too many elements for people to easily wrap their heads around. Still another problem stems from communicating too little information about the *how* of the vision. The further the vision is from the current state of affairs, the greater the need for some indication of the path the organization will take to get there. Without this path, staff may dismiss the vision out of hand—a risk made far more likely if there is recent history of abandoned visions.

### Lacking Meaning for the Audience

The challenge of making a broad organizational vision meaningful at department and subdepartment levels is usually beyond the capabilities of any individual leader. Effective leaders know this and work with managers to develop local interpretations of how the efforts of a given division, department, or team will fit into this broader vision. Without this careful linkage, staff may only receive the corporate take on the vision and may have difficulty viewing their roles as part of that vision.

Another frequent problem is the articulation of a vision that does not clearly express how the vision affects everyone, and how everyone affects the vision. This risk exists any time a vision communication places special emphasis on a specific aspect of operations. Common examples include vision statements that draw special attention to the physicians, nurses, profitable service lines, or quality improvement initiatives. If poorly communicated, the vision will leave the counterparts (e.g., nonphysicians, non-nurses) feeling excluded.

### Communicating Infrequently

Although communication plans can (and should) be designed to be highly efficient, they are still typically time and resource intensive. Communications is a tempting place to cut corners, and so corners are often cut. The best prevention here is to arrange a review of all internal communications coming from the corporate level to ensure they make some mention of future plans. Think about it this way: Any time the vision of the future state of the organization is *not* mentioned, the status quo will take center stage.

---

**When Communicating Vision Is Not All It Could Be**

Communication in the realm of strategic vision can fall short for any of the following reasons:

- Lacking clarity, focus, or information
  - A visual picture is not created, either because it is unclear or it contains too many elements.
  - Lack of thought about the *how* makes the vision seem too far-fetched.
- Lacking meaning for the audience
  - The importance of individual roles is not adequately addressed.
- Communicating infrequently
  - The vision is rolled out and then rarely referred to again.

---

## MISUSE AND OVERUSE: HOW COMMUNICATING VISION CAN WORK AGAINST YOU

Overcommunication of the vision is not nearly as frequent as undercommunication. When communication fails, it is usually because of a problem with the communication itself rather than it being too frequent. The following patterns will cause your communication to be ineffective, regardless of frequency.

## Communicating Vision as an End Rather Than a Means

Occasionally, leaders may be accused of talking a great game and getting people excited about an idea or strategy that they are ultimately unable to implement. Leaders may routinely be caught up in the excitement of thinking (or dreaming) about what the future could be like, but the actions needed to make this future happen are conspicuously absent. The vision is thus discussed as a concept permanently divorced from the present day—a beautiful mirage across the wide chasm of inaction. The danger of this pattern is greatest in groups where no great sense of urgency has been cultivated to overcome the comfort of the status quo.

## Viewing Vision as the Program du Jour

Some leaders do not fully recognize both the power and the responsibility associated with setting and communicating organizational vision. For some, the vision is viewed more trivially, a slogan for the occasional staff pep rallies rather than a beacon by which to set direction. For others, particularly high-energy leaders who pride themselves for turning on a dime, the vision may change too rapidly over time, causing confusion and frustration among their staff. Leaders may try out so many different kinds of visions that staff and physicians may view them as just another gimmick program. Healthcare has been known for this, and leaders need to be cautious about falling into this trap.

## Communicating Too Specifically

Communications about vision can be too specific in a number of ways. Consider an organization that develops a vision with specific, objective goals (e.g., "We will gain 40 percent of the inpatient market share in the area," or "We will be the top provider of heart surgeries by market share in our market"). What if your organization achieves those types of measured goals? Your vision would dissolve, and you would need a new one.

Another example of communicating too specifically relates to timelines. Timelines are terrific for operational goals, but putting a vision on a timeline is often a mistake. Say you set "three years from now" as the time your vision will be achieved. You have just turned the vision into something that can be proved or disproved. People can start to decide early on whether they think the vision will be achieved; if it starts to look undoable, it may be abandoned prematurely. In short, it devolves into an operational goal and loses some of its original power to unite and energize.

**Misuse and Overuse: How Communicating Vision Can Work Against You**

When your communication is ineffective, regardless of frequency, one of the following is most likely the cause:

- Communicating vision as an end rather than a means
  - Communication is emphasized at the expense of implementation.
  - Too much time is spent talking about doing instead of doing.
- Viewing vision as the program du jour
  - Motivation building rather than direction setting is the primary goal.
  - Visions change too frequently and are thought of as gimmick programs.
- Communicating too specifically
  - Setting a timeline for the vision will eventually force the need to develop a new vision.
  - Vision becomes something that can be proved or disproved.

## HOW TO BETTER COMMUNICATE VISION

### Finding Role Models

The best way to find mentors in this area is to ask yourself, Who do I find most compelling to listen to? Who paints the most vivid, most exciting, and most believable pictures of the future? Once you have identified these individuals, take note of what they say, how they say it, and what really reaches you about their communication. These individuals need not be people you know personally—for example, politicians and religious leaders are some of the most powerful communicators. What is most important in this exercise is to develop the discipline of attending to the elements that make these communications really work.

Another approach you can take is to identify people (your peers and direct reports, for example) others seem to listen to the most. They need not be leaders you find particularly compelling; sometimes zeroing in on people who surprise you with their ability to captivate others can be useful. In these cases, try to learn what it is about this person's communication style that others find so intriguing and look for elements that you can adopt to your advantage.

### Additional Opportunities for Personal Development

Many excellent books have been written on improving your communication style. For clear and concise writing, the single best source we have seen is *Revising Prose* by Richard Lanham (1999), in any edition. It is a concise, well-written, enjoyable read emphasizing clarity and economy of words. For communication more generally, an excellent collection of ten "must read" articles is available from the archives of Harvard Business Review (2013).

To develop your skills in turning analyses into compelling graphical statements, we highly recommend the works of Edward Tufte. Tufte has published a series of books on how to present data in captivating ways, including the classic *The Visual Display of Quantitative Information* (2001). He has developed a cult following among some of the more powerful strategic speakers we know. A good place to start is his monograph *The Cognitive Style of PowerPoint* (Tufte 2003), followed by his more recent work. All are available via online booksellers or through www.edwardtufte.com.

The process of Communicating Vision in ways that facilitate change are well described in John Kotter's (2012) book *Leading Change*. Originally released in 2006, this book is widely regarded as a classic on this topic; we highly recommend it, as well as two other books, *Our Iceberg Is Melting: Changing and Succeeding Under Any Conditions* (Kotter et al. 2006) and *A Sense of Urgency* (Kotter 2008).

If you are interested in fine-tuning your public speaking skills, there is no better method than practice followed immediately by candid feedback. Because this can often be very difficult to drum up in the workplace, consider a course with the local chapter of Toastmasters International (www.toastmasters.org). (If you have no local chapter, consider starting one.) The sole focus of this group is to improve the speaking skills of its members. We are told that the quality of the experience does differ depending on the chapter's membership; however, in general, leaders' and professional speakers' experiences with this organization have been favorable.

## SUMMARY

As important as vision is, it will not move an organization where it needs to go without systematic and compelling communication. In this chapter we described what effective vision communications can look like, as well as the ways in which these communications can miss the mark. Learning how to craft and systematically convey visionary communications will help you achieve exceptional leadership outcomes.

## Consider This

St. Nicholas just purchased another rural hospital. Located two hours' drive from Barkley, Hummingbird Hospital had once been a vibrant center of activity. To run the hospital, Elizabeth Parris appointed Rosemary Ruiz, who had worked under Dave Damron, the senior business development officer at St. Nicholas.

Rosemary was excited to be in her first CEO position. Because she had done all the study that led to this acquisition, she was well versed on the issues faced there and knew that she needed to make significant changes. She had mapped out a detailed plan of action she called The Hummingbird Vision. As her first activity two weeks after she arrived, she gave a presentation with more than 100 PowerPoint slides to a mixed meeting of the local board, the medical staff leadership, and her senior team at Hummingbird. Her slides were excellent and to the point. The presentation mapped out specific strategies and tactics for the next three years at Hummingbird. She had provided 24 strategies and more than 250 tactics. She was pleased that she had "thought of everything" and after concluding, felt that she had presented with great clarity. She knew that the next essential step was to ensure that the entire physician and employee community be totally engaged in the plan and change initiatives.

What did Rosemary do wrong?

## Consider This

**Vision One.** Our vision is to be a health center of excellence and to provide the highest quality patient care at the lowest cost so that all citizens of our area can benefit from our programs and services and our area will be recognized for being a national leader for excellence and innovation in the delivery of healthcare, quality, and patient safety, and our organization can also be an employer of choice, providing a highly rewarding and enriching environment for our employees, physicians, and volunteers. (Fictitious vision statement but similar to those of many healthcare organizations.)

**Vision Two.** We are making cancer history. (Part of the vision statement from MD Anderson Cancer Center.)

- What advantages and disadvantages do you see in each of these vision statements?
- Which vision do you think will be better communicated? Why?

# REFERENCES

Harvard Business Review. 2013. *HBR's 10 Must Reads on Communication.* Cambridge, MA: Harvard Business School Press Books.

Kotter, J. P. 2012. *Leading Change.* Cambridge, MA: Harvard Business Review Press.

———. 2008. *A Sense of Urgency.* Cambridge, MA: Harvard Business School Press.

Kotter, J. P., H. Rathgeber, P. Mueller, and S. Johnson. 2006. *Our Iceberg Is Melting: Changing and Succeeding Under Any Conditions.* Cambridge, MA: Harvard Business School Press.

Lanham, R. 1999. *Revising Prose,* 4th ed. New York: Longman.

Tufte, E. 2003. *The Cognitive Style of PowerPoint.* Cheshire, CT: Graphics Press.

———. 2001. *The Visual Display of Quantitative Information.* Cheshire, CT: Graphics Press.

## CHAPTER FIVE

# Competency 5: Earning Trust And Loyalty

Don Wilson was nearing the end of his career and was starting to struggle with it. His tenure as the CEO of Academy Health, the large academic medical center in Barkley, began 15 years ago, during a time of plentiful resources. Wilson had practiced as a general surgeon with the academic medical center for decades before entering management. He carried considerable social capital throughout Academy Health; his wit, charm, and people skills had served him well throughout most of his tenure. Most important, early in his career as CEO, Wilson had been able to create and sustain highly compelling strategic visions. One of his strategies involved developing a strong affiliation with St. Nicholas Health System, which allowed him to greatly expand his teaching hospital footprint without incurring additional expenses. People were excited to work with him and follow him. Wilson's medical center had consistently experienced remarkable success. It recruited world-renowned physicians, grew a vast outreach program, and amassed significant cash reserves.

All of this was beginning to change. National policy changes were calling Academy Health's operating model into question, but Wilson's read on the future did not seem to be keeping pace. In public forums, he continued to reassure people that things were going well and getting better—a story the Barkley business papers regularly refuted and many of his senior executives quietly questioned. The staff of the hospital liked him and wanted to believe him, but they were finding it harder and harder to do so. In fact, the medical center had lost 10 percent of its market share, no longer had a top-ten transplant program, and had lost several leading clinical researchers. Financial results were also in question, with the organization needing to use cash

*(continued)*

*(continued from previous page)*

reserves to cover operating losses. Wilson had also started to become unapproachable and communicated less and less with his direct reports. The warm and close relationships he had with many of the leading physicians also started to deteriorate. Working with his office door closed much more than was typical, he also became isolated. The bottom line was that, despite his vision, Wilson had lost credibility with his followers.

As this vignette illustrates, having and articulating a vision is not enough to ensure successful development and implementation of that vision. A trust level with stakeholders must be established first, and maintained throughout any change process.

Success in communicating vision depends strongly on the receptivity of the audience. Receptivity, in turn, depends heavily on trust. This chapter is about developing, cultivating and, as necessary, repairing these relationships of trust.

## WHAT IS EARNING TRUST AND LOYALTY, AND WHY IS IT IMPORTANT?

People are naturally suspicious of those in leadership roles. The greater the distance between individuals and leaders, the more room for interpretation there is and the more likely the leaders may be mistrusted. *Earning Trust And Loyalty* is vital for highly effective leadership; in many ways, it is the glue that holds work groups and organizations together. Conversely, mistrust can create a tremendous sinkhole of time and energy on activities irrelevant to the organization's mission.

**Earning Trust And Loyalty** means you are a direct and truthful person, are willing to admit mistakes, are sincerely interested in the concerns and dreams of others, show empathy and a general orientation toward helping others, consistently follow promises with promised actions, maintain confidences and disclose information ethically and appropriately, and conduct work in open, transparent ways.

## WHEN HIGHLY EFFECTIVE LEADERS EARN TRUST AND LOYALTY

Given what we have noted about the natural tendency toward suspicion, leaders in some ways start with a burden of proof. However, leaders can easily rack up trustworthiness points by simply improving their accessibility to staff. The more that leaders are seen as real, authentic people who are available to and concerned for the problems of their staff and colleagues, the more difficult it will be to view them with suspicion. The following are ways in which exceptional leaders earn their staff's trust.

## Being Accessible

Trust development is facilitated when leaders are open, frank, and share information freely. They develop confidences with others and share their feelings—even their fears and concerns. The leaders whom people will trust the least are the ones who are cold and distant. Stepping out of the executive suite frequently will enhance trust.

## Fostering Openness

As one well-known CEO once said, "Trust develops over the long haul—there are no quick fixes." Trust begins as leaders and followers gain a sense that each other's actions are predictable. Trust then builds over time in cycles involving increasing familiarity and comfort with interpersonal risk taking. The evolution takes place from both sides of the relationship; leaders take some personal risks when they reveal themselves, and followers take risks when they rely on their leaders.

Exceptional leaders care about their staff and will try to minimize the risk for their followers. They will actively cultivate an environment of considerable psychological safety, in which people feel they can speak openly and honestly without fear of their comments coming back to haunt them. Leaders accomplish this not only by demonstrating themselves to be capable of openly receiving feedback but also by thanking their staff for showing the courage to put their concerns on the table.

## Being Authentic

Authenticity is a critical component of trust. Many senior leaders talk frequently about engaging the hearts and minds of employees and physicians. That ability requires that those individuals *first be connected* to the heart and mind of the leader. This is the ultimate "walking the talk." Leaders who do this best accept their own personal ability to grow and then live their values by connecting authentically to what they do in their work.

The relationship between care and ability is another aspect of being authentic. Highly effective leaders care about their followers, and the followers know that their leaders have the ability and capability to do what is needed. Trust involves leaders who fulfill their promises; they display what one might call a high "do/say ratio." Staff, physicians, and other stakeholders want to know their leaders are not only willing to do what they say they will but also are *capable* of doing it.

When exceptional leaders learn that they will be unable to keep a promise, they address it as proactively as possible and give people the heads-up right away. Whenever possible, reparations are made, even if the reparations need to be of a token nature. You can think of this as a symbolic gesture to convey that you take your promises seriously. Highly effective leaders know the worst response is to say nothing and hope the transgression goes unnoticed. It is most often noticed, and trust takes an extra hit in the process.

## Modeling Behavior

Breakthrough leaders demonstrate role modeling throughout all aspects of their workplace interactions. If there are sacrifices to be made, they will step up first. If there are rewards to be doled out, they will allow others to step forward first.

Willingness to chip in is another area that sends a strong, implicit message about the leader's character. By being willing to help out in times of stress or crisis and in handling tasks they normally would not do, leaders communicate their fundamental positive regard for the contributions their coworkers make to the workplace. The implicit message is, "I wouldn't ask you to do anything I wouldn't be willing to do myself."

Indeed, exceptional leaders are just as likely to chip in with the tasks their coworkers enjoy the least as they are to chip in where their contributions will be greatest.

## Turning Trust into Loyalty

Trust is best considered a necessary but not sufficient condition for loyalty. Trust becomes loyalty when followers experience the leader as supporting their own interests over a period of time. Exceptional leaders are capable of taking these individual interests and finding ways to bring them into alignment with the organization's goals. As in military parlance, the followers bind themselves to the course of action that is being taken.

# WHEN EARNING TRUST AND LOYALTY IS NOT ALL IT COULD BE

As we previously noted, most people are naturally wary of individuals in positions of authority. As such, no baseline of trust and loyalty is automatically granted with a particular leadership role. The opposite is usually more accurate: a person's baseline loyalty is to the role or the job rather than to the leader. Development of trust and loyalty will be impaired if a leader demonstrates any of the following.

## Being Unavailable

Some leaders are most comfortable staying in their offices. They may describe themselves as having an open-door policy but may send subtle signals that you had better have a good reason for interrupting them. Leaders who are described as difficult to approach usually have lower levels of trust from their staff.

Other leaders may engage their staff more regularly but still fail to convey a genuine concern about challenges they are facing. The difference between *having* and *showing* concern is important here: Most leaders have concern, but not all of them are adept at showing it. Some leaders find listening to their staff's complaints so discomforting that they feel compelled either to jump to an immediate fix or to push for a change of subject. While a change of subject has a more obvious effect, the fix approach also fails to convey a true sense of engagement; the unintended message staff may hear from the leader is, "How can I get this off my to-do list as quickly as possible?"

Still other leaders may show concern to their staff but will fail to go to bat for them as much as they should. A leader might tell staff, "I'll see what I can do" and then either not follow up or not circle back to staff to tell them what happened. In both cases, the result is the same: Staff will assume the leader did not care enough to do anything about their concerns.

## Lacking Follow-Through

Perhaps no more common barrier to trust building exists than a lack of follow-through. Lack of follow-through will often appear callous or even malicious, though this is rarely the intent. More often, the cause is an overwillingness to make promises without considering what it will take to make good on them. (In referring to trust-building, one exceptional leader once told us, "Great leaders find it very easy to say no, and very hard to say yes.") Other leaders simply have not mastered their organizational skills to the point where they can keep track of what they told people they would do for them.

Of course, we all face situations where we have agreed to do something only to find out later we cannot honor that promise. In general, people can forgive such transgressions, assuming they do not become regular patterns. However, people are much less forgiving of leaders who do not accept personal responsibility for failing to live up to their commitments.

## Assigning Credit or Blame to the Wrong Person

Leaders chip away at trust and loyalty whenever they assign credit or blame to the wrong individuals. Leaders often do this with no willful intention whatsoever; they may simply be in the habit of describing the work of their group by saying "I" and may forget to acknowledge the team's contributions when they are in the room. Conversely, in the heat of the moment of learning about a failure on the part of team members, some leaders may be quick to harshly note individual accountabilities rather than to take the time to fully understand why the problems occurred, or they may fail to understand and acknowledge their own role in the problems.

In the moment, any one of these oversights may seem relatively benign. Over time, however, people get the message that there is a less certain payoff (and, in the case of blame, a greater risk) to the efforts they put forth on that leader's behalf. Typically, they will adjust their efforts accordingly.

## Failing to Lead by Example

We define leading by example according to two fundamental behaviors: (1) modeling the approach to work and the workplace that you request of others and (2) being willing to lend one's efforts to the work responsibilities of others.

Over the years, people have begun to interpret the phrase *leading by example* as though it were a description of a particular leadership style. In our view, leading by example is not a style but a practice. Leading by example means that the behavior of leaders corresponds with their statements. For example, autocratic leaders can lead by example; they may be autocratic, but their behavior reliably reflects this style. In similar fashion, participative leaders can lead by example by being participative on a consistent basis. They key is predictability; others must be able to rely on you.

Leading by example is essential to highly effective leadership, regardless of the other aspects of the person's style. Indeed, in our review of leadership models, we were unable to identify any that appeared incompatible with leading by example.

Role modeling is fundamental not only to leadership but also to every facet of human relationships. We all are constantly attentive to the social cues of the people we interact with, and we are continuously modifying our behavior accordingly. If a person says one thing and does another, we are more likely to attend to what they did rather than what they said. (We will also be less likely to trust them in the future.) Leaders who do not remember this basic lesson in human nature will repeatedly undercut their effectiveness in building relationships of trust.

---

### When Earning Trust And Loyalty Is Not All It Could Be

Leaders who do not build trust and loyalty to their full potential may have fallen short as a result of any of the following behaviors:

- Being unavailable
  - Leaders are not available to staff when they are needed and appear unconcerned about staff's challenges.
  - Leaders are unwilling to go to bat for staff.
- Lacking follow-through
  - Leaders lose track of what was promised to others or make promises that cannot be delivered.
  - Leaders do not acknowledge these as failures on their part; others are blamed or the failures are not acknowledged at all.
- Assigning credit or blame to the wrong person
  - The contributions of team members are not acknowledged.
  - Personal responsibility for decisions and actions is avoided.
- Failing to lead by example
  - Others are held to standards that the leader does not demonstrate.
  - Leaders are unwilling to go first into uncharted waters or to chip in when help is needed.

---

## MISUSE AND OVERUSE: HOW EARNING TRUST AND LOYALTY CAN WORK AGAINST YOU

We have seen a number of instances where leaders have overemphasized trust and loyalty to the eventual detriment of better performance. When this happens, one of the following patterns is usually present.

## Communicating Too Directly

On the one hand, open and candid communication is essential to maximizing performance. Without such dialogue, performance problems cannot be discovered and addressed. On the other hand, we all have a core self-concept that we guard jealously; we can only handle so much truth about ourselves at once. Leaders who fail to understand this are at risk for overcommunicating about performance deficits, which results in an environment that can feel harsh and punitive, and is simply not enjoyable to work in.

Candor must be tempered with considerations about how feedback will be received by an individual or group. A simple but often overlooked tip is to deliver criticism in one-on-one dialogue rather than in a group context. Another suggestion is to address interpersonal conflict by first acknowledging the value that the working relationship holds for you.

## Discouraging Dissenting Opinions

In some cases, open communication may be viewed as a challenge to loyalty. For example, when substantial organizational change efforts are implemented, such a premium can be put on being on board that dissenting opinions are actively discouraged. In these cases, employees may learn to keep their concerns to themselves for fear of being viewed as disloyal.

In other cases, leaders may be so successful in their compelling communications that employees become overly faithful. Employees may view the leader's actions in purely emotional rather than rational terms, so much so that groupthink sets in and they start to distrust their own independent judgment. Speaking up starts to feel like a failure on their part, and they begin to follow the leader's directives blindly.

## Overemphasizing Loyalty

Some leaders may create a cult of personality around their roles such that loyalty to those leaders is viewed as superordinate to the mission that the leaders are employed to support. Leaders may place special emphasis on loyalty, holding it in higher regard than other elements of job performance that may be more central to the organization's mission. Sometimes this is done by creating an "us versus them" mentality within a given group. Not surprisingly, such an approach will often do more to grow the leader's power base than it will to improve the organization; in the long run, the approach is difficult to sustain at all.

A less insidious but still problematic shortcoming involves leaders who attempt to foster loyalty within their teams by devaluing other groups within the organization. For example, support departments sometimes fall into a pattern of externalizing service problems by blaming the customer. Leaders who fail to challenge (or who may even encourage) the view that other departments are inferior in any way (e.g., less talented, less professional) also indirectly create barriers to the development of useful cross-departmental working relationships as well as the resolution of challenges the departments may face in working with each other.

---

**Misuse and Overuse: How Earning Trust And Loyalty Can Work Against You**

The following can be symptoms of misuse or overuse of this competency:

- Communicating too directly
  - Frankness takes precedence over tact, diplomacy, and timing.
  - The leader fails to temper feedback.
- Discouraging dissenting opinions
  - Employees fear being viewed as disloyal and succumb to groupthink.
  - Critical thinking and dialogue are not actively encouraged.
  - Employees become overly faithful and begin to distrust their own judgment.
- Overemphasizing loyalty
  - Loyalty is overvalued in comparison to other elements of job performance.
  - Loyalty to a leader or team is valued above loyalty to the organization's mission.
  - There is a distrust of people outside the department, group, or inner circle.

---

## HOW TO BETTER EARN TRUST AND LOYALTY

### Finding Role Models

Although loyalty could be measured in many ways, one of the most straightforward is employee retention. Within your organization, who has the best record of retaining staff? Have any new leaders to your organization brought a number of people with them? A human resources executive will likely know the answers to these questions and thus may have the names of some good potential role models. Top performers on employee engagement surveys are another great source.

Also consider any specific leaders whom you have trusted greatly. These may be good people to reconnect with or good experiences to reflect on. What was it exactly about their behavior that inspired that level of trust? What specifically might you do that will help others trust you to that same extent? Reflect also on leaders who recovered well from commitments they couldn't honor—in particular, how they managed these situations and the relationships they affected.

## Additional Opportunities for Personal Development

Getting an accurate read on the trust and loyalty people have in you can be difficult. In most cases, the only way to get at this may be to ask people, directly or indirectly, for this feedback. The direct approach involves finding an opportunity to talk with staff one on one to ask them about their experiences. Here are some model questions you might use as a starting point, depending on the specific nature of your relationship with the person you are meeting with.

- It's important to me that I follow through on my commitments. I try hard to do this, but I'm probably not perfect. Can you recall any times when I may have missed the mark in the last year?
- I want you to feel that you can talk openly and candidly with me and that I will be respectful of what you tell me. How well would you say I have done in achieving that goal? Are there any situations you can remember in which you would have preferred that I handled things differently?
- I want to make sure that I am being an effective role model in my approach to our work. Of course, it's difficult for me to know how effectively I am coming across to others in that regard. Can you give me some feedback on how I have been as a role model—in particular, any areas in which I might improve?

A classic book on trust in leadership is Kouzes and Posner's (1993) *Credibility: How Leaders Gain and Lose It, Why People Demand It.* Chapter 2 of their book ("Credibility Makes a Difference") provides a compelling view of leadership from the follower's perspective. In Chapter 7 ("Serving a Purpose"), there is a useful section on losing and regaining credibility. Bill George, former CEO of Medtronic and Harvard Business professor, has written two books, *Authentic Leadership— Rediscovering the Secrets to Creating Lasting Value* (2004) and *True North: Discover Your Authentic Leadership* (2007), with the overall theme that people trust you when you are genuine and authentic, and that this authenticity is a hallmark of exceptional leaders. Finally, Dye's (2010) book *Leadership in Healthcare: Essential*

*Values and Skills* provides additional guidance on developing trust (Chapter 13, pages 151–69).

## SUMMARY

An exceptional leader's ability to develop and communicate vision is what gets others to follow them initially; the leader's ability to establish and maintain trust is what keeps them following through the most challenging times. For most followers, loyalty is slow to be established and quick to lose. Exceptional leaders develop the competency to know where risks to trust are most likely to be; they work actively to safeguard trust and to repair it when it's damaged.

### Consider This

Human resources VP Jim Batten was talking with Barbara Buczinski, VP of patient care services, about gaining trust with staff. Buczinski stated, "It really is all about being yourself. I find that I have to put in a lot of time and help people get to know who I am and what makes me tick. In doing so, I think I will gain their trust."

Batten replied, "How true. And yet so many leaders seem to orchestrate their actions and how they are seen. It is almost like a political campaign. You know that the people who are running for election are not really letting us see their true selves."

- Debate the two sides of this issue. Should leaders let their guard down and let followers see *everything*? Or should they be cautious in what is seen and what is known about them? In other words, are there circumstances in which some withholding of information or even manipulation may be best?

### Consider This

Jim Batten, vice president of human resources, and Elizabeth Parris, CEO, were talking one day about trust. Parris commented, "I just don't believe that you can measure trust. I know that people say you cannot manage what you do not measure, but trust is one of the concepts that I do not see a way to measure."

*(continued)*

*(continued from previous page)*

Batten replied, "Well, I think you can measure trust in two ways. The first is quite simple. You ask if there is a trust relationship—and ask for a yes or no answer. In an employee engagement survey, we often include the item 'I trust my supervisor.' I also think that you can measure those behaviors that come out of trusting relationships. Again, if we conduct an employee engagement survey, we might include items such as 'I trust what my supervisor tells me' or 'I can trust the information that I receive from senior management.'"

Parris commented, "I see what you mean. I only wish there was a deeper level of science to this topic."

- How might trust be measured? Use your Internet search skills to examine the concept of trust.

## REFERENCES

Dye, C. 2010. *Leadership in Healthcare: Essential Values and Skills*. Chicago: Health Administration Press.

George, B. 2007. *True North: Discover Your Authentic Leadership*. San Francisco: Jossey-Bass.

———. 2004. *Authentic Leadership—Rediscovering the Secrets to Creating Lasting Value*. San Francisco: Jossey-Bass.

Kouzes, J. M., and B. Z. Posner. 1993. *Credibility: How Leaders Gain and Lose It, Why People Demand It*. San Francisco: Jossey-Bass.

# Part III

# A REAL WAY WITH PEOPLE— THE THIRD CORNERSTONE

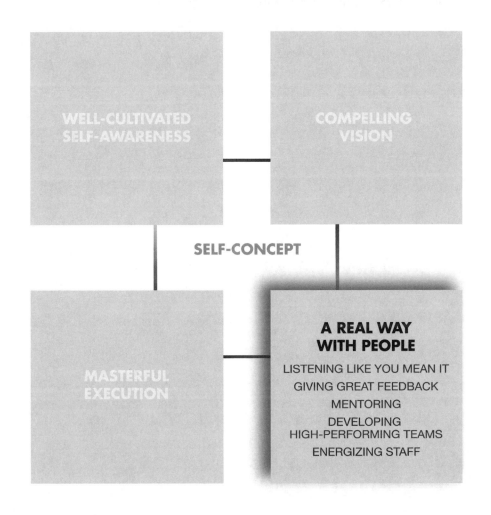

THE THIRD CORNERSTONE, A Real Way With People, involves the competencies most closely related to interpersonal effectiveness on a day-to-day basis. It includes competencies that build staff engagement ("Listening Like You Mean It" and "Energizing Staff") as well as their skills ("Giving Great Feedback," "Mentoring," and "Developing High-Performing Teams"). As Kaitlin Madden (2011) writes, "Relationship building is the most fundamental element of leadership. Establishing strong relationships with people enables them to trust and respect you, in turn giving them a reason to follow your lead."

Relational skills are the most important abilities in leadership.

*John C. Maxwell (2005)*

## CHAPTER SIX

# Competency 6: Listening Like You Mean It

Nancy Groves, the chief marketing and public relations executive for St. Nicholas, reviews her notes while she waits for Emily Gohara to come out of her office. She has been waiting for almost 20 minutes, but she does not mind too much; she knows Gohara has many other demands on her time, and she is grateful to be having the meeting at all. Groves has been under pressure to develop a comprehensive marketing communications program, and she needs Gohara's support for it.

Meanwhile, Gohara is meeting with her controller and the outside auditor. The news is not good: The cost overruns on several new projects will likely pull the health system into the red this month. Inpatient admissions were also down, and the losses in the employed practices were greater than budgeted. Emily will need to inform the board about these items later this week. In the best case scenario, she will hear a few "I told you so" comments. She would rather not think about the worst case scenario.

Gohara comes out of the meeting and sees Groves waiting. It has been a long day, but she does not want to put her off again. Groves comes in and excitedly begins outlining the ambitious marketing campaign. A less-seasoned executive, she jumps right to her ideas for splashy TV ads and a billboard campaign without first building her business case. In her mind, Gohara sees only another big sinkhole of cash opening up in front of her. She has already decided she will not support the initiative, but she lets Groves continue out of a mixture of courtesy and inertia. Her silence quickly turns to seething as Groves continues her image-driven presentation; Groves, thinking Gohara is growing impatient, picks up her pace. She

*(continued)*

*(continued from previous page)*

finishes his presentation with, "I'm getting the sense that the timing isn't right for this. Yes?"

"Yes," says Gohara, relieved that Groves arrived at the conclusion herself.

ALTHOUGH THIS VIGNETTE describes a specific dialogue between two leaders, the nature of the exchange is common in healthcare: different perspectives coming together awkwardly in an inadequately planned, poorly executed meeting. We can see the frustrations and disappointments on both sides, and we can probably relate to the experiences of one or both individuals.

Throughout the conversation each had opportunities to engage differently that would have increased learning, enhanced mutual understanding, and improved the outcomes. These opportunities were lost for lack of better listening skills.

## WHAT IS LISTENING LIKE YOU MEAN IT, AND WHY IS IT IMPORTANT?

*Listening Like You Mean It* distinguishes true active listening from all other forms. Many people like to think of themselves as good listeners, but we all know there is a difference between waiting for your turn to talk and really hearing what a person is trying to say to you. Listening, and demonstrating that you are listening, are skills that can be cultivated. As a leader, it is worth your while to do so; it will increase the trust people put in you, and it will enhance your ability to lead them effectively, especially during times of significant uncertainty and change.

**Listening Like You Mean It** means you maintain a calm, easy-to-approach demeanor; are seen by others as warm, gracious, and inviting; are patient, open minded, and willing to hear people out; see through the words that others express to the real meaning (i.e., cut to the heart of the issue); maintain formal and informal channels of communication; and build strong rapport over time.

Active listening improves a leader's effectiveness in several key ways. Perhaps foremost, the investment in listening can help you to better understand the goals, priorities, and perspectives of the people you work with. This understanding equips you to have more helpful and more meaningful dialogues about the work you do together, which in turn can foster deeper levels of interpersonal trust.

Listening also pays dividends in facilitating your role as a change agent. With a better mental map of your peers, direct reports, and superiors, you will have an easier time understanding how individuals relate to their work as well as how organizational changes can help and harm them. When you propose changes, you will have an easier time anticipating fears and concerns and addressing them proactively. This capacity for problem solving affords these leaders an easier time creating and sustaining high-energy organizations.

## WHEN HIGHLY EFFECTIVE LEADERS LISTEN LIKE THEY MEAN IT

Highly effective listeners grasp a great deal from a speaker's message. However, they also grasp a lot from the messenger. Exceptional leaders understand the motivations behind the message and value the speaker's unique perspective.

### Understanding the Message

Beyond the surface content, highly effective listeners will also understand the *why* behind the message—what it is about the speaker that has led to the statement, presentation, or request. They will hear the emotion or passion, and they will perceive the level of concurrence or disagreement in the ongoing dialogue.

In honing your listening skills, keep in mind that every message is crafted by a person who is trying to get a set of needs met—perhaps her own, the department's, or the patient's. These speakers are expressing needs and revealing something about themselves in the hope that the listener will better understand them.

### Valuing the Messenger

What if the message is one you disagree with? Effective listeners will still demonstrate they value and respect the thoughts, opinions, and ideas of speakers. In expressing disagreement, they will present the possibility that the speaker's perspective is valid and make the speaker feel heard. Rather than say the speaker is wrong, effective listeners will view the disagreement as a difference in opinion or perspective: something to be explored in such a way that both parties gain a better understanding of each other.

# WHEN LISTENING LIKE YOU MEAN IT IS NOT ALL IT COULD BE

Leaders often vary widely in their listening effectiveness depending on the circumstances at hand. The following are some of the ways listening can fall short of being effective, and why.

## Listening Inattentively

Inattentive listening can come from different causes. For example, some leaders inherently enjoy interacting with people throughout the day; others prefer working in solitude. Leaders with the latter tendency (sometimes called introverts) can be particularly vulnerable to problems with inattentive listening. They may send indirect messages that they would rather not be bothered, or they may appear impatient when people do seek them out.

Another type of inattentiveness can arise from failing to set up dependable communication channels. Leaders who do not set up regular meetings with their staff (or who routinely cancel them), who do not reliably respond to voicemails or e-mails, or who do so in ways that make it clear they did not take the time to fully read and understand the message, can create the same implicit (albeit unintended) message to others: Your communications are not that important to me.

The widespread availability of smart phones and other communications devices has made the problem of inattentive listening much worse. Some leaders find it difficult to set these devices aside when they are with others. In doing so, the message people get is that their needs are not worthy of the leader's full attention.

## Hearing Selectively

*Hearing selectively* refers to the tendency to tune out information the listener disagrees with. We all have this tendency to some degree. In fact, some measure of this tendency is probably functional; leaders do not have the luxury to stop in their tracks every time someone disagrees with them to work through the disagreement on the spot. However, this tendency also works against us in two important ways: (1) it can prevent us from being able to take in useful new information, and (2) it can prevent us from taking appropriate time to acknowledge divergent opinions as having some legitimacy. Taking the time to understand *why* a staff member does not agree with you can be an important part of building and maintaining the working relationship. People are usually less upset by being disagreed with than by being dismissed.

## Being Impatient

Impatience is a pervasive barrier to effective listening. Almost all leaders in health-care work under extraordinary time pressures, and listening can sometimes feel like an unproductive use of time. The ever-present temptation is to find ways to "listen more efficiently." Efficiency can be virtuous, but it is often pursued in the wrong ways.

In situations of acute time pressure, effective leaders will tell speakers how much time they have available so the speaker can manage that time wisely. The less effective approach is to try to reach a speaker's conclusion before the speaker is finished talking. This might involve finishing the speaker's sentences or, even worse, assuming you have the "gist" of it and simply cutting the comments off and taking your own turn. In some uncomfortable dialogues, or those in which the leader cannot productively respond in the moment, she may even change the subject without warning.

## Being Emotionally Volatile

Emotional volatility goes by a number of names: "short fuse" and "hair trigger" come to mind. It represents a basic failure of listening in that the leader's emotions are overtaking her ability to objectively hear what the speaker is saying.

The consequences of being volatile can be severe. At a minimum, it decreases people's trust to the point that they may actively hide bad news from the leader to avoid being scolded. At worst, it will cause people to withdraw from the working relationship altogether.

## Providing Time Rather Than Attention

Some leaders master the art of "listening without listening." They do all the right things to ensure their peers and direct reports have adequate access to them, and they do not rush people or cut them off. But the listening is ultimately a façade; silence is provided for politeness' sake, with all mental energy wandering elsewhere or formulating rebuttals rather than considering what the speaker has to say.

**When Listening Like You Mean It Is Not All It Could Be**

In leadership roles, listening can fall short for any of the following reasons:

- Listening inattentively
  - Direct reports are given the impression that their communications are bothersome intrusions.
  - Few or no routine settings are provided in which listening can take place.
  - The listener is attending to his devices rather than giving others his full attention.
- Hearing selectively
  - Divergent opinions are ignored.
  - Time is spent formulating counterarguments rather than listening.
- Being impatient
  - The listener jumps to erroneous conclusions and cuts people off prematurely.
  - The listener changes the subject rather than concluding it.
- Being emotionally volatile
  - The listener reacts with visible anger, disgust, or disappointment.
- Providing time rather than attention
  - The listener is effective at taking turns but substitutes silence for genuine listening.
  - The listener focuses on formulating rebuttals rather than on taking in what is being said.

## MISUSE AND OVERUSE: HOW LISTENING LIKE YOU MEAN IT CAN WORK AGAINST YOU

It is difficult to conceive of leaders getting themselves into trouble for listening too much. Indeed, former US President Calvin Coolidge was famously quoted as saying, "No man ever listened himself out of a job." In our experience, if leaders are viewed as overdoing it on listening, it is usually because they are engaging in one or more of the following.

### Taking Too Passive an Approach to Listening

Some leaders do not actively manage the listening process enough. An example that most of us can relate to is a meeting in which the conveners provide too little structure, allowing individuals to monopolize the dialogue and/or direction of the process. Leaders who are overly focused on avoiding disagreements may also fall into this passive pattern. Such leaders may allow others to air their views but will offer no public challenge to them, even if they hold conflicting views. In the end, these leaders will do what they originally intended regardless of the input they received, leaving those around them with puzzling mixed messages.

### Using Listening to Avoid Action

When leaders are faced with difficult decisions, listening can sometimes become a stall tactic. Collecting stakeholder opinions is an important step in many difficult decisions, but it is also a step that can be overdone. If you have ever been involved in a never-ending survey process (i.e., a survey that leads only to the conclusion that additional surveys are needed), then you are familiar with this dynamic.

**Misuse and Overuse: How Listening Like You Mean It Can Work Against You**

Listening is rarely viewed as an overused skill. However, perceived overuse is usually a symptom of one of the following problems:

- Taking too passive an approach to listening
  - People are allowed to take the podium without regard to time or efficiency, particularly in meetings.
  - Points of disagreement are not expressed or explored.
- Using listening to avoid action
  - The leader listens too acutely when a decision must be made (and may not listen enough at other times).
  - The need for additional input, opinions, and discussion is used as an excuse to delay taking needed action.

## HOW TO IMPROVE AT LISTENING LIKE YOU MEAN IT

### Finding Role Models

Where do you find good listening mentors—people who can help you hone your listening skills? One approach is to look for people who are professionally trained in listening, such as counselors and therapists. However, while these professionals may be terrific listeners, they may not be as effective at balancing listening against the other time constraints managers regularly face. People who are likely to be good at balancing attention against time pressures include executives in human resources management, marketing and communications, community relations, and philanthropy and development. These roles often involve the need to carefully attend to agendas that may or may not be compelling or personally relevant, and that they may personally disagree with, and often under considerable associated time constraints.

## Additional Opportunities for Personal Development

We recommend to all readers, no matter how seasoned, that they seriously consider working on their listening skills. Our experiences and those of others who provided input for this chapter suggest most of us have more room for improvement in this area than we may believe and will see more payoff from improving these skills than we may realize.

As with many of the skills discussed in this book, the best approach to improving your listening skills involves a small amount of education and large amounts of practice with feedback.

### Seek Feedback

Feedback is essential for rapidly developing listening skills. None of us are consistently effective or ineffective listeners. Depending on factors such as the topic, audience, and time of day, we may do better or worse. Also, because ineffective listening is never our goal, it is hard for us to initially pinpoint when we are listening more or less effectively.

Trusted colleagues can be very helpful in this regard. If someone says to you that he feels like you do not listen to him, ask him to help you identify specific examples. Start by looking backward, but then ask also for his help in moving forward.

If a colleague agrees to give you this feedback, pledge to yourself to work extra hard to capitalize on it. If he has genuinely caught you at a listening low point, thank him for his help. If there are other circumstances that you feel prevent you from taking the time to listen, take the time to at least explain these to him: "I see how you didn't have the chance to finish describing your concerns. Unfortunately, your description was putting the meeting agenda behind, and I felt we needed to move on in order to give the other attendees' items adequate attention."

### Develop a Clear, Active Listening Posture

Displaying active listening involves more than silence—body language also plays a substantial role. If you have ever seen someone roll their eyes after hearing something, you have a sense of body language associated with poor listening; others include checking the time, sighing loudly, looking away, or looking at a mobile device. Body language associated with effective listening includes facing the person who is talking, sitting up straight, maintaining good eye contact, nodding in acknowledgment, or reacting to key points the speaker is making, and taking notes.

### Summarize

Summarizing is a particularly useful technique in situations where your own opinions disagree strongly with someone else's. In these situations, challenge yourself to summarize the speaker's comments back to him: "If I understand you correctly, you think you are more qualified for this project than I am because you have prior experience with their department's VP, and I do not. Is that correct?" Challenging yourself to take this step serves several goals. First, and most importantly, it forces you to listen to what the other person is saying at a deep enough level that you are able to represent it back. Second, it helps you decentralize from your own perspective long enough to gain a glimpse of the speaker's perspective. Third, if you still disagree with the speaker, he is less likely to believe it is because of a lack of understanding.

Summarizing can also be helpful in less heated dialogues. You can think of them as checkpoints that provide you with the opportunity to be sure you and others are still proceeding with a common understanding.

### Ask Probing Questions

Probing questions are follow-up questions designed to elicit a deeper understanding of a subject. One style of probing—requesting specifics—focuses on clarifying the message: "You said employees are upset about this change. How many employees are we talking about? How upset are they? Do they want to resign? Do they feel betrayed or merely inconvenienced? How would you compare their reactions to the premium increase (or other example)—stronger, weaker, or about the same?" A time-based probe can help clarify whether an issue seems to be a flare-up versus an ongoing trend that may be building steam: "How long has this been going on? How consistent has the trend been?"

### Monitor Your Emotions

Strong emotional reactions can quickly derail good listening practices. This can play out in several common ways.

- *Shock*. You might react with shock when you find news or ideas difficult to believe. In these situations, it is important to guard against the tendency to dismiss the information or to react too strongly to it. A good way to handle this reaction is to put it on the table in a nonthreatening way: "This comes as a surprise to me. I may need a few minutes to take this in."

- *Anger or disgust.* Reactions of anger and disgust can happen when you believe someone is thinking or acting incompetently or in a way that is not in the best interests of your department or organization. In these situations, there is often a need to convey an important learning point or to foster a better understanding between yourself and the other person; however, this need may be competing with an instinctive feeling of being threatened and a commensurate reflex to strike back. A more moderate, and typically more effective approach, is to use questions instead of attacks: "Can you help me understand how this would positively affect our department?" or "How would this resolve the problem?"

- *Elation.* We can all come up with examples of when our negative feelings toward someone else interfered with our ability to attend to their communication. The same is true about positive emotions. If you find yourself getting overly excited about an idea, you may find your own internal thought process triggering at such a fast pace that you lose the thread of what is being said.

- *Boredom.* A reaction of boredom most often comes from judging the communication to be irrelevant, unimportant, or not delivered efficiently (e.g., unnecessary or overly elaborated details). Sometimes, particularly if the speaker is anxious, both the communicator and the listener will be well served by some assistance in framing the message: "Let me see if I understand the heart of the matter here." Other times, however, the meta-communication the speaker may need to hear is, "I want to feel you value my opinion and will take the time to hear me out." In these cases, the challenge is more internal: Find the anchors to keep yourself appropriately and mentally engaged in the dialogue. Balancing your focus between the content of the message and the personal meaning behind the content can be a useful approach.

### Schedule Time with Smaller Groups

Large group meetings, while effective for many purposes, do limit participants' comfort in disclosing points of disagreement. You can facilitate the flow of feedback by finding occasions to meet with smaller groups of staff. Smaller group meetings also allow you more opportunities to build individual relationships of trust.

### Find Opportunities for One-on-One Conversation

Just as small group meetings can enhance feedback over large groups, so too can one-on-one communication over small groups. Think for a moment about the people you count on most in your organization. Do you have opportunities to meet with each of them individually on a periodic basis? If you do not, you should consider finding these opportunities from time to time. Meeting with someone individually gives you a unique opportunity to reflect not just on the work you do with this person but also on the quality of your working relationship.

### Visit the Troops

Highly effective listening involves going beyond a "my door is open" policy to a "let me knock on your door" policy. While staff usually appreciate responsiveness of their leaders to concerns they express, there are few actions that demonstrate concern more concretely than planned and purposeful visits to worksites.

### Mind Your Limits

Despite your best efforts, at times you will not be as effective a listener as you would like to be. Fatigue can be a barrier to effective listening—for example, at the end of a hard day or week, or after difficult conversations or disappointments. Another key barrier is role conflict—someone coming to talk with you about a concern at a time when your mind is firmly pointed elsewhere, or when you need to be preparing for your next meeting.

How you handle those situations depends partly on your ability to overcome your fatigue or distraction, as well as how fatigued you are. On the one hand, concentration, like other skills, improves with practice—if you push yourself to listen through your fatigue, you will continue to get better at it. For this reason, taking the time to listen can sometimes be better than putting a conversation off.

However, there may be times when you are too tired or distracted to have any hope of listening effectively. In these situations, efforts to overcome your fatigue will not pay off, and diplomatically delaying the conversation is the better move. You can do so by first acknowledging the importance of what the speaker has to say before requesting a postponement: "I can see this is an important concern to you, and it deserves my full attention. However, right now I won't be able to give you the attention you deserve. I will be too distracted by this meeting coming up later today. I'd like to find a time when I can give you my undivided attention on this matter. What does tomorrow morning look like for you?"

Given how important listening is to interpersonal effectiveness, there are also numerous books that provide an in-depth treatment on this topic. Two excellent reference books that go into greater detail on listening practices are physician Mark Goulston's (2009) book, *Just Listen: Discover the Secret to Getting Through to Absolutely Anyone* and Edgar Schein's (2013) *Humble Inquiry*.

# SUMMARY

There are few more powerful tools for building staff engagement than giving employees the sense that their leader hears and understands where they are coming from. Exceptional leaders are particularly adept at sending this message to the people they work with through their body language and actions in the context of listening.

## Consider This

By the age of 45, Dr. Linda McKenzie was the top surgeon in Barkley. She graduated from a top-tier med school, did a world-class residency, and had been selected for one of the top fellowship programs in the country. A quick learner with a great work ethic, she was always at the top of her class. She also relished taking the toughest cases with the toughest attendings. She had a rapid climb up in surgery and ultimately became vice chair of the department. If you asked people what Dr. McKenzie was like, their inevitable response was "brilliant." It wasn't just pure intellectual ability. Dr. McKenzie was a skilled surgeon, could flex in tough situations, and also had the knack for cutting through all the information and honing in on just the right approach to some of the more complicated surgeries. She was a leader in the classic mode: assertive, decisive, and highly motivated. It wasn't a question of whether she'd become the first female chair in history at St. Nicholas; it was just a question of when. Yet the more position power and influence she gained within the organization, the more assertive (some would say aggressive) she became. It reached the point where, according to a number of the residents and nurses, "Linda was no longer able to manage her own arrogance." Her conversations became lectures and her team meetings became a forum for her to belittle others. Interestingly, this is not to say that Dr. McKenzie changed in any way. In fact, she became too intensely like herself. She still was one of the top surgeons in the country and her referral base was continuing to increase. But with all this success, there was a cost. She stopped reading social cues. She didn't get it when her team sat there quietly as she droned on. Slowly but surely, Dr. McKenzie lost trust and respect among her team and some of her peers. She became so convinced of the rightness of her perspective that she turned others off. People no longer sought her out or wanted to work with her. Not only did she start to lose some valued and experienced nurses but residents started to avoid her and latched on to other surgeons. She started to become embroiled in petty

*(continued)*

*(continued from previous page)*

feuds with other top executives over direction and resources. Each argument ended with others saying something along the lines of, "You seem to be certain that you're right," and Dr. McKenzie responding, "That's because I am."

She was shocked, therefore, when the chair and Dr. James, the CMO, met with her to tell her she was no longer in line to become chair. In fact, Dr. James suggested that she consider another hospital in which to practice. It wasn't as if she'd never received a signal; the chair and other senior surgeons had talked to her about the problems her overly confident stances were causing. Dr. McKenzie claimed that she thought they were just coaching suggestions; she assumed her considerable contributions to the medical center made her invulnerable.

- What impact do factors such as expertise, power, or stature have on the ability to listen?
- How would you coach Dr. McKenzie to make needed changes in her style?

## Consider This

Review the material presented in the Introduction to this book about Self Concept (pages xxx-xxxiv). What are the various ways in which a negative self-concept can harm listening? What are the various ways in which a positive self-concept can help listening?

## REFERENCES

Goulston, M. 2009. *Just Listen: Discover the Secret to Getting Through to Absolutely Anyone.* New York: AMACOM.

Madden, K. 2011. "What Makes a Good Leader at Work?" Published October 1. www.careerbuilder.com/Article/CB-2062-Leadership-Management-What-makes-a-good-leader-at-work/.

Maxwell, J. C. 2005. *Developing the Leaders Around You: How to Help Others Reach Their Full Potential.* Nashville, TN: Thomas Nelson.

Schein, E. 2013. *Humble Inquiry: The Gentle Art of Asking Instead of Telling.* New York: Berrett-Koehler.

# Competency 7: Giving Great Feedback

It is 11:20 a.m., and the nursing leadership team is waiting for Stockard Smith to arrive for their weekly meeting. Smith took over the nursing leadership group a few months ago, having been made interim VP of patient care services and chief nursing officer (CNO) following the unexpected illness of the prior CNO, Barbara Buczinski. It is unlikely that Buczinski will return, but St. Nicholas is not planning to start a search for a replacement yet.

Several years earlier, Buczinski and the nursing leadership team had established a strict promptness rule for their meetings, resulting in these meetings starting and ending on time. The leadership team cannot get started without Smith, so the other members use the time however they can—checking back with their units, reading e-mails, or pulling other members out into the hall for conversations. When Smith finally arrives, she looks quite frustrated. She stomps in, sits down, lets out a loud sigh, and says, "OK, let's go."

Clearly, it is taking all of Smith's energy and patience to learn this new role and still cover her other responsibilities, but she is doing a reasonably good job with it overall. The rest of the team knows this, and so no one wants to say anything to her about coming in late.

The meeting continues but time runs out before the last agenda item is addressed—an action item from Rick Kramer, the director of surgery, concerning the new quality program that he wants to kick off in the coming week. Patti Juniper, the nurse manager in the emergency department, recognizes there will not be adequate time to discuss such a critical matter and suggests tabling it until the following week. Kramer, who is now furious, turns to Smith and says, "This is ridiculous. I want you to remember we

*(continued)*

*(continued from previous page)*

did not get to this because you couldn't be bothered to come to this meeting when you were supposed to. If we have any sentinel events this week, I hope you feel personally responsible!" (For the record, Smith's response to Kramer's outburst was even less measured.)

THIS VIGNETTE ILLUSTRATES a number of exchanges in which the delivery of feedback was not nearly as effective as it could have been. Smith's failure to come to this meeting on time is inconveniencing the nursing team and impairing the productivity of the group. However, the team has been reluctant to address the problem with Smith, at least in part because of their sympathy regarding the challenges she is facing in her new role. In fact, Smith had not been part of the group years earlier when the punctuality rule had been set, and no one had told her about it. When one of the team told her about the rule a couple of days after the meeting, it was said in a caustic manner. Smith did not internalize the matter, and once more the problem led instead to an unproductive counterattack.

However, this team can hardly be described as dysfunctional. They are productively moving the hospital forward, and over time Smith is successfully learning her role. However, with better approaches to giving and receiving feedback, Smith would most likely adapt to her role more rapidly, and the team's decision-making processes could become even more efficient.

## WHAT IS GIVING GREAT FEEDBACK, AND WHY IS IT IMPORTANT?

*Giving Great Feedback* can be most concisely defined as the effective delivery of information about performance. For our purposes, we are referring to interpersonal feedback, which is feedback that is transmitted from one individual to another, and by "effective," we mean that the feedback provides both the pathway to and motivation for higher levels of performance.

**Giving Great Feedback** means you set clear expectations, bring important issues to the table in a way that helps others hear them, show an openness to facing difficult topics and sources of conflict, deal with problems and difficult people directly and frankly, provide timely criticism when needed, and provide feedback messages that are clear and unambiguous.

If you have ever taken a human resources or leadership skills course, you have probably learned some rules of thumb about delivering feedback. Some useful and familiar guidelines are to give feedback as soon as possible after the event, to describe objectively what you observed, to suggest a specific course of improvement, and to end on a positive note. All are good tips for feedback, but they are less helpful in thinking through context: the relationship in which the feedback takes place.

Interpersonal feedback messages *always* occur within the context of a relationship. We choose whom we want to give feedback to and when, based on our prior knowledge of the person and how we think he will react. The receiver's reactions, in turn, will be governed by his self-concept and expectations about us. If leaders fail to recognize and draw on these relationship factors in setting up the feedback they provide, the feedback may still work—but it will usually lack the power and utility that it might otherwise have had.

## WHEN HIGHLY EFFECTIVE LEADERS GIVE GREAT FEEDBACK

Leaders with exceptional feedback skills are better at attending to contextual factors. Whenever they are considering providing feedback, they will routinely start with an examination of their own motives by working through a process like the following.

### Defining the Real Issue

Highly effective leaders know that the core issue and the appropriate target for feedback may not be the same as the presenting problem. Too often, busy leaders are not explicit when defining problems. They may dance around the meaning or fail to use precise words. In contrast, highly effective leaders zero-in on the real issues and focus on the true concerns by using more specific and direct language. For example, let us return to our vignette, in which Kramer told Smith off for being late. Had Kramer taken more time to think about why he was upset, he may have gained a better understanding of the complex context in which these events were occurring. For instance, perhaps he resented being last on the agenda, which he may have taken to mean that Smith did not care as much as she should about rolling out the new quality program. Or perhaps Kramer had bitten his tongue about Smith's lateness in a few prior meetings, and he was now reacting to the pattern more so than to the individual event. In failing to recognize either of these possibilities, Kramer's feedback is probably far out of proportion to Smith's immediate offense.

## Evaluating the Issue

Exceptional leaders ask themselves if the *return* on addressing the issue is likely to be higher than the *cost* of addressing it. One leadership development book featured a section entitled "Feedback: Give It Often." We disagree with this premise. Highly effective leaders assess the value or return for addressing an issue before discussing it with the individual involved. They often let matters drop because of their lack of importance in the overall scheme of things. As one wise CEO once told us, "You have to determine if the juice is worth the squeeze." This evaluation is less straightforward than it may initially sound because of how subjective it can be.

In the vignette, some of the nursing team members might have chosen to let the lateness issue fester because of their own fears that pushing Smith too hard might cause her to make their lives more difficult. Some may have wondered whether she might be given the role permanently since no search had been started. Some actually may not have cared that much about the meetings starting late. If these were indeed legitimate concerns, it may make sense to have allowed passive support to win out over constructive feedback. (In reality, the likelihood that Smith would resign over this feedback is probably quite low.) Conversely, leaders can sometimes view behaviors as more problematic than they really are. Such a leader might address both a misspelling in an e-mail and a careless patient safety violation with the same harsh tone.

## Setting the Stage

Once a decision has been made to deliver feedback, highly effective leaders will make sure they give adequate thought to setting the stage for delivery. If the climate of the discussion is safe, there is a much better chance the receivers will be able to accept the feedback without getting overly defensive, and then productively use it to improve their performance. If the leader is particularly upset, she may decide to delay the conversation rather than risk failing to deliver the feedback in a measured way.

## Balancing Feedback

Highly effective leaders make sure the people they work with receive an appropriate balance of positive and constructive feedback. Some go as far as to mentally pencil in a small chunk of time during the workday to develop and deliver positive feedback to their staff. People appreciate receiving positive feedback, which is perhaps reason enough to pursue this practice, but positive feedback also serves another purpose: It helps staff have greater resilience to the constructive feedback they receive. If a person feels like he is generally doing okay, he will usually feel less of a sense of personal vulnerability when he receives constructive feedback and will be more able to hear and productively use the feedback he receives.

## WHEN GIVING FEEDBACK IS NOT ALL IT COULD BE

Problems with the delivery of feedback can stem from motivation or from the need for better methods. Here are some common reasons feedback can fall short.

### Being Reluctant to Critique

Some leaders view critiques as punitive measures and will avoid them until they feel they have no other option. This bias can be compounded by the recognition that many healthcare staff work extraordinarily long hours and under considerable pressure—what kind of monster would needlessly add pain and suffering to the mix?

In reality, critiques are needlessly painful only if they are delivered poorly or too infrequently. The latter is a lesson often associated with the wait-and-see approach (i.e., holding off on giving feedback in the hope that the performance problem will self-correct). When the problem persists, a leader may not only be on the hook for confronting the problem but also for explaining the sudden interest in a problem that has persisted for so long.

### Hesitating to Praise

At least as frequent a problem is hesitating to praise. Leadership roles tend to focus on fixing things, and it is easy to forget to bring attention to what is going well. Most leaders will acknowledge extraordinary performance, but the praise is frequently expected in such situations and so has less emotional impact on the recipient than receiving praise for more routine successes.

### Structuring Feedback Poorly

Feedback can also fall short if it is not well delivered. If the focus is too narrow, it may not be taken seriously by the recipient; if too wide, it can come across as an attack. If it is too vague, the recipient will leave feeling puzzled, or worse, helpless, about how to improve. Another important consideration is the amount of emotional force behind the message. As the saying goes, "Leaders cast long shadows"; what feels like a slap on the wrist in delivery can come across like a bullet in receipt. Conversely, leaders who find themselves in great pain when delivering critiques may overly sugarcoat a message and then feel frustrated when the recipient does not seem concerned about the problem performance.

## Giving Judgmental Feedback

Sometimes focusing a feedback message just on behavior is difficult, particularly when the behavior is either part of an ongoing pattern or seems so common-sense that it is hard to believe the person would not know better. However, going any deeper than the observed behavior can quickly render a feedback message less effective; it creates a level of defensiveness that becomes a potent distraction from the feedback itself. Exceptional leaders are certain to describe the situation factually, refrain from expressing opinions or value judgments, and focus on the actual behavior and consequences (i.e., keep focused on the *what* of the situation); on the other hand, less effective leaders tend to create a debate about the *why*.

---

**When Giving Feedback Is Not All It Could Be**

In leadership roles, listening can fall short for any of the following reasons:

- Being reluctant to critique
  - Critiques are viewed as punishments and not delivered until someone "really deserves it."
  - There is a bias toward the wait-and-see approach for performance problems.
- Hesitating to praise
  - Leaders fail to provide positive feedback as a routine part of work.
  - Leaders are reluctant to deliver praise except in unusual circumstances.
- Structuring feedback poorly
  - Critiques are too focused on the individual rather than on the problem behavior or performance.
  - Feedback is delivered with too much or too little force or is too vague.
- Giving judgmental feedback
  - Critiques are focused on the *why* of the behavior rather than the *what*.
  - The feedback recipient's defensiveness distracts him from hearing the feedback.

---

# MISUSE AND OVERUSE: HOW GIVING FEEDBACK CAN WORK AGAINST YOU

For leaders who are described as giving too much feedback, often one or more of the following patterns is present.

### Giving Feedback Too Quickly

Some leaders have too much of a hair trigger when it comes to delivering feedback. Leaders who do not stop to ask themselves, "Is this an issue worth addressing?" fall into this category. In a similar vein, leaders can be too quick to jump to action after hearing about problems from a third party. If leaders do not first inquire about the "offender's" side of the story, they set themselves up for a lot of defensiveness from the feedback receiver.

### Delivering Feedback Too Frequently

It is possible to give feedback too often. This can happen when leaders have unrealistic expectations about performance improvement. Some skills and behaviors, particularly the more complex and ingrained ones, take more effort to change than we may realize. The best antidote is to set mutually agreed-on goals and timelines for performance improvement and to limit constructive feedback on the focal issue during the interim periods. For some leaders, the sense of loss of control associated with backing off for a while is too much to bear. If this is the case, the leader's need for excessive control may be the real issue that should be addressed.

### Giving Imbalanced Feedback

Sometimes when leaders are described as providing too much feedback, the real concern is an imbalance between positive and negative feedback. Positive feedback often helps staff to be more resilient to critiques; conversely, if they are not receiving positive feedback, the critiques sting all the more. Of course, the imbalance can also happen on the positive side; some leaders indeed overuse the "strokes" to the point where they come across as perfunctory or gratuitous. If this is the case, it may suggest some general problems with the leader's ability to read her direct reports.

> **Misuse and Overuse: How Giving Feedback Can Work Against You**
>
> Leaders are sometimes described as giving too much feedback. Typically, that will look like one or more of the following:
>
> - Giving feedback too quickly
>   - Attention is drawn toward unimportant performance problems.
>   - Feedback is based on hearsay alone.
> - Delivering feedback too frequently
>   - The leader has unrealistic expectations about the velocity of performance improvement.
>   - Feedback is used as an excuse for micromanagement.
> - Giving imbalanced feedback
>   - Constructive feedback is overemphasized and positive feedback is lacking.
>   - Critiques are delivered with too strong a tone or emphasis.

## HOW TO IMPROVE AT GIVING FEEDBACK

### Finding Role Models

Because so much of the most transformative feedback happens one on one rather than in public, identifying good mentors can be difficult. The best approach may be peer nomination: Ask people who they would identify as particularly good at providing feedback. Another approach is to ask a senior human resources executive for his recommendations; he should have both the mental framework for such an assessment and the broad knowledge of leaders in your organization from which to make informed suggestions.

### Additional Opportunities for Personal Development

The best way to learn more skillful feedback approaches is to practice and to get feedback yourself. Often the best place to start is with someone you already feel you have a solid working relationship with. Enlist this person's help in crafting effective feedback dialogues. You might also ask them to role play with you any particularly challenging feedback sessions you need to have with others.

For managing the delivery of constructive feedback in the context of your relationship with others, we recommend two books, *Crucial Conversations* (2011) and *Crucial Accountability* (2013), by Kerry Patterson and colleagues. These books provide structured approaches to some of the trickiest kinds of conversations, as well as walk-through examples from which to learn.

If you think you need to provide more positive feedback in addition to your critiques, try setting aside five minutes per day for this specific task. You might add this as a note in your PDA or on your calendar. At first this exercise may feel forced, but over time you should find it easier to identify positive things your staff have done and find opportunities to express your appreciation.

## SUMMARY

Delivering feedback in the right ways and at the right times makes a big difference in improving performance over time, which is why leaders who are particularly skillful at it tend to be viewed as exceptional. Practicing feedback using structured approaches may feel awkward at first, but it can quickly improve your effectiveness at this crucial skill. Finding the right balance of positive and constructive feedback, as well as when to deliver each, takes even more practice, but its mastery can be even more rewarding in terms of overall effectiveness.

### Consider This

According to research done by *The Journal of Consumer Research* and reported in the *New York Times* (Tugend 2013), "As people gain expertise, feedback serves a different purpose. When people are just beginning a venture, they may not have much confidence, and they need encouragement. But experts' commitment 'is more secure than novices, and their focus is on their progress.'"

This means that giving feedback is far more complex than many leaders think.

- Based on your own experiences receiving feedback, do you agree with this description?
- What are some memorable examples of feedback you've gotten, positive or otherwise?

### Consider This

Revisit the opening vignette at the beginning of this chapter in which the new chief nursing officer, Stockard Smith, dealt with the feedback situation.

- If you were Smith's executive coach and you had been sitting in this meeting, how would you counsel her? What other underlying problems might be going on in this scenario?

# REFERENCES

Patterson, K., J. Grenny, and R. McMillan. 2013. *Crucial Accountability: Tools for Resolving Violated Expectations, Broken Commitments, and Bad Behavior,* 2nd ed. New York: McGraw-Hill.

Patterson, K., J. Grenny, R. McMillan, and A. Switzler. 2011. *Crucial Conversations: Tools for Talking When Stakes Are High,* 2nd ed. New York: McGraw-Hill.

Tugend, A. 2013. "You've Been Doing a Fantastic Job. Just One Thing. . . ." Published April 5. www.nytimes.com/2013/04/06/your-money/how-to-give-effective-feedback-both-positive-and-negative.html?pagewanted=all&_r=0.

## CHAPTER EIGHT

# Competency 8: Mentoring

Mary Moses was new to the role of chief administrative officer (CAO) for the Suburban West Hospital in the St. Nicholas Health System, but she knew full well the challenges she would face in the coming years. Suburban West had been incredibly successful, most of her department heads had long tenures in their roles, and many had become complacent during the long stretch of sound financial times. Some were good with their people skills but not as strong with their financial ones. Others had great budgeting and revenue management skills but failed to invest appropriately in developing their leaders, often to the detriment of their staff. There also were a host of individual challenges: one department head always hired from the outside and never promoted staff, another was not able to retain people, and still another seemed to spend more time in grievance hearings than he did in meetings with his staff.

The previous CAO had been more of a public figure—a visible presence in the community but scarcely available to his direct reports. He took a laissez-faire approach to his staff: "Perform well, and I'll leave you alone; perform poorly, and you're out of here." Moses knew she would need to take a different approach.

IN THIS VIGNETTE, Moses has concluded that a number of her new direct reports are underperforming at least in part because of a variety of skills deficits. Moses has the advantage of being a newcomer; she has no old expectations to renegotiate or habits to unlearn. She also faces a number of challenges: She may not have the time to meet regularly with everyone who could benefit from additional mentoring, and she may herself not have some of the skills her direct reports need to learn. Beyond these basic concerns are a host of more subtle considerations: How strongly should she push people? Whom should she give slack to? How long should she give it to them? And how can she ensure mentoring is deepening, rather than weakening, her working relationships? Exceptional leaders can often be distinguished from good leaders according to how well they recognize and address these questions.

## WHAT IS MENTORING, AND WHY IS IT IMPORTANT?

In this context, we define *Mentoring* as all of the actions leaders take to support the long-term growth of their direct reports. Of particular concern are the career goals these individuals have. Do staff members feel they are moving ahead in their jobs and careers? Are they able to increase their responsibilities, either in their present positions or in expanded positions? Do they feel free to openly explore opportunities in other areas of the organization or even outside the organization?

> **Mentoring** means you invest the time to understand the career aspirations of your direct reports, work with direct reports to create engaging mentoring plans, support staff in developing their skills, support career development in a nonpossessive way (e.g., support staff moving up and out as necessary for their advancement), find stretch assignments and other delegation opportunities that support skill development, and model professional development by advancing your own skills.

We focus particular attention on the relationship and the goals rather than the means because the activities will differ depending on both the direct report's needs and the leader's capabilities to personally address those needs.

Returning to the vignette, Moses's framing of her direct reports' performance problems leads her to conclude that a focus on mentoring is necessary. However, in our experience, providing mentoring is a staple for all exceptional leaders, not just for those in situations that so obviously need this attention. This is true regardless of the overall performance level of the department or organization; in fact, mentoring is more likely to happen in teams that are already high performing—it may be how they got that way in the first place.

## WHEN HIGHLY EFFECTIVE LEADERS MENTOR

In our experience, the following qualities are hallmarks of mentorship in highly effective leaders.

## Taking a Comprehensive Approach

The most effective mentors focus attention on *all* of their direct reports. Returning to the vignette that started this chapter, Moses recognizes the need to mentor this group of leaders but appears to be in some danger of falling into a common trap: focusing on the "problem children." The departments in the red are likely to be the ones she herself will be under scrutiny for, so a bias toward attending to these groups is understandable. But what about the departments that are performing well? In addition to fixing problems, a highly effective mentor will also seek ways to make good departments great and to turn great departments into world-class operations.

## Building on Relationships

For you to be a highly effective mentor, your direct reports must come to believe their individual interests will be well served by listening to you. The first step in this process is developing a clear understanding of your direct reports' interests and goals. Mentoring will be most powerful when it focuses on individuals' needs as well as the needs of the organization.

Highly effective leaders meet routinely with each of their direct reports to explore career goals. Once they gain an understanding of how individuals would like to see their jobs, careers, and areas of accountability over the next several years, they can then discuss areas for improvement, simultaneously looking for ways by which these improvements can also serve the individual's goals.

## Emphasizing Clear, Consistent Follow-Through

As our emphasis on the relationship suggests, high-performance mentoring requires a long-term commitment to the process. In addition to starting strong, exceptional leaders robustly build the mentoring process into their workflow. Many of these leaders have regularly scheduled meetings with their direct reports to focus on mentoring; the meetings may not be frequent, but they are held consistently.

## Participating in Staff Development

In a high-performance approach to staff development, the leader will actively work with staff on skill development. For example, if an off-site educational program is called for, the leader will have some involvement in helping the staff select an appropriate one. When the program is complete, the leader will find time to discuss what was learned with the staff. Forethought will also be given to opportunities in which the new skills could be practiced on the job, so that these opportunities for application and reinforcement of learning are taken.

### Encouraging Growth

Exceptional leaders recognize that higher-performing staff are also more employable elsewhere, but that does not stop them from developing their staff. They understand that the value of being viewed as a powerful mentor exceeds the cost of replacing staff when they outgrow their roles. How can this be? Consider the references coming from previous employees. A job with a strong mentor is described as a valuable learning opportunity—one that helped them prepare for the even better position they now hold. A job with a weak mentor is described as a dead end—one that the former staff members "escaped" to accept their new position.

## WHEN MENTORING IS NOT ALL IT COULD BE

In several common situations, mentoring is not as effective as it might be. The ones we have encountered most frequently include the following.

### Undervaluing Mentoring

If leaders do not view mentoring as an essential part of their roles, chances are it will fall by the wayside. For some leaders, the driving force is left too much in the hands of their staff; they mentor the direct reports who make a point of demanding it, and they are far less attentive to everyone else. The typical result is that the vocal high performers continue to develop their skills, the quiet high performers get frustrated about being passed over, the low performers are ignored until they become serious problems, and the B players never get any better. Some leaders do not even make the initial investment in learning their staff's career goals—or, if they do, they fail to internalize them or at least write them down somewhere accessible.

Another way mentoring can fall short is if leaders view mentorship as about supporting training rather than about the relationship. We see this in leaders whose automatic reactions to performance improvement needs are to send staff to an off-site conference, workshop, or class. While these approaches can be very helpful in improving knowledge, they usually do little to develop skills and even less to ensure that skills transfer successfully to the staff's workplace.

## Undervaluing Staff Development

Some leaders take a more fatalistic "you either have it or you don't" view of skill development. These leaders may not have well-developed abilities to track performance improvement over time, or they may take an overly informal approach to this process. As a result, these leaders tend to think performance levels are more static than they really are.

For some leaders, this tendency shows up as a bias toward replacing people rather than mentoring them. In senior-level positions in particular, many organizations show a bias toward hiring outside talent rather than developing it from within.

## Being Too Possessive

Some leaders are overly possessive of their staff. These leaders may actively avoid mentoring staff out of fear that they will outgrow their positions and leave. Other leaders create barriers to their staff working on some developmental projects out of a fear that other departments will poach them. They may mistakenly believe that if they don't develop their team members, those members are more likely to stay put; in reality, their higher-performing staff in particular are more likely to leave if they don't feel that they are developing in their job.

## Lacking Mentoring Skills

Mentoring can also fall short because of a lack of skills in the mentoring process itself. Some of these skills relate back to our discussion of feedback in Chapter 7. Others relate to the leader's ability to recognize the naturally occurring opportunities for direct reports to develop skills.

Let us consider the latter point in more depth. Think about how you decide who does what in your own department or organization. Chances are, most work goes to the individuals you believe will do the best job, either because of past experiences or relevant skills. Indeed, our industry's approach to human resources is essentially designed to ensure that this is the case. With this in mind, it becomes easier to see how mentoring involves some unnatural approaches to work, at least on occasion. From the mentoring perspective, the question is not always "Who will be most *successful* at this task?" but rather "Who stands to *learn* the most from working on this task?"

## MISUSE AND OVERUSE: HOW MENTORING CAN WORK AGAINST YOU

If mentoring was taken to the logical extreme, we would no longer have a place of productive work. Instead, we would have a place of education. Of course, an organization can stay in business only if the economic contributions of staff exceed the size of their paychecks, so the learning aspects of a job can be taken only so far. The ideal balance finds the sweet spot that maximizes both organizational performance and individual development. But when this balance either leans too far toward mentoring or is not well executed, the following pitfalls might be seen.

### Miscommunicating Developmental Decisions

Developing highly effective mentoring relationships requires regular communication, and sometimes not just with the individual receiving the mentoring. Direct reports are often quick to view learning opportunities, even developmental assignments, as being doled out unfairly. Developmental decisions often make good sense, but their rationale is often not well communicated to staff. In these situations, sometimes the best remedy is simply to better articulate how these decisions are made, attending in particular to any skill development needs that a staff member may feel are not receiving appropriate attention. However, leaders should also avoid dismissing concerns about fairness too quickly; uneven attention to developmental needs is a reality in many leadership teams.

## Overemphasizing Star Performers

When it comes to mentoring, star performers represent a mixed blessing. On the positive side, they tend to yield the highest returns on the time their leaders invest in them. But for this reason, they also tend to receive more of the leaders' focus to the detriment of other staff. Some leaders have a misguided notion that focusing attention on the stars will inspire the now-jealous B players to try harder so they can also reap their rewards. While this tactic may work for some direct reports, others may become less motivated, and their efforts may actually decline.

## Failing to Address Performance Problems

The one area in which some leaders face a genuine risk of overdoing mentoring is in working with staff who are chronically underperforming in their roles. In some cases, the cost of mentoring someone into a role definitely exceeds the return. Sometimes the problem stems from escalating commitment: Leaders may start to view the considerable time they spent building the staff's skills as a sunk cost that they need to recoup; giving up on a staff member's ability to learn a given skill set begins to feel like a personal failure on the leader's part. For other leaders, the problem may stem from discomfort in addressing performance problems and/or transitioning poor performers out of roles that are beyond their capabilities. A leader who overidentifies with her staff or who overpersonalizes her role is at particular risk for this vulnerability.

---

### Misuse and Overuse: How Mentoring Others Can Work Against You

A focus on mentoring can work against a leader in any of the following ways:

- Miscommunicating developmental decisions
  - The rationale for mentoring is not well explained or justified to the team.
  - The leader is viewed as playing favorites.

*(continued)*

*(continued from previous page)*

- Overemphasizing star performers
  - Development opportunities are too imbalanced toward star performers.
  - Other team members receive little or no mentoring and become demoralized.
- Failing to address performance problems
  - People are given too much time and too many opportunities to improve.
  - The leader fails to recognize when termination or redeployment should be pursued.

## HOW TO BECOME A BETTER MENTOR

### Finding Role Models

We have described mentoring as a complex, multifaceted aspect of the leader–direct report relationship; as such, the most appropriate people to help you develop your skills will depend on the specific skills for which you have the greatest need.

In the broadest sense, the best mentors are leaders who have promoted many direct reports. If your organization has a more formal mentoring program in place (e.g., a program that matches junior managers with senior leaders who are not typically in their direct chain of command), strong mentors may have been identified already by whoever is in charge of the program. You might check first with that person for his recommendations.

For help in developing your skills in the mechanics of the mentoring process, leaders who are also educators are often good people to seek out. Examples include department chairs who regularly work with post-docs (particularly if their placement record is strong), executives who work with administrative fellows (assuming the placements are favorably evaluated), or senior clinicians who have reputations as outstanding preceptors. Mentoring is also the stock and trade of many executive coaches; in addition to using these skills in their practices, they are often called on to teach leaders these skills.

### Additional Opportunities for Personal Development

Mentoring is a skill that develops only with practice. If you are not currently in a role where you have direct reports, find analogous opportunities to work with others on developing their skills. Agreeing to work with an intern (paid or unpaid) can be an excellent way to practice and to learn; leadership roles in community organizations can also provide valuable mentoring experience. If your organization has a mentoring program in place, inquire about participating.

Attending local professional education events, especially the shorter lunch or dinner sessions, can also provide mentoring opportunities. These events are frequently attended by younger professionals who are actively seeking professional and career growth. Visiting with them over dinner or during receptions can provide good opportunities to provide counsel and respond to questions.

We encourage you to visit the American College of Healthcare Executives (ACHE) website (www.ache.org) to review its information on mentoring. ACHE supports a virtual mentorship program called the Leadership Mentoring Network. Using its resources or accessing the ACHE local chapter and/or the area ACHE Regent can provide a great opportunity to find a mentor or to become one yourself.

Although coaching is the kind of skill that can be difficult to convey in a book, several good books are available. One is *Coaching for Performance* by John Whitmore (2002). In this technique-focused book, Whitmore adapts sports coaching approaches for use in the workplace.

If you want to work on your relationships with poor performers, we recommend *Crucial Confrontations* by Patterson and colleagues (2005). This text argues compellingly for addressing performance problems proactively and provides approaches to doing so for the most challenging of circumstances.

## SUMMARY

In recent years, the considerable pressure to do more with less has translated into fewer managers doing the same or more work. It also means a larger number of entry-level leaders must compete for the mentoring attention of fewer senior-level leaders. Thus investing in the development of more junior staff through mentoring relationships is all the more difficult but all the more valuable. If you find yourself questioning the time you spend mentoring, we encourage you to spend a few minutes reflecting on the help you received as an early careerist, and let these memories energize you about paying it forward.

### Consider This

Develop a business case for a mentoring program in an organization. Answer the following questions:

1. How will mentoring be defined? How will the program's success be measured?

*(continued)*

*(continued from previous page)*

2. Should mentors come from inside the organization or from the outside?
3. Will mentors be paid any stipend or bonus for their service?
4. Should any individual be eligible to receive mentorship?
5. What training should mentors receive?
6. How often should mentors meet with their mentees?
7. Should the mentoring program be separate from the organizational succession plan?
8. Should the mentorship program be run by human resources or by an outside expert? Should an individual be empowered to intervene if problems surface between mentors and mentees?
9. Should the mentoring program be built into the leadership development program? The high-potential leadership program?

## Consider This

Elizabeth Parris held this conversation with human resources VP Jim Batten: "Jim, we really do not have much of a succession plan for either our senior leaders or our middle managers. I think this is a serious weakness. At minimum, I think we need to start setting our potential leaders up with some senior-level mentoring. Come to the senior team meeting in the next couple of months and present a plan of action that the group can discuss."

Assume you are the consultant helping Batten develop this plan. Identify some key action steps and milestones for implementing a mentoring program at St. Nicholas, as well as any issues or concerns to keep in mind along the way. (For more resources on succession planning, see the additional readings for this chapter on page 268.)

## REFERENCES

Patterson, K., J. Grenny, R. McMillan, and A. Switzler. 2005. *Crucial Confrontations: Tools for Resolving Broken Promises, Violated Expectations, and Bad Behavior.* New York: McGraw-Hill.

Whitmore, J. 2002. *Coaching for Performance: Growing People, Performance, and Purpose.* London: Nicholas Brealey Publishing.

## CHAPTER NINE

# Competency 9: Developing High-Performing Teams

Mary Moses's promotion to the role of chief administrative officer (CAO) at Suburban West Hospital gave her the opportunity to restructure their leadership team to better serve the organization's needs. With considerable support from the system, she successfully brought in several new middle managers, all of whom were top-flight and all hired within the space of about 18 months. She now felt the team was set to pursue the system's ambitious goals to expand the organization's square footage, build two additional outpatient sites tied to Suburban West, open an urgent care center, build a new outpatient surgery center, open a new seven-story multispecialty building, and prepare to serve as one of the system's models for the future.

Her tenor changed just a few short weeks later, when the new team began experiencing serious problems. Each new initiative seemed to end in a bitter and divisive conflict. Initiatives involving major changes to the status quo inevitably pitted the veteran members of the leadership group against the "new kids on the block," and new program initiatives turned new members against each other. Discussions about strategic direction started to seem like multinational arms talks. As a result, everything was taking much longer than anyone thought it should.

Moses wanted to support the autonomy of the individual group members, but she was increasingly fed up with their constant, unproductive conflicts. She set aside time at the end of the next meeting to express her disappointments. She made an impassioned speech about how the vision for Suburban West, one that they had all subscribed to, was now at risk because the group could not figure out how to work together.

The speech did serve to quiet the meetings down. The conflicts raged on, but now they took place in the halls rather than the meeting room. As

*(continued)*

(continued from previous page)
more time passed, Moses sensed the members of the team becoming increasingly stiff and formal toward each other. She tried another pass at raising the issue for discussion. When she did, everyone agreed the group was not making progress as rapidly as they needed to; still, no one seemed to have any good ideas for how they could get any better at working together.

THE SITUATION DESCRIBED in this vignette highlights a number of dynamics commonly found in senior leadership groups. All members of the group have an understanding of the organization's goals—the greater good—which conflict from time to time with their individual roles as advocates for their department's goals. This tension leads to the formation of allegiances, both opportunistic and long-term, as leaders find common interests and opportunities to "horse trade" to marshal support. The dimension of history also exists, in which memorable and regrettable transactions from the past become filters through which the contemporary challenges these leaders grapple with are viewed.

We can encapsulate this enormous complexity in the deceptively simple concept of teamwork.

## WHAT IS DEVELOPING HIGH-PERFORMING TEAMS, AND WHY IS IT IMPORTANT?

For our purposes, we define a *team* as a group of leaders having both of the following characteristics: (1) they have goals in common, and (2) their success in achieving those goals involves their interdependence.

This definition is purposely broad. Most senior leadership groups do not technically fit a narrow definition of teams and still manage to perform quite well. Our

**Developing High-Performing Teams** means you select executives who will be strong team players, actively support the concept of teaming, develop open discourse and encourage healthy debate on important issues, create compelling reasons and incentives for team members to work together, effectively set limits on the political activity that takes place outside the team framework, celebrate successes together as a unit, and commiserate as a group over disappointments.

focus is not on forming the optimal team per se, but rather on pursuing the greatest productivity with the team in whatever form it takes and on examining how exceptional leaders use their teams to their maximum potential.

## WHEN HIGHLY EFFECTIVE LEADERS DEVELOP TEAMS

In the development of a highly effective team, five critical activities stand out:

1.  Get the best people for team roles.
2.  Develop their orientation toward a common vision and collective goals.
3.  Develop trust among team members (as discussed in Chapter 5).
4.  Develop cohesiveness between team members.
5.  Help team members productively work through the inevitable conflicts that come with group interaction.

With these five activities in mind, we have observed that the following competencies often distinguish the highest performing leaders.

### Getting the Best People for Team Roles

In his book *Good to Great*, Jim Collins (2001) describes the fundamental importance of "getting the right people on the bus." To accomplish this goal, leaders must have a solid focus on hiring team-oriented performers. Strong leaders are deliberative in their hiring practices; they seek to develop a thorough and critical understanding of candidates and are willing to take the time necessary to make the best possible hiring decisions.

What distinguishes exceptional leaders in this category? In great part they emphasize hiring as a continuous process. These leaders think regularly about talent acquisition and management, and they will routinely try to identify talent before they need it. They make a point of developing robust networks of professional contacts, and they keep those networks active throughout their careers. They keep in touch with the high performers they have worked with in the past; those people become their prime recruiting sources in the future. If these contacts are not themselves interested in a given role, they will still be available to provide high-value references. These leaders also make sure to monitor the succession planning processes going on inside their organizations, keeping an eye out for those with high potential whom they may need in the future.

## Building a Sense of "We"

In senior leadership teams in particular, collective goals are a tricky business. On one hand, leaders need to establish them and ensure they are pursued; on the other, these goals need to be balanced against the need for individual accountability. Additionally, the natural tension between supporting the executive team and advocating for one's own staff must be balanced thoughtfully.

The best leaders recognize these tensions and will find effective ways to help the group maintain an optimal balance. Tools that can be highly effective in improving a team emphasis include team goal setting and team-based incentive compensation; a balanced scorecard can also help ensure that the team goals do not overpower individual accountabilities.

## Developing Cohesiveness

Attending to team effectiveness also means attending to the cohesiveness of the team. Techniques that can help to build team cohesiveness include the following:

- *Increasing the frequency of interaction.* The more teams interact, both formally and informally and both on and off the job, the more opportunities members have to know each other as people and the more cohesive they can become.
- *Providing opportunities to discuss group goals, and how they can be best achieved.* Providing incentive compensation goals that are tied to group efforts can also help focus the team toward greater cohesiveness.
- *Developing a healthy sense of competition against other teams.* To the extent that individuals can be rallied around a common "enemy," even if that enemy exists mostly in fun, cohesiveness is likely to increase.

## Working Through Conflicts

Every team has conflicts. Carson Dye (2010) wrote in *Leadership in Healthcare: Essential Values and Skills* that many healthcare CEOs try to stifle conflict among their senior teams. Exceptional leaders, in contrast, learn to expect conflict and will lead their teams to develop rules of engagement that guide them in their debates and deliberations.

To minimize harm in conflict, highly effective leaders work hard to do the following:

- ensure there is fairness in resource allocation among team members,
- minimize the growth of smaller intragroup cliques (often by keeping the group size small in the first place),
- keep personal reactions out of the bounds of the conflict,
- ensure team members have minimal role ambiguity, and
- ensure team discussions take place within the confines of the team.

## WHEN DEVELOPING HIGH-PERFORMING TEAMS IS NOT ALL IT COULD BE

Team development falls short in a number of ways. The most common are outlined as follows.

### Using the Team for the Wrong Reasons

If teams are used for the wrong reasons, they will not yield the benefits normally attributed to teamwork. Leaders may fail to use the power of the many and may not see the value that can come from group discussion and problem solving. Instead, they may use teams solely for show-and-tell–type meetings, where group members merely report on their individual activities. Another less effective approach is to use teams as congregations, with an expectation that members rally unquestioningly around the leader's decisions rather than providing healthy skepticism and skillful contribution.

### Maintaining Too Much Control

Teams will not reach their full potential if leaders are unwilling to cede enough control to allow members the chance to weigh in on issues and ask questions. Some leaders place too much emphasis on ensuring that meetings proceed smoothly and without debate. Without these critical opportunities for input and dialogue, decisions are inevitably less thought through and tend to have less overall buy-in from the team.

### Overemphasizing Individual Roles

One of the greatest barriers to fully developing teams is viewing team members more as individual contributors and less as team contributors. If leaders place primary emphasis on achievements that are individually oriented, then team members will respond in kind. This can also happen when there is little setting of team goals or incentive for achieving these goals. Superior teams are constantly focused on both team development and on team performance.

## Underemphasizing Team Development

Although most senior leaders have had at least some exposure to team-building efforts, too often the approach is event-driven; rarely does it involve methodically implementing lessons learned into the regular team meeting settings. Although team-building exercises can be informative, they will not build a team for you or even improve team performance.[1] These types of interventions are helpful only to the extent that they are woven meaningfully into an effective, ongoing commitment to team development.

If teams have no routine way to discuss processes and decisions, they will have little chance to grow and develop as a group.

## Treating Others Unequally

For teams to work effectively, the team needs to perceive a level playing field for all members. Maintaining equitable treatment requires active work on the part of the leader; a natural tendency often exists to create an in-group/out-group within the team, particularly when leaders work more closely with some members than with others. Power imbalances within the team can also be a source of conflict; if they are allowed to continue unchallenged, they can create significant barriers to smooth team functioning.

---

**When Developing High-Performing Teams Is Not All It Could Be**

Team development can fall short for any of the following reasons:

- Using the team for the wrong reasons
  - Team meetings are only "show and tell."
  - Team members are expected to confirm support rather than provide healthy skepticism.
- Maintaining too much control
  - Meetings do not allow creative input on ideas and problem solutions.

*(continued)*

---

*(continued from previous page)*

- – Disagreement and conflict are not allowed to surface.
- Overemphasizing individual roles
  - – Staff are regarded as individual contributors.
  - – There is too little setting of team goals or incentive for achieving team goals.
- Underemphasizing team development
  - – Team building is too event-driven (e.g., too much reliance on Myers-Briggs assessments or other facilitated team-building exercises).
  - – No regular forum exists in which team processes can be discussed.
- Treating others unequally
  - – The tendency exists to create an in-group/out-group within the team.
  - – Some staff receive clear preferential treatment without clear justification.
  - – Power imbalances within the team are allowed to continue unchallenged.

## MISUSE AND OVERUSE: HOW DEVELOPING TEAMS CAN WORK AGAINST YOU

While many executive groups can benefit from a more team-oriented approach, the risk of misuse and overuse also exists. This risk can show up as any of the following problems.

### Using Teams to Avoid Decision Making

The team approach can be misused to avoid making decisions or to avoid accountability for them. For example, a decision that would be best handled unilaterally by the CEO may instead be discussed for weeks on end. Team protocols can also evolve a rigidity that ends up precluding timely decision making. We have seen team structures limit themselves by historical policy; a fast decision might be avoided for no better reason than overemphasizing protocol or simply thinking it feels too rushed.

### Creating a "Country Club" Team

A particularly dysfunctional example of team overuse involves the attempt to create a "country club" environment—one in which security and comfort of team members become the primary objectives. While the working environment should not be uncomfortable, too much stability creates a stale culture. Highly effective teams, in contrast, will frequently challenge the status quo and will always be on the lookout for how they might improve.

## Overemphasizing the Need to Keep the Peace

Placing too much emphasis on teams can discourage healthy tension and disagreements that arise over different points of view. To keep the peace, less effective leaders may actively discourage healthy competition among team members. They will try to place too much attention on treating everyone the same rather than acknowledging diversity in efforts, ideas, and abilities. Conflicts often present opportunities for improvement; avoiding conflicts rather than addressing them just to maintain harmony will significantly impair team performance over time.

## Overemphasizing the Team

Sometimes leaders act as though the team is everything. Their constant references to the team take precedence over ensuring both individual accountability and a clear understanding of roles within the team. A lack of individual accountability often becomes a barrier to addressing individual performance problems and is thus another source of productivity loss.

---

### Misuse and Overuse: How Developing Teams Can Work Against You

- Using teams to avoid decision making
  - Situations that call for individual leadership are overdiscussed.
  - Decisions are extended unnecessarily because of protocol.
- Creating a "country club" team
  - Team member happiness is overvalued.
  - Security and stability are overemphasized.
- Overemphasizing the need to keep the peace
  - Healthy competition among team members is actively discouraged.
  - Too much attention is paid to treating everyone the same rather than acknowledging diversity in efforts and abilities.
- Overemphasizing the team
  - The team lacks individual accountabilities and clear roles.

---

# GETTING BETTER AT DEVELOPING HIGH-PERFORMING TEAMS

Most of us do not enter our professional careers with a refined set of team development skills. Team leadership, like teams themselves, evolves to higher levels of performance through a combination of skill development, practice, and open, candid dialogue about opportunities for improvement.

### Finding Role Models

Role models for high-performing team development are best found by joining and participating in a number of teams and task forces. Many organizations use temporary task forces to address problems and tackle projects. Participating in these can provide many opportunities to learn both the helpful and harmful approaches to team development.

Many operations executives are adept at forming and sustaining effective teams. They often need to accomplish multiple actions by pulling together a diverse group of contributors. Medical services corps leaders who run the hospitals and clinics for our armed forces also tend to be talented in developing and using teams.

Joining boards or other outside groups in the community can provide opportunities to study effective team performance. Participation in church or synagogue leadership teams can give you insights, in particular, into managing volunteers and using persuasion in team management.

### Additional Opportunities for Personal Development

There are many team development books on the market. Some of the better ones are listed at the end of this chapter. Many of these books take a theoretical or mechanical approach, which can make for difficult reading. A noteworthy exception is Patrick Lencioni's (2002) highly readable *The Five Dysfunctions of a Team*. Lencioni also suggests, as we do, that trust is a critical foundation for superior team performance.

## SUMMARY

The work of healthcare leaders is becoming increasingly team-based. We anticipate this trend will continue and quite possibly escalate as our emphasis on population health and value-based care increases in the coming years. When formidable time pressure to move through an agenda exists, carving out the time to reflect on team process and work on improving it can be particularly difficult. But in our experience with exceptional leaders, that time is very well spent.

## Consider This

Many organizations use team-building exercises and programs, often done at a retreat away from the workplace. Some of these exercises can be quite controversial because they may violate team members' dignity or privacy. Activities that involve physical activities or athletic games may create discomfort for some. Peer pressure and feeling the need to conform often cause hard feelings. Some individuals feel that team-building exercises have little relation to what they do in their jobs the other 364 days of the year.

- Identify at least three approaches to team building, and weigh each against the others in terms of how relevant and useful you think they would be for use by a specific team.
- Interview one or more friends or colleagues about their experiences with team-building exercises. Ask for their honest opinions about how helpful the exercises were and in what ways.

## Consider This

Building teams presents several complex challenges. The first is that many teams are brought together solely on the basis of functional skills (CEO, COO, CFO, CNO, and so on). These individuals play these formal technical roles because of their expertise and position title. Because of this, the impact that the personality plays in individuals playing informal roles (e.g., persons who function as idea generator, the conscience, the devil's advocate, the caretaker, the comedian, and so on) is often overlooked. Moreover, the role that individual values play in team functioning presents a complex set of dynamics. Finally, there is no universally recognized way to measure team effectiveness.

- Research the effect of individual factors (e.g., values, personality, diversity) on team effectiveness. What seems to make the biggest differences?
- Develop several methods to improve team effectiveness through a deeper understanding of individual factors.

## NOTE

1. A meta-analytic review concerning the effects of team-building interventions on performance, the largest ever published, concluded that team building tends to make teams feel like they are accomplishing more, while in reality they are accomplishing the same amount or less. See Salas, E., D. Rozell, B. Mullen, and J. E. Driskell. 1999. "The Effect of Team Building on Performance: An Integration." *Small Group Research* 30: 309–29.

## REFERENCES

Collins, J. 2001. *Good to Great: Why Some Companies Make the Leap…and Others Don't*. New York: Harper Business.

Dye, C. 2010. *Leadership in Healthcare: Essential Values and Skills*. Chicago: Health Administration Press.

Lencioni, P. 2002. *The Five Dysfunctions of a Team: A Leadership Fable*. San Francisco: Jossey-Bass.

## CHAPTER TEN

# Competency 10: Energizing Staff

After another disappointing drop in patient satisfaction scores, Barbara Buczinski decided she needed to back off from driving her improvement initiatives to spend some time learning how other hospitals were getting it right. Her organization's patient satisfaction survey vendor offered to put her in touch with a particularly high-performing health system in another market similar to hers. During her flight there, she found herself thinking of all the ways this other organization must differ from hers; for starters, they probably did not have the same labor shortages or union headaches. Certainly, they could not have the same financial pressures. Most likely they were serving a more affluent population, too.

But what she saw in the other organization nearly made her jaw drop.

The health system she visited was actually far worse off than hers in many ways. Their pay structure was below market, their facilities were much older than hers, and the payer mix was even more challenging than what St. Nicholas worked with. Yet the clinical staff seemed quite cheerful, the customer service scripts were followed consistently, and the patients clearly felt they were well cared for.

At the end of the day, Buczinski had a meeting with Marcia Lahey, the vice president of quality at the health system she was visiting. Buczinski only had one question: "How on earth do you do it?" Lahey's answer seemed incredibly straightforward: The team worked together to find meaningful goals, they communicated progress pervasively and consistently, and they used both success and failure to drive more progress. Lahey was quick to add their department indeed had many of the same challenges Buczinski described, but the group had become good at keeping their individual needs separate from the group's goals.

THIS VIGNETTE CONTRASTS two hospitals in terms of the energy level of their staff. Although staff motivation may not explain all the differences in performance outcomes, it could very well be playing a central, albeit indirect, role. By ensuring that staff maintain a positive outlook on their work, Lahey is also increasing the likelihood that they would be willing to try new approaches, give people the benefit of the doubt, and weather disappointments.

In Cornerstone 2, we examine how leaders can most effectively communicate their vision to get people's buy-in excitement about their participation. We also mentioned the importance of ongoing communication, and how challenging this can be to pull off consistently. In this chapter, we expand on this theme, looking at how exceptional leaders pursue not just commitment but *high-energy commitment* from the people they count on. Developing and sustaining a high-energy workplace may indeed be one of the most difficult tasks healthcare leaders are charged with. Success in this area often very clearly differentiates the truly great leaders from the good leaders.

## WHAT IS ENERGIZING STAFF, AND WHY IS IT IMPORTANT?

We characterize *Energizing Staff* as the activities leaders pursue to heighten levels of motivation in the people they work with. Motivation, in turn, can be defined as the amount of effort an individual wants to put into a particular initiative. In healthcare, energizing staff often involves helping people stay in touch with the service orientation that brought them to the field in the first place as well as helping them see how their efforts are paying off in the service of others.

**Energizing Staff** means you set a personal example of good work ethic and motivation; talk and act enthusiastically and optimistically about the future; enjoy rising to new challenges; take on your work with energy, passion, and drive to finish successfully; help others recognize the importance of their work and find it enjoyable; and have a goal-oriented, ambitious, and determined working style that others find infectious.

Leaders have more of an effect on staff motivation than they may realize; it is therefore an area that separates high-performing leaders from average performers, and the highest performers from the merely good ones. Indeed, the extent to which leaders inspire their staff has well-documented positive effects on job performance (Lowe, Kroeck, and Sivasubramaniam 1996).

# WHEN HIGHLY EFFECTIVE LEADERS ENERGIZE STAFF

The most energizing leaders have usually mastered the following aspects of the process.

## Understanding Individual Goals and Priorities

Exceptional leaders thoughtfully tailor their approaches to differences in individual needs. They know that what motivates one individual can be meaningless or even demotivating to another. A common example is public recognition; some individuals enjoy being singled out and publicly acknowledged for their accomplishments, while others shun the spotlight and feel embarrassed or ashamed if it is thrust on them. Another example relates to the relative value of extra-role experiences—the opportunity to present about a successful change initiative during a professional association's evening meeting may be much more rewarding for a single, career-minded up-and-comer than for a seasoned, family-minded manager.

## Celebrating and Sharing Successes

Highly effective leaders work to ensure that both individuals and the teams supporting them are appropriately acknowledged for their accomplishments. They capitalize on the energy that flows naturally from successes by mining it and spreading it around.

In the abstract, this point may seem obvious; in reality, this rarely happens anywhere near as often as it could, for a host of reasons. For one, health administration tends to involve constant, unexpected change; the emergency of the afternoon rapidly draws attention away from the success of the morning. For another, the managerial role tends to frame accomplishments as basic expectations of the job; it becomes very easy to view these accomplishments as just what you are paid to do. Strong leaders resist this temptation and work to ensure that recognition and celebration are an ongoing part of the workplace.

## Having a Sense of Humor

Given the business of healthcare, the risk of becoming—and remaining—gravely serious at all times is constant. Certainly aspects of the job are poor choices for lightheartedness (less-than-desirable patient experiences or clinical outcomes;

difficult but necessary job changes); however, an overemphasis on seriousness can itself drain staff's energy levels.

Many leaders are described as having a good sense of humor. What distinguishes exceptional leaders in this area is not so much how fun or funny they are, but rather their ability to use lightheartedness to their strategic advantage. Humor can be a particularly potent device for breaking through unproductive tension; it can also help people find the distance they need from a problem to make more objective decisions and can boost creative thinking about challenges a team may be facing.

Beyond humor, highly effective leaders strive to make their workplaces enjoyable. They want their staff to be excited to come to work; they take a serious interest both in the concerns staff have about the workplace and also in the ideas they provide about making the workplace more fun.

## WHEN ENERGIZING STAFF IS NOT ALL IT COULD BE

Walk into any department or organization that is low energy, and you will see a group that is not working to its full potential. When this happens, the leader may be contributing to the problem in the following ways.

### Undervaluing Motivation

Some leaders simply do not view staff motivation as part of their job. They assume people come to work to earn a paycheck or to further their careers, and they leave it at that. This perspective tends to coexist with poor habits related to staff feedback and staff relations more generally. These leaders fail to recognize their potential to positively influence staff's energy and motivation levels.

As with most barriers, there is a grain of truth to the perspective: The single greatest force affecting an individual's level of motivation is the individual, and some people will always be more motivated than others. Still, the environment plays a strong role in an individual's motivation level, and the person most responsible for the work environment is the leader.

### Underdeveloped Motivational Skills

Some leaders do understand the role they can play in their staff's motivation but may have limited skill in energizing their staff. For leaders who themselves tend to be low-energy or highly introverted, energizing staff may not come very naturally.

High-performing leaders who are introverted or have lower energy recognize this barrier and overcome it by delegating elements of energizing staff to someone better at it. Less effective leaders, in contrast, may try to fake it by taking a one-size-fits-all approach.

### Tolerating Cynicism

Efforts to energize can be undercut by staff cynicism. Higher performing leaders will address cynical comments to contain the damage they can inflict on enthusiasm. Lower performing leaders will let cynical comments go, either out of discomfort with confrontation or a lack of skill in tactfully addressing them. They may justify their inaction by telling themselves, "Everyone is entitled to her opinion," or by convincing themselves the comments are not a big deal—"Everyone knows he's a cynic. No one will listen to him." In our experience, neither rationale is particularly accurate nor helpful to the team's functioning. In the most serious cases, the leaders may not recognize the cynicism because they themselves have grown cynical; in these cases, unless leaders confront their own cynicism, little hope exists of raising the enthusiasm of the team.

---

### When Energizing Staff Is Not All It Could Be

Leaders can misuse or misapply energizing, in any of the following ways:

- Undervaluing motivation
  - Leaders do not view energizing staff as an important part of their job responsibilities.
  - Leaders fail to understand or appreciate how they can influence others' energy and motivation levels.
- Underdeveloping motivational skills
  - Leaders take a one-size-fits-all approach to motivating staff.
  - Leaders may be too introverted or too low-energy themselves.
- Tolerating cynicism
  - Cynical behavior among staff is allowed to go unchallenged.
  - Leaders may be cynical about their own roles.

---

## MISUSE AND OVERUSE: HOW ENERGIZING STAFF CAN WORK AGAINST YOU

Leaders can misuse and also overuse their emphasis on energizing. Rather than creating energy, they end up creating discomfort; the result is usually a net loss of productivity. This can occur because of any of the following.

## Having Too Much Energy

Many successful leaders have unusually high energy levels. Energy is a considerable asset for enduring the long and stressful days associated with many of the more senior roles. However, if a leader's energy level is too far above that of her direct reports, she can leave them feeling worn out rather than energized. Leaders must be able to gauge the energy levels of their direct reports to ensure their own energy levels are experienced as bringing them up rather than wearing them down.

A related concern can occur when a leader is overzealous about continuously raising the bar. Here, leaders must be careful to ensure performance targets are meaningful to the organization or department's needs and do not come to be viewed as performance for performance's sake or performance only for the sake of the leader.

## Being Too Excitable

We have also seen some leaders overemphasize energizing staff while underemphasizing performance. Leaders with a strong affinity for energizing are at risk for falling into this trap. Such a leader may, for example, err on the side of ensuring the achievement of goals rather than the achievement of performance. They will be sure to celebrate the accomplishment of these successes, but the inevitability of the successes may make these celebrations seem hollow for staff.

Another way leaders risk overemphasizing energizing staff is in the creation and institutionalization of perfunctory celebrations. Celebrations that become routine quickly lose their motivating power, as does the proliferation of recognition awards. The first award is always the most powerful; adding more awards decreases their overall impact. Any celebrations of a repeating nature (e.g., employee of the month) should be monitored carefully and discontinued when they reach the point of diminishing returns.

### Misuse and Overuse: How Energizing Staff Can Work Against You

If a leader is viewed as overdoing it on energizing, it could suggest any of the following problems:

- Having too much energy
  - Enthusiasm crosses the line to grandiosity.
  - Reaching the bar is underemphasized and setting the bar higher is overemphasized.

*(continued)*

*(continued from previous page)*

- Being too excitable
  - Expectations are set so low that success is certain, yet still celebrated.
  - Staff feel obligated to go along with too many perfunctory celebrations.

## WHAT TO DO TO BETTER ENERGIZE STAFF

### Finding Good Mentors

One group of leaders who are particularly adept at energizing staff are successful entrepreneurs. Many entrepreneurs, particularly in the early stages of their companies, have little in the way of material reward to provide their staff; the currency they do have is the hopes and dreams people have about their future success. Another group to consider is leaders of successful volunteer organizations; success in these positions is particularly dependent on skill in helping volunteers put in effort to further the organization's social mission.

### Additional Opportunities for Personal Development

In the realm of customer service improvement, Quint Studer describes a number of proven approaches in his books *Hardwiring Excellence* (2004) and *Straight A Leadership* (2009). An implementation of Studer's methods at Delnor Hospital is described in a chapter of *Best Practices in Leadership Development and Organizational Change* (Carter, Ulrich, and Goldsmith 2005). The story of Herb Kelleher and Southwest Airlines is also a classic of customer service. A detailed account of many of their energizing approaches has been collected in the book *Nuts!* (Freiberg and Freiberg 1996). Although not about healthcare per se, these companies' success stories have many lessons that can benefit healthcare leaders. Jim Haudan's (2008) book *The Art of Engagement* provides additional useful approaches to energizing staff across a variety of industries. Lastly, for a perspective on using leadership assemblies to drive cultural change, we recommend Tim Rice and Joan Evans's (2012) presentation, "Culture Transformation Drives Breakthrough Performance," available on the National Center for Healthcare Leadership YouTube channel.

## SUMMARY

No matter how important an organization's work and mission, staff will face ebbs and flows of their energy in response to the personal and organizational challenges they face. Exceptional leaders are in tune with their staff's energy levels, and are skillful at raising enthusiasm when it needs to be raised, and keeping it going when it's already high. The strategies suggested in this chapter can help you in developing your own approach to energizing your staff while still keeping true to your own personal style.

---

### Consider This

Healthcare organizations typically are very process-oriented. However, process and arduous use of policies and procedures reduce the energy and enthusiasm that staff have about their work and their level of engagement in the workplace.

- How might leaders best balance process with outcomes?

---

### Consider This

Alfie Kohn (author of *Punished by Rewards*, 1999) contends that money is not always a motivator. He suggests that "rewards are most damaging to interest when the task is already intrinsically motivating" (Brandt 1995).

- Research some of Kohn's thoughts and premises.
- How might his ideas conflict with some of the ideas presented in this chapter?
- How might these apparently conflicting perspectives be reconciled?

---

## REFERENCES

Brandt, R. 1995. "Punished by Rewards? A Conversation with Alfie Kohn." www.alfiekohn.org/teaching/pdf/Punished%20by%20Rewards.pdf.

Carter, L., D. Ulrich, and M. Goldsmith (eds.). 2005. *Best Practices in Leadership Development and Organizational Change: How the Best Companies Ensure Meaningful Change and Sustainable Leadership.* San Francisco: Pfeiffer.

Freiberg, K., and J. Freiberg. 1996. *Nuts! Southwest Airlines' Crazy Recipe for Business and Personal Success.* Austin, TX: Bard Press.

Haudan, J. 2008. *The Art of Engagement: Bridging the Gap Between People and Possibilities.* New York: McGraw-Hill.

Kohn, A. 1999. *Punished by Rewards: The Trouble with Gold Stars, Incentive Plans, A's, Praise, and Other Bribes.* Boston: Houghton-Mifflin.

Lowe, K. B., K. G. Kroeck, and N. Sivasubramaniam. 1996. "Effectiveness Correlates of Transformation and Transactional Leadership: A Meta-Analytic Review of the MLQ Literature." *Leadership Quarterly* 7: 385–425.

Rice, T., and J. Evans. 2012. "Culture Transformation Drives Breakthrough Performance. Presentation at the Annual Conference of the National Center for Healthcare Leadership." www.youtube.com/watch?v=h4haGu7PLCw.

Studer, Q. 2009. *Straight A Leadership: Alignment, Action, Accountability.* Gulf Breeze, FL: Fire Starter.

———. 2004. *Hardwiring Excellence: Purpose, Worthwhile Work, Making a Difference.* Gulf Breeze, FL: Fire Starter.

# Part IV

# MASTERFUL EXECUTION— THE FOURTH CORNERSTONE

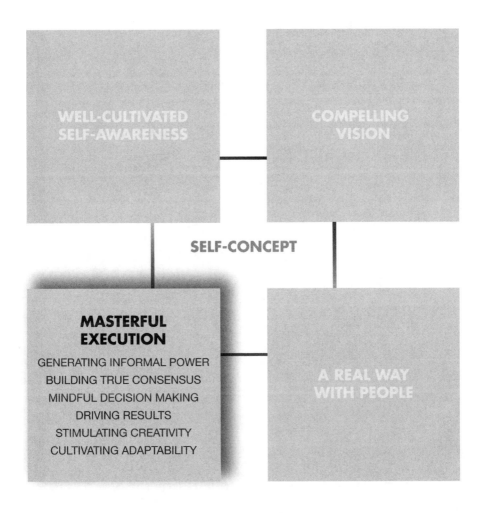

WELL-CULTIVATED SELF-AWARENESS

COMPELLING VISION

SELF-CONCEPT

**MASTERFUL EXECUTION**

GENERATING INFORMAL POWER
BUILDING TRUE CONSENSUS
MINDFUL DECISION MAKING
DRIVING RESULTS
STIMULATING CREATIVITY
CULTIVATING ADAPTABILITY

A REAL WAY WITH PEOPLE

THE FOURTH AND final Cornerstone, Masterful Execution, involves the competencies most directly tied to the day-to-day work of leadership. It includes competencies that emphasize leveraging the goodwill within working relationships ("Generating Informal Power") and finding common ground on which to move forward ("Building True Consensus"). It also includes optimally balancing information and intuition in charting the path forward ("Mindful Decision Making"), ensuring people are appropriately challenged to maximize their performance ("Driving Results"), and helping people expand their capacity to innovate and look beyond conventional solutions ("Stimulating Creativity" and "Cultivating Adaptability").

## CHAPTER ELEVEN

# Competency 11: Generating Informal Power

Looking at her watch, Elizabeth Parris realized that her executive in charge of the employed physician group, Dr. Bob Borman, was probably wrapping up his meeting with Dr. Bruce Red about now. She was at an impasse with Dr. Red on several fundamental decisions about the new strategic plan, and she was looking for a way to avoid a confrontation on the matter.

Dr. Borman's last meeting with Dr. Red had not gone as well as they had hoped; Dr. Red raised many objections that Dr. Borman was not prepared to address. This time, Borman had been preparing for this meeting for days, and he had developed as strong a case for his requested changes as possible. He had researched every single issue Dr. Red brought up in their last meeting as well as a host of others he thought Dr. Red could potentially bring up. But after an hour with Dr. Red, which seemed to last a week, he felt the negotiations had actually gone backward several steps.

A few minutes later, Dr. Borman called in to Parris to report his lack of progress. She listened patiently for a while, then interrupted him.

"Bob, how's your relationship with Dr. Randy Carl?"

"The chair of surgery? Fine, why?"

"What I mean is, would you say you have a positive 'bank account' with him?"

Dr. Borman thought a moment and said, "Not sure. I think so. We gave him a lot of support when the ambulatory surgery center he and his group owned ran into trouble. We created a good comanagement agreement, helped him recruit new docs, and gave him prime space in our new building."

*(continued)*

(continued from previous page)

> Parris smiled. "We may need to make a withdrawal."
>
> Dr. Borman was skeptical about the suggestion but followed Parris's advice. He arranged a lunch meeting with Dr. Carl to see whether he might be able to help persuade Dr. Red to see things differently. Not only did Dr. Carl say he would support them, he said he was glad to have the chance to repay his "debt."
>
> Sure enough, by the end of the week, Dr. Red e-mailed Parris and Dr. Borman to say he thought perhaps he had been taking too hard a line with them. He had decided to support several of the most critical requests, although he remained firm on a number of other (relatively trivial) ones. Dr. Borman breathed a sigh of relief. He also filed away a mental note about the connection between Dr. Carl and Dr. Red for future reference.

THIS VIGNETTE ILLUSTRATES a curious reality in every organization: Getting things done often requires more than rules and reason; it requires knowledge of the nature of people's relationships and the capacity to use that knowledge creatively. The more complex the initiative, the more of a role these informal relationships are likely to play. Success in building and navigating these networks is another way in which the highest performing leaders often stand out from their peers.

## WHAT IS GENERATING INFORMAL POWER, AND WHY IS IT IMPORTANT?

*Informal power* can be defined as the capacity to influence others without resorting to formal authority (i.e., without saying "Do it because I'm the boss").

> **Generating Informal Power** means you understand the roles of power and influence in organizations; develop compelling arguments or points of view based on a knowledge of others' priorities; develop and sustain useful networks up, down, and sideways in the organization; develop a reputation as a go-to person; and effectively affect others' thoughts and opinions, both directly and indirectly.

Formal power allows leaders to directly influence their direct reports and may also let certain leaders (e.g., a corporate compliance officer) influence people by appealing to a set of universally accepted rules. Informal power captures everything outside of that recognized formal structure and is generally where most power resides.

The classic research of French and Raven (1959) identified six fundamental sources of power, each with a greater or lesser association with formal authority:

1. *Legitimate power* comes from the position a person holds and the formally recognized authority associated with that position.
2. *Coercive power* comes from the threat of sanctions. (This is the type of power viewed most critically when considered as a part of leadership.)
3. *Reward power* is derived from the ability to provide benefits or rewards (e.g., compensation, praise, promotion).
4. *Expert power* is derived from knowledge or special expertise.
5. *Referent power* comes from the admiration or high regard that is held for someone.
6. *Information power* is derived from holding information or data.

Both types of power—formal and informal—are related to the ability to gain access to and activate cooperation, support, information, resources, funds, and opportunities inside the organization.

## WHEN HIGHLY EFFECTIVE LEADERS GENERATE INFORMAL POWER

Exceptional leaders tend to share the following approaches to informal power generation.

### Approaching Power Strategically

Highly effective leaders will be selective about who they invest in developing informal power relationships with. They seek out the individuals most likely to be helpful to them in the future. For example, a high-performing leader will typically seek out the most skilled individual or individuals in each department as their contacts rather than assume the appointed head of the department is the best contact to have.

This is not to say that high-performing leaders will only work with the top performing individual in any department; their approaches to relationship building are not scheming and manipulative. However, in terms of the proactive steps they take to build their networks, high-performing leaders know the value of prioritizing their efforts, and they will focus on where the talent is and where the opportunities for relationship development are richest.

### Taking an Efficient Approach

Although the concept of having a relationship "bank account" with people is widely recognized, the accounting of favors and support is at best imprecise. Some kinds of support are more valuable than others, and some require more effort than others. Highly effective leaders learn how to develop these relationships with an eye toward efficiency.

Some of the most efficient approaches to informal power involve a leader's ability to influence a person's decisions on behalf of another person, as in the case of Dr. Borman influencing Dr. Red through the help of Dr. Carl. The brokering of support, particularly when the costs to the leader are low, can yield substantial returns in informal power.

### Reciprocating

Returning favors is at least as important as requesting them in the first place. Exceptional leaders recognize the debt they owe others for their support and welcome the opportunity to repay it. Interpersonal relationships typically involve some amount of quid pro quo, or exchange process. One well-known leader has called this process "interpersonal economics."

## WHEN GENERATING INFORMAL POWER IS NOT ALL IT COULD BE

Leaders who do not have informal power bases may be impaired by one or more of the following.

### Undervaluing Informal Power

Some leaders, even in more senior leadership roles, remain uncomfortable with the idea of doing anything outside of formally recognized policies and hierarchies. Leaders may be particularly sensitive to fairness and due process—and in many cases, formally recognized channels are the best ones to follow. However, the view can also be taken too far, to the point where *any* informal action is viewed as categorically unethical or underhanded.

A less extreme view held by some leaders is that politics are a regular part of organizational life; leaders tolerate them but fail to see them as potentially helpful tools they themselves might use. In the process, they are overlooking important opportunities to be more effective in pursuing their goals.

### Involving the Wrong People in Networks

Leaders who do take their informal networks seriously may still fall short if they do not invest their efforts in the right people. Some leaders do not give enough thought to why they are building a network in terms of the capacity it should yield. Alternatively, some leaders focus too much on quantity and not enough on quality; as a result, their network is too diffuse, and the return on their efforts declines. Finally, leaders may focus too specifically on the formal power positions (e.g., the heads of departments), which may or may not always yield the ideal power sources or the most efficient networks to maintain.

### Using Ineffective Approaches

Some leaders are not as effective as others in network building. For example, a more strategic networker will recognize the kinds of contacts or networks they may need in advance of actually needing them. Many leaders will instead build their networks only once the needs have presented themselves. Examples include making contacts in the philanthropy department only *after* deciding to embark on a fundraising campaign, or finding a contact in employee relations *after* an employee discipline problem presents itself. Although this approach can work fine for most leaders, we would hardly call it highly effective; because well-tended connections tend to grow in strength over time, leaders are usually in a better position if they develop networks proactively.

In addition to falling short on early identification, informal power will also be less potent if leaders are not as skillful in their relationship development efforts. For example, some leaders focus too much of their energy on the social aspects of their relationships. They may make a point of attending office parties and sending cards, thinking this is helping them build an effective working relationship. In developing an effective informal network, the message you want to send is "I am helpful to know." By focusing solely on the social side of the relationship, you only send the message "I am your friend." When it comes to generating informal power, a year's worth of dutiful attendance in office social events pales in comparison to a single, well-timed assist with a difficult workplace challenge.

Another way in which leaders' network-building efforts can run into trouble is if they fail to recognize and honor the need for reciprocity. This may seem an obvious point; indeed, in our experience, the failure is rarely willfully intended. We again return to the topic of trust building: Good leaders may do well enough that they can be forgiven the occasional oversight; great leaders strive to avoid the oversights in the first place.

Lastly, leaders must recognize that people differ in their general orientation toward reciprocity. While most people within healthcare are oriented toward helping others, some seek to gain what they can out of their relationships with little thought to returning whatever support they have received. These relationships must be managed especially carefully, so the leaders' support is not coming at the expense of their own goals.

---

### When Generating Informal Power Is Not All It Could Be

If informal power does not reach its full potential, the cause can be any of the following:

- Undervaluing informal power
  - Informal power is viewed as unethical or underhanded.
  - Politics are tolerated but not proactively used to the organization's benefit.
- Involving the wrong people in networks
  - Leaders do not effectively prioritize relationships to develop.
  - Formal power structures are overly relied on.
- Using ineffective approaches
  - Leaders do not develop networks in advance of needing them.
  - Leaders fail to reciprocate assistance or fall short in follow-through.
  - Leaders don't hold others accountable for reciprocity.

---

## MISUSE AND OVERUSE: HOW GENERATING INFORMAL POWER CAN WORK AGAINST YOU

Some leaders place too much emphasis on the pursuit of informal power than is necessary to support their role. What follows are some of the more common patterns this is associated with.

## Focusing Too Much on Personal Agenda

For leaders who are particularly adept at building relationships, the temptation can arise to use the networks to support decisions that are more in the leader's interest than in the organization's. In some extreme cases, a leader's job security may be based primarily on who they know. In other cases, leaders have used their informal networks to stage a mutiny against senior leadership.

Any time leaders set out to build informal power on the basis of individual agendas rather than organizational goals, badly imbalanced networks can result. These leaders may find themselves comfortably in the loop on key decisions and actions that affect them, but they will have far less useful power bases for ensuring effective performance in their roles.

## Overvaluing Relationship Building

For leaders who really enjoy the relationship-building aspects of their roles, this process can become the end rather than the means. Earlier, we mentioned the problem of overemphasizing the nonwork aspects of relationship building. We are not suggesting that attending office social functions is poor practice, only that it can be overdone. Deservedly or not, creating the perception that one always has time for social functions can be viewed as slacking or self-aggrandizing by peers and direct reports: "She's off schmoozing again." The attention paid to networking can also take too much attention away from other essential aspects of the job. Effective leaders attend to the norms of their peers regarding how often they attend social functions, and how much time they spend at them. They also tend to plan more strategically for the opportunities these functions provide to efficiently touch base with people they may not regularly see.

## Playing Power Politics

Leaders who move too far along this spectrum of relationship building may find themselves involved in power politics. They begin to see the workplace as a competitive arena with winners and losers. Their political activities become a way to stand out and be noticed. The development of relationships and the ability to call in chits become too central to their work.

## HOW TO IMPROVE ON GENERATING INFORMAL POWER

### Finding Role Models

Informal power generation tends to be an intentional activity, and as such, people who are particularly good at it can often articulate how they approach developing these relationships. Finding these people can be a little tricky, however. By definition, the people most skilled with informal power are the individuals in the organization whose power is far higher than would be expected by virtue of their formal job title. However, informal power often tends to be a quiet art. The most effective leaders will not bring attention to their informal power, except when it is necessary to do so. However, there are some telling indicators, including the following characteristics:

- *Faster or more varied career trajectories.* Leaders who are better at generating informal power tend to be promoted more quickly than their peers. Also, for leaders who have worked in a number of different organizations (or in consulting firms), generating informal power is more of a survival skill.
- *Cross-departmental roles.* Leaders whose success most depends on organization-wide or cross-organizational collaboration also tend to have well-honed informal power skills. This is especially true for roles with

neither legal/policy stipulations nor strong senior-level endorsements to fall back on. These people must truly exercise influence without authority to be successful.

## Additional Opportunities for Personal Development

If you are interested in learning more about how to develop informal power, a classic text on this topic is Cohen and Bradford's (1990) *Influence Without Authority*. This book provides excellent formulas to help you evaluate your assumptions, consider the interests and needs of others, and negotiate mutually beneficial exchanges to achieve your goals. Thematically, their book emphasizes the principle of building relationships by assuming everyone is a potential ally. For more modern examination of the role helping others tends to play in one's own success, we recommend *Give and Take* by Adam Grant (2013). Chapter 7, "Chump Change," is particularly helpful in considering approaches to working with people who have trouble understanding the importance of reciprocity in their working relationships.

Because informal power is such a mainstay of organizational behavior research, almost any college-level textbook on organizational behavior will provide useful material. A favorite of ours is Henry Mintzberg's (1983) classic, *Power In and Around Organizations*.

If thinking strategically about informal power is new to you, we recommend trying out some of the formal tools that are available for assessing and diagnosing influence networks. The tools can be helpful in quantifying and visualizing what your networks look like, including areas that may be providing relatively lower or higher payoffs and areas in need of further development. *The Hidden Power of Social Networks* (Cross and Parker 2004) is a particularly good practitioner-oriented text that contains many tools for assessing social networks.

## SUMMARY

The dynamics of informal power and politics are realities in all organizations. Attempts to deny their existence or minimize their impact are not always energy well spent. Exceptional leaders are skillful at capitalizing on these realities to support rather than undermine their organization's goals as much as possible. By understanding how decisions are really made, and by whom, as well as who the most helpful resources across the organization are, leaders will find themselves much more capable in their roles.

## Consider This

The phrase *office politics* describes efforts individuals pursue to support their personal power within an organization.

- What are some of the ways that leaders can minimize the negative effects of this phenomenon?

## Consider This

Most successful leaders build many networks or alliances. Yet many negatives can surface with alliances. Some alliances are not as powerful as others. Some seem to be dominated by individuals who are not that respected. Other alliances are tied strictly to the control of finances and can rapidly dissipate if the budgets get tight. And often individuals find that they are doing more favors for people than they received.

- What are some steps that can be taken to manage alliances so that benefits are maximized and negatives are minimized?

## REFERENCES

Cohen, A. R., and D. L. Bradford. 2005. *Influence Without Authority,* 2nd ed. New York: John Wiley & Sons.

Cross, R., and A. Parker. 2004. *The Hidden Power of Social Networks: Understanding How Work Really Gets Done in Organizations.* Boston: Harvard Business School Publishing.

French, J. P., and B. Raven. 1959. "The Bases of Social Power." In *Studies in Social Power,* edited by D. Cartwright, 150–67. New York: Institute for Social Research.

Grant, A. 2013. *Give and Take: A Revolutionary Approach to Success.* New York: Viking Adult.

Mintzberg, H. 1983. *Power In and Around Organizations.* Englewood Cliffs, NJ: Prentice Hall.

## CHAPTER TWELVE

# Competency 12: Building True Consensus

**Scenario A.** Alicia Zielinski was frustrated. As the new CEO of one of St. Nicholas Health System's rural hospitals, she had spent the past 15 months rebuilding her executive team. The group had been in place for five months now, and although each executive had outstanding credentials, decision making on key strategic initiatives was scarcely any better. Alicia valued input from her executive team members and did not want to simply listen to them and then make the final decision. She had hoped that in forming this team, they would make many decisions together by consensus. She wanted to exploit the collective knowledge of the team and use the group discussion process to enrich the quality of their decisions. But each member seemed entrenched in his or her functional areas. Discussions regularly devolved into a focus on turf issues and attempts to clarify their own roles.

**Scenario B.** Randall Repito, president of the St. Nicholas Health Plan, was overseeing his first budget process at the insurance company. He had given his leadership group great latitude, and yet the last three iterations of the budget had shown increasingly greater losses. The mandate to show at least a 2 percent profit on operations had been clear from the start. Repito called the leadership council together for a meeting in his office on Friday afternoon. He stated, "Folks, our goal could not be clearer: We need a budget that shows a 2 percent profit on operations. You have spent the past week revising the budget, and each time the loss gets worse. I meet with the system CEO next Tuesday and then have the board meeting next Thursday night. I would suggest you come in tomorrow and use the weekend to complete

*(continued)*

*(continued from previous page)*

the budget. If I don't have a budget that shows a 2 percent profit by Monday morning, I don't need you. I will find other executives who will reach their targets."

THESE SCENARIOS DESCRIBE just two examples of how well-meaning executive teams can fail to work together toward the best outcomes. There are no obvious problem performers, just problem processes. In our last chapter, we discussed the importance of stockpiling informal power as well as the methods that seem to work most effectively for doing so. This chapter is about using that power, along with other negotiating skills, to help people move toward consensus. In the process, we investigate how groups can better work together in collective decision making.

## WHAT IS BUILDING TRUE CONSENSUS, AND WHY IS IT IMPORTANT?

*Consensus* can be defined as general agreement or accord. *Building True Consensus* involves the use of group decision making and other techniques to ensure a critical threshold of general agreement is reached and maintained concerning both the decision at hand and the consensus-building process itself.

**Building True Consensus** means you frame issues in ways that facilitate clarity from multiple perspectives, keep issues separate from personalities, skillfully use group decision techniques (e.g., Nominal Group Technique), ensure that quieter group members are drawn into discussions, find shared values and common adversaries, facilitate discussions rather than guide them, and ensure the consensus-building process itself is viewed as fair and appropriate.

Most decisions that leaders must make do not yield equal outcomes for all who are affected. As such, leaders rarely have the luxury of developing initiatives or finding solutions that everyone favors equally. The art of consensus building involves developing the levels of support needed to move initiatives forward without causing some individuals to feel left behind, slighted, or otherwise powerless to affect the organization—or causing other individuals to feel too powerful. Consensus building can be a labor-intensive process, requiring careful planning to ensure it involves the ideal amount of time and attention. Spend too much time on it, and you have too little time for other aspects of your role. Spend too little, and your initiatives will not receive the long-term support they need for success.

## WHEN HIGHLY EFFECTIVE LEADERS BUILD CONSENSUS

Leaders who are skilled at building consensus have the following traits in common.

### Knowing When to Count Votes and When to Weigh Them

Not every decision made within an organization requires consensus. Exceptional leaders understand this and will convey this to their leadership teams. They also let their teams know in advance how their input will or will not affect the ultimate decision. Sometimes, they will seek their team's input but will reserve the right to make the final decision. Other times, they will inform their leadership groups that the decision will be a purely democratic process. Still other times, they will ask the group to actively participate in a consensus process to move toward a decision that will involve a synthesis of the viewpoints of the entire group.

When consensus is called for, effective leaders ensure the following factors each receive appropriate attention:

- *Balance.* In this context, balance refers to the level of consensus a leader seeks for a given decision or initiative. The most effective consensus builders do not attempt to maximize agreement, but instead to reach "good enough" agreement. They will continue to build consensus until they reach the good enough point, and they will stop their selling shortly after that.
- *Efficiency.* Given how labor intensive the consensus-building process can be, exceptional leaders can distinguish themselves according to how efficiently they make it work. For example, most leaders have a sense of when a battle is winnable and when it is not; however, even for battles that can be won, most of us could improve our ability to know when the effort will be worth it and when it will not be.
- *Technique.* In addition to deciding who to work on and who to give up on, the most effective consensus builders have a well-developed portfolio of approaches to address the *how.* The approach a leader uses to get buy-in from any given individual will be well informed by a clear understanding of

that person's goals and priorities, related to both the decision at hand and also the individual's need for power and social standing among her peers. The most effective consensus builders make it easy to say yes—for example, by finding ways for dissenters to change their minds without losing face.

In terms of the process itself, consensus building does not involve just going around the table to listen to everyone's opinions and then taking a vote on the final decision. Such an approach risks leaving the less verbal or less persuasive group members feeling slighted, and it may create second-rate decisions.

While voting is a quantitative process involving a count, consensus building is more qualitative, involving actively synthesizing diverse needs and perspectives. While it does not mean everyone will feel the ultimate decision is the optimal one, all should feel their perspectives are heard and considered.

## WHEN BUILDING TRUE CONSENSUS IS NOT ALL IT COULD BE

True consensus building is more art than science; no one gets it right all the time. However, there are some common barriers that can impair a leader's overall results.

### Using a Command-and-Control Approach

Some leaders lean too heavily on their formal authority in making decisions that affect others. As a result, they lack an understanding or appreciation for consensus building. Some of these leaders will stifle consensus-building efforts because they do not view them as valuable. Others believe using consensus building will legitimize others' disagreements with them, diminishing their own power along the way. The command-and-control style is becoming less and less accepted; most people want the opportunity to question and even challenge authority and will not tolerate having their input stifled.

### Approaching Consensus Unevenly

Even leaders who understand the importance of consensus building can get themselves into trouble by failing to maintain a clear focus on their goals for the process.

Some leaders find it particularly challenging to face vocal opposition; as a result, they tend to give in disproportionately according to how loudly a dissenter complains rather than considering how central the dissenter's role is or how powerful his influence may (or may not) be. Leaders do not need to give in many times before their colleagues recognize this weakness and begin to use it as a tool when it suits them.

Some leaders only seek consensus from those most likely to provide it. These leaders have a bias toward approval seeking rather than support seeking; they may have an easier time getting initiatives started, but these initiatives will move forward with less support, which is often reflected in the lower quality or speed of their eventual results.

## Lacking Sensitivity to Interpersonal Process

For some leaders, the consensus-building process itself is the greatest bottleneck. This can be caused by a lack of experience with consensus building, a lack of knowledge about the players and their histories, or occasionally a more basic lack of understanding of interpersonal process. At times, leaders may not want to offend a team member by pushing for a decision. There may also be occasions when certain individuals within a team may have certain sensitivities to specific issues (e.g., the chief financial officer and the budget; the chief nursing officer and nurse staffing) and the team leader does not allow discussions related to these topics to be managed by the group.

---

### When Consensus Building Is Not What It Could Be

- Using a command-and-control approach
  - Leaders do not recognize the value of consensus in building long-term support.
  - Leaders view others as obliged to go along with decisions because it's their job.
- Approaching consensus unevenly
  - Too much ground is given to the most vocal individuals.
  - Getting approval is emphasized over getting support.
- Lacking sensitivity to interpersonal process
  - Leaders lack experience with the consensus-building process.
  - Leaders lack a clear understanding of the needs and priorities of the people involved.

---

## MISUSE AND OVERUSE: HOW BUILDING CONSENSUS CAN WORK AGAINST YOU

Many leaders overuse or misuse consensus building. In our experience, the following patterns are usually to blame.

### Being Biased Toward Universal Agreement

Whenever leaders are described as overdoing consensus building, it is usually because they place too much emphasis on getting everyone to agree. For most initiatives of any complexity, universal agreement is an impossible goal; still, some leaders press on pursuing it, wasting time and energy to push as closely as they can to all-inclusive buy-in. Along the way, they may too quickly redesign plans in a misguided effort to capture additional votes, leading to unnecessary and inefficient cycles of reworking and diminishing returns.

### Building Unnecessary Consensus

Even leaders without a universal agreement bias may overuse consensus building. For example, at times leaders face decisions that will negatively affect *all* stakeholders—decisions that no one is likely to support but that still must be made for the good of the organization. To seek consensus on such a decision is unproductive at best and, at worst, will lead to much effort and time being spent on a hopeless cause.

Other leaders overuse consensus building in working with their direct reports. For some leaders, the real issue is their discomfort in saying no to their staff. Rather than taking a harder line, they resort to pleading; as a result, staff are extended an inappropriate amount of power in their roles. Although leading through inspiration and encouragement is often best, staff still need to respect the formal authority of the leader's role.

---

**Misuse and Overuse: How Building Consensus Can Work Against You**

- Being biased toward universal agreement
  - Too much effort is devoted to getting every person on board.
  - Leaders are too quick to redesign plans to accommodate disagreeable individuals.

*(continued)*

---

*(continued from previous page)*

- Building unnecessary consensus
  - Consensus is sought when it is not needed or helpful.
  - Consensus is sought even when a decision outcome is already clear.

## HOW TO ENHANCE CONSENSUS BUILDING

### Finding Role Models

Several common organizational roles require highly skilled consensus builders and therefore tend to have good role models for this competency. Internal consultants, particularly those with stellar reputations for getting things done, are often good choices. Strategic planning consultants are often quite adept at consensus building, as are Six Sigma and Lean Management specialists. Training and education managers are also often well versed in consensus-building tools, and they may also have some experience in teaching these skills to others.

### Additional Opportunities for Personal Development

One of the best ways to enhance skills in this area is to volunteer to lead a strategic planning or other group process in a community not-for-profit organization, association, church, or synagogue. Members in these settings often hold passionate views and feel far less need to express agreement (particularly if their jobs are not at stake).

Given that consensus building is both widely recognized as important but also difficult to master, many workshops and books are available to support skill development. Among our favorites is *Team Decision-Making Techniques: A Practical Guide to Successful Team Outcomes* by Kelly and Kelly (1996).

Effective consensus building also involves the use of group process techniques. Readers are encouraged to learn more about the many resources that teach the following techniques:

- Nominal Group Technique
- Brainstorming
- Force field analysis
- Affinity mapping
- Fishbone diagrams
- Scenario sketching

These techniques are used so widely that information and instruction on many of these techniques can be easily found through an Internet search.

## SUMMARY

Building True Consensus is difficult to master and distinguishes exceptional leaders for at least two reasons. First, for any given initiative, a higher level of consensus will translate into greater effort and energy supporting that initiative. Second, across initiatives, if staff feel their voice was heard, they will show greater support even for those initiatives they didn't personally endorse. For these reasons and others, developing your effectiveness as a true builder of consensus is a worthwhile undertaking.

---

### Consider This

Recall the group and subgroup dynamics among the senior team at St. Nicholas. Elizabeth Parris has traditionally used a hands-off leadership style and has not worried that much about how consensus was developed. Usually she let senior VP of medical affairs Dr. Howard James, CFO Sam Stoman, and senior VP of business development Dave Damron drive the decision making in the team. Over several years, the rest of the team began to yield the floor to these three, especially on topics of strategic importance.

As St. Nicholas started to face the enormous changes brought about by health reform legislation, the need to develop a more robust strategic direction became evident. Parris's regional executive vice president, Duhal Malinka, took her to lunch one day and said, "Liz, we've known each other for several years and I have great respect for you. But I find it important for me to call out a serious issue I think is harming our ability to move forward strategically. I do not know if you realize it, but you have given practically all the authority to shape future strategic vision to Dr. James, Stoman, and Damron. And while I think all three are fine leaders, none are strategic. Howard has grown up in a tertiary environment and knows practically nothing about primary care. Sam is a true old-school finance guy, and he too is an acute care–oriented manager. And Dave's only focus has been primary care acquisition. The fact is, we have no one with any strategic knowledge about population health and managing care across the continuum. Quite frankly, we seem to still be acting as though adding more inpatient beds is our sole strategy. And the real issue is that our decision-making processes are not ones of consensus."

*(continued)*

---

(continued from previous page)

Parris listened intently to Malinka and after a pause, responded, "Duhal, I totally agree with you. This has been a concern of mine for some time now. But I just do not know how to address it."

- Put yourself in Malinka's shoes and draft a set of recommendations to Parris on how she can begin to turn her senior team around and build a more consensus-oriented approach to strategy development. Think about the St. Nicholas senior leadership team or another team you are familiar with that needs to make rapid decisions.

## Consider This

Many healthcare organizations have adopted such rigorous consensus-type processes into their decision making that they often seem frozen in time, unable to make crisp decisions when needed. This often happens when multiple meetings and discussions have to take place over a period of time. Compounding these processes are the supposedly helpful electronic communications tools that often replace face-to-face meetings. All this repeatedly causes frustration for many leaders.

- Draft a set of guidelines for decision making that support consensus but do not allow it to be frozen ("analysis paralysis").

## REFERENCE

Kelly, P., and K. Kelly. 1996. *Team Decision-Making Techniques: A Practical Guide to Successful Team Outcomes*, 2nd ed. San Francisco: Jossey-Bass.

## CHAPTER THIRTEEN

# Competency 13: Mindful Decision Making

After her staff meeting, Judy Flores, the president of the St. Nicholas Ambulatory Services Corporation, returned to her office, still feeling a bit agitated but much better than earlier that morning. She had spent most of the meeting undoing a set of policies and procedures related to unscheduled absences and overtime that she had implemented just weeks before. The changes had arisen in the first place because Kim Brown, one of her managers, had complained to her that the current system was particularly unfair to the many working mothers in her department. Kim had proposed the changes to Flores, suggesting they would be cost-neutral and guaranteeing that it would a no-brainer for everyone in the division to support them.

Flores approved the changes, only to learn later that the other two managers strongly opposed them. They believed the changes would make it much more difficult to discipline staff with attendance problems, and the overtime policy, which was abused already, would be doubly so under the new standard.

The incident reminded Flores of a workshop she had attended a year or so ago on decision making. The instructor had made a strong case for keeping a journal of key decisions to help her notice patterns in her judgments and to avoid "selective remembering." Given the traps she had fallen into recently, she decided she ought to give the exercise a more concerted try than she had at the time.

When she finally located the decision journal file from the workshop and got ready to write, her jaw dropped at what she saw. Her last entry, from about ten months ago, ended with the following analysis, in two points:

*(continued)*

*(continued from previous page)*

"(1) I have too much of a soft spot when it comes to work–life balance, and my staff know it. I need to be very careful when this is thrown in as a rationale for anything. (2) If I'm presented with a problem and I am told 'all my staff agree' about it, I need to double check to be sure that's true." She smiled to herself as she considered cutting and pasting those two learning points to the end of today's entry.

THIS VIGNETTE HIGHLIGHTS three key aspects of leadership decision making. First, it illustrates how decision-making biases can surface in day-to-day operations over time. Second, it depicts a fundamental reality of decision making as a highly complex but patterned process, the steps of which often unfold largely outside of our full and reflective awareness. Third, the outcome is one many of us can identify with: having to learn the same lesson multiple times to break a habit.

In this chapter, we take a reflective look at executive decision making. Becoming mindful of your decision making takes some deliberate effort, but it will pay off in improved decision-making habits and higher decision quality.

## WHAT IS MINDFUL DECISION MAKING, AND WHY IS IT IMPORTANT?

Broadly defined, *Mindful Decision Making* involves developing a clear awareness of how you make choices between multiple actions or directions. In the leadership context, we restrict the definition to the process of choosing an action or direction that will affect other people as well as the organization.

**Mindful Decision Making** means you are conscious of the approach you take to decisions; you make decisions based on an optimal mix of ethics, values, goals, facts, alternatives, and judgments; use decision tools (such as force-field analysis, cost-benefit analysis, decision trees, and paired comparisons analysis) effectively and at appropriate times; and show a good sense of timing related to decision making.

There is a tendency to think of decision making as an immutable quality, and to think some leaders are simply better decision makers than others. Although the quality of leaders' decisions does depend in part on their intelligence and experience, it is also strongly affected by the intentional approaches they take to decision-making processes. That aspect of decision making involves learnable, refinable skills.

## WHEN HIGHLY EFFECTIVE LEADERS MAKE DECISIONS

Leaders who are described as highly effective decision makers are particularly attentive to the following dimensions of their decisions.

### Gauging the True Urgency

At the senior executive level, many decisions are habitually described as requiring immediate action. A highly effective decision maker will have a solid sense of when a decision truly requires immediate action and when it does not. If a decision does require immediate action, mindful decision makers have the capacity to move forward with whatever information is available and are comfortable living with the results. For decisions not requiring immediate action, these leaders might still act on them immediately, but only after considering whether the decision would benefit from more time, analysis, and/or input.

### Evaluating the Best Approach

No single best approach exists for making all decisions. As a first step, the best decision makers decide how to decide. They will ask themselves questions such as the following:

- Who will be affected by the outcome of this decision?
- How much of a role, if any, should these individuals (groups) have in the decision-making process?
- What are the most critical things I need to know to make an informed decision?

The answers to these questions will then influence how they go about making the decision—who gets involved and how, how much time is devoted to the process, how much consensus is required (see Chapter 12), and when the decision gets made.

### Analyzing the Decision

Analysis refers to the collection of information, identification of courses of action, and weighing of costs and benefits related to a particular decision. Highly effective analyzers take a systematic though not necessarily comprehensive approach to their analyses. Because analysis can be very resource intensive; the good-enough analysis is often more desirable than the all-inclusive one. In many cases, taking additional time to collect more data or ponder the planned course of action can cause failure. Making decisions without complete information is a required skill in healthcare. Leaders who can effectively leverage their experience, track record of judgment, and collegial trust tend to be the most efficient decision makers.

### Using Good Judgment

The quality of a leader's judgment is determined by how effectively she draws on experience and information to arrive at a decision. Two qualities in particular tend to distinguish the judgment of exceptionally skillful decision makers. First, they select from a broader array of options. In other words, a highly effective decision maker will see more options, including innovative choices. Second, they are more effective in explaining *why* they arrived at a particular conclusion, a point we elaborate on next.

### Acting with Consistency and Integrity

Exceptional decision makers are often described in terms of consistency and integrity. Both of these qualities relate to transparency; these leaders tend to be better at explaining and, as necessary, justifying their decisions. In doing so, their goal is not to argue that their judgments are always correct; instead, it is to represent their *process* as methodical, measured, and fair. Here, the trust-building competencies discussed in Chapter 5 are particularly relevant. Leaders who are viewed as excellent decision makers will also be described in terms of trust: "I know that whatever she decides will be in the best interest of the patients we serve."

## WHEN MAKING DECISIONS IS NOT ALL IT COULD BE

Most leaders have developed good decision-making skills and habits. People would not refer to them as bad decision makers; however, they would not say they are outstanding decision makers either. A number of these leaders could be outstanding decision makers, but they are held back by one or more of the following barriers.

## Being Overly Fearful of Making a Bad Decision

For some leaders, the key challenge is their fear of making a wrong decision. We must put this one in proper context: All leaders make mistakes, and, from our experience, most leaders know this. However, they differ in how comfortable they are with being wrong. Some can admit it, freely and unapologetically; others try whatever they can think of to wriggle out of appearing to have made a mistake. These latter leaders risk losing sight of which decisions are important and which are trivial. Decisions involving greater uncertainty and ambiguity will be especially tough calls for them.

## Unwilling to Take Risks

Some leaders routinely fail to consider options that are out of the mainstream. This unwillingness is particularly prevalent in healthcare; many managers choose this route at least in part for the perceived stability the career path provides.

The unwillingness manifests itself in several steps of the decision-making process. During the brainstorming phase, when the goal is to generate a breadth of options, leaders may fail to lead by example with creative options. They may also step in early to rule out particularly creative or innovative ideas. The move can be as subtle as chuckling at someone for being "way out there" with a suggestion; the message staff will hear is "I'm not willing to consider anything innovative or daring."

In the later stages of decision making, the unwillingness can show up again in how much of a calculated risk leaders are willing to take as well as how large a change leaders will tolerate. Their bias may be toward taking things slowly, giving themselves lots of room to back out later if they care to.

## Lacking Good Decision-Making Methods

A leader's decision-making process may itself be problematic in several ways. One surprisingly common example is reliability—the consistency of the process as experienced by others. Even if leaders are methodical in their decisions, they may overlook the need to explain their approach to others. If coworkers do not understand the process behind the decisions, they may view the decision making as puzzling or haphazard.

For some leaders, the decision-making process is itself truly lacking; for example, they may fumble one or more of the fundamental steps on a regular basis. For some, the most challenging steps involve identifying the potential effects of a decision on key stakeholders. While outcomes of complex decisions are often not fully predictable ahead of time, some leaders are more effective than others in thinking through and managing these effects. Such leaders may fail to reach out to stakeholders for their input into the decision-making process at times when that input would improve the quality of the decisions as well as the buy-in.

Framing is another step that causes problems for some leaders. Framing involves coming up with useful, clear articulation of the problem and the options that may be available to address it. Leaders who are exceptionally good with details can at times find themselves overwhelmed by this step; they may see a decision as a problem to be carefully worked through, when a "good enough" decision is what is needed.

The analysis step can be another stumbling point. For example, some leaders rely too much on past experiences in informing their judgments. Giving up what has worked in the past can be difficult, particularly when it is still working fine in the present. The strongest decision makers regularly challenge themselves and their coworkers to consider new options, recognizing that although a past decision may still be a good option, it may not continue to be the best option.

---

**When Making Decisions Is Not All It Could Be**

- Being overly fearful of making a bad decision
  - Too much time is spent on trivial decisions.
  - Leaders have trouble admitting when they are wrong.
- Being unwilling to take risks
  - Leaders fail to generate innovative options or to take them seriously.
  - Leaders focus on incremental options to the exclusion of potentially transformational ones.
- Lacking good decision-making methods
  - Leaders seem to take an unclear or unsystematic approach to decision making.
  - Leaders fail to consider repercussions of decisions or reactions of stakeholders.
  - The approach to collecting information necessary to support decisions is disorganized and haphazard.

*(continued)*

---

*(continued from previous page)*
- Past experience is relied on too heavily.
- Leaders have difficulty establishing appropriate scope and options (e.g., getting overwhelmed with the details).

## MISUSE AND OVERUSE: HOW DECISION MAKING CAN WORK AGAINST YOU

Even leaders with well-honed decision-making skills may not be regarded as exceptional decision makers if they focus their time and energies in the wrong places. Here are some common ways in which good decision makers hold themselves back from better outcomes.

### Making Decisions for Decisions' Sake

Earlier, we made a case for good-enough decision making. But while some leaders get into trouble overanalyzing decisions, other leaders habitually underanalyze them. These same leaders may pride themselves in their ability to make rapid decisions, and they may have a harder time recognizing how their rushes to judgment create the need to rework plans later.

Often this problem is related to a leader's discomfort with having decisions in their inbox for very long. Leaders in this category are well served to improve their tolerance for ambiguity as well as their comfort in spending more time to make decisions when it is warranted.

### Overanalyzing Decisions

Some leaders take an overly cautious approach to decision making, using more resources or time than the decision requires. Common patterns include tabling decisions without a coherent rationale, adding analysis steps that do not clearly yield additional useful information, and asking for additional opinions from stakeholder groups who have already provided input. The pattern can drive peers and direct reports crazy; worse, it often will not improve the quality of the decisions, and may make them worse.

This pattern can be symptomatic of a basic discomfort with making and taking responsibility for decisions. Efforts to perpetually seek additional input sometimes suggest that the leader is trying to dodge accountability by crafting decisions as "what they asked for." Leaders who are overly fearful of being wrong sometimes display this pattern.

## Overconfidence

Some leaders have too high a comfort level with their own decision-making skills. The quality of their decisions may suffer because of a tendency to skip steps in the process. For example, they may fail to actively seek out devil's advocate opinions that would help them clarify and sharpen their rationale for a given decision. When they do receive dissenting opinions, they may too quickly dismiss these naysayers without taking the time to understand their concerns. (Even if the quality of the decision at hand does not suffer from missing this step, buy-in surely will.) A related issue is selective memory, where some leaders tend to forget about or discount how this decision-making pattern has brought them trouble in the past.

---

**Misuse and Overuse: How Decision Making Can Work Against You**

- Making decisions for decisions' sake
  - Decisions are rapid but lack sufficient analysis.
  - Input is not sought, or it is sought but not attended to.
- Overanalyzing decisions
  - Redundant steps in analyzing options are taken (e.g., multiple sources of the same information or multiple surveys addressing very similar questions).
  - The leader seeks more input than is necessary.
- Displaying overconfidence
  - The devil's advocate step in making decisions is skipped.
  - Leaders fail to see the importance of others' contrary perspectives.

---

## HOW TO IMPROVE MINDFUL DECISION MAKING

### Finding Role Models

If you are interested in identifying role models for Mindful Decision Making, look for leaders who are successful in positions that call for both a high quantity and a high quality of decisions. Chief operating officer and executive vice president roles come immediately to mind, as do leaders who oversee multiple discrete service lines or departments. Executives in strategic planning roles tend to be particularly skillful in analytic approaches to decision-making, as well as in seeking input from key stakeholders. (For more suggestions on the consensus-building component of decision making, see Chapter 12.)

## Additional Opportunities for Personal Development

If you have never formally tracked or evaluated the decision making that you or your team do, we recommend trying this for a while. Building a brief lessons-learned step into your decision-making process can be particularly helpful for uncovering the patterns in your approaches and identifying opportunities to improve these approaches over time.

Leaders with problematically high risk aversion or fears of being wrong can usually benefit from investing time in examining and understanding these fears. Often the fears stem from unrealistic assumptions about consequences: "If I'm wrong about this decision, I'll surely lose my job." Testing these assumptions against reality can be very helpful in overcoming this overly cautious pattern.

Many books focus on improving decision making. In our experience, serious books on this subject do not make for quick reads. They can take a fair amount of time to slog through, and implementing their recommendations takes no small amount of discipline. For those motivated to do so, we have several recommendations.

An excellent book on developing your intuitive decision-making skills is Gary Klein's (2003) *Intuition at Work*. The emphasis of this book is on using experience to inform decisions and using the outcomes of past decisions to inform future ones. You might think of it as total quality management for your decision making.

A more in-depth treatment of decision making, but still with a practical, how-to orientation, is available in J. Edward Russo and Paul Shoemaker's (2002) *Winning Decisions*. It is a more engaging read than *Intuition at Work*, and it gives a broader scope of application (including much more material on group decision making), though the topics are covered in less depth.

For more specific healthcare application and a more quantitative focus, we recommend the popular *Evaluation and Decision Making for Health Services* by James Veney and Arnold Kaluzny (2005).

Lastly, a substantial volume of research in recent years has come from the field of behavioral economics, providing some useful perspectives on how people make decisions, the common biases that these approaches often contain, and strategies for keeping these biases in check. Several popular books have made many of these concepts much more accessible, including Daniel Kahneman's (2013) *Thinking, Fast and Slow,* and Dan Ariely's (2010) *Predictably Irrational.*

## SUMMARY

Decision making is central to most leader's roles, yet many leaders spend little time systematically reflecting on how they have approached decisions in the past and may do so more effectively in the future. Developing a mindfulness about your approach to decisions can help you improve decision quality over time, by revealing the biases and blind spots we all have but few of us take the time to identify.

---

### Consider This

Ralph Warren was a self-confident and decisive CEO. He spent the first ten years of his career working for Crimson Judge, a legendary CEO who had been in charge at his hospital for more than 30 years. Warren served first as a vice president and then COO under the tutelage of this superstar. After 20 years of serving as CEO of three other community hospitals, he took a new position in a large and complex academic medical center with a strong research focus and a parent university of international renown. Warren felt that his greatest strength as a leader was his decisiveness. He felt he had modeled his style after Judge's and this had served him well. When asked what his decision-making style was, Warren once said, "I think it is summed up by four key points: first, it is likely I have had every experience a CEO could possibly have in the field. I have seen it all. Second, decisions to me are like math—there really are clear-cut paths to take. Third, I feel that the courage to act and to act decisively sends a clear message to those in the organization that they can trust me and where we are going. And finally, I simply do not believe in mistakes; yes, I may make course corrections at times, but they are usually minor."

- Clearly Ralph Warren can articulate his decision-making philosophy. What might be wrong with it? How might Warren encounter problems in his new job?

---

### Consider This

A great deal of decision making takes place in a group setting. This requires expert communications skills. One of the suggested steps in the book *Crucial Conversations* (Patterson et al. 2011) is to "State Your Path"—in other words, disclose your own personal point of view and conclusions, and create an atmosphere that helps others feel secure telling their stories as well.

*(continued)*

*(continued from previous page)*

- Research the topic of "rules of engagement" in group interaction and detail how these can help the conversations described in the *Crucial Conversations* approach.

## REFERENCES

Ariely, D. 2010. *Predictably Irrational: The Hidden Forces That Shape Our Decisions.* New York: Harper Perennial.

Kahneman, D. 2013. *Thinking, Fast and Slow.* New York: Farrar, Straus and Giroux.

Klein, G. 2003. *Intuition at Work: Why Developing Your Gut Instincts Will Make You Better at What You Do.* New York: Doubleday Business.

Patterson, K., J. Grenny, R. McMillan, and A. Switzler. 2011. *Crucial Conversations: Tools for Talking When Stakes Are High,* 2nd ed. New York: McGraw-Hill.

Russo, J. E., and P. J. H. Shoemaker. 2002. *Winning Decisions: Getting It Right the First Time.* New York: Crown Business.

Veney, J. E., and A. D. Kaluzny. 2005. *Evaluation and Decision Making for Health Services,* 3rd ed. Frederick, MD: Beard Books.

## CHAPTER FOURTEEN

# Competency 14: Driving Results

As the new vice president of support and facility services, Bill Sutor asked each of his new direct reports to provide him with their most recent annual summary of accomplishments and goals. They had not historically been required to prepare formal summaries of this type; fortunately, the outgoing SVP had given them the heads-up that Bill would be expecting these reports, so most of the staff had a good start on them by the time he arrived on the job.

As Bill pored over the reports, he noted everyone was meeting or exceeding their performance targets. Collectively, the departments were the most efficiently run they had been in their history. In their goals for the coming year, each described raising the bar in a measured fashion, ensuring some continuous improvement while avoiding setting expectations so high that their direct reports would dismiss the goals as impossible to reach. The report from plant facilities seemed to be a particularly strong success story, with substantial progress made on the formidable challenges of staff absenteeism and turnover. Employee development was another department describing substantial improvements, including doubling the amount of training provided to employees without adding any new trainers—essentially halving the per-unit delivery cost.

All this would seem like good news. Yet when Sutor emerged from his office, he had a noticeably stern look on his face. He turned to George Boucher, the administrative director of plant facilities, and asked him to step into his office.

"Let me start by first thanking you for preparing this annual report, particularly on such short notice," Sutor said. "It really helped me understand some of the strengths of your department, as well as its limitations. Now then, we're going to need to revise your goals moving forward . . . ."

AMONG THE MANY dynamics this vignette suggests is the apparent gap between Sutor's expectations and those of his direct reports. On the surface, each of the departments seems to be doing well. But from Sutor's experience in prior roles, he knows the departments could be doing even better. Sutor has elected to raise performance expectations as a top priority, capitalizing on the natural tension and uncertainty that comes with his newness to the role.

The focus of this chapter is how leaders most effectively move their staff and departments toward higher levels of performance. Leaders who do well in this area have mastered a collection of skills that we refer to collectively as *Driving Results*.

## WHAT IS DRIVING RESULTS, AND WHY IS IT IMPORTANT?

*Driving Results* encompasses all activities leaders engage in to define, monitor, and ensure high performance from themselves and their staff. You can also think of Driving Results as a set of performance habits—patterns of interacting with others to ensure goals are clarified and reinforced, progress is regularly discussed, and accomplishments are acknowledged and used to redefine expectations.

> **Driving Results** means you mobilize people toward greater commitment to a vision, challenge people to set higher standards and goals, keep people focused on achieving goals, give direct and complete feedback that keeps teams and individuals on track, quickly take corrective action as necessary to keep everyone moving forward, show a bias toward action, and proactively work through performance barriers.

The habits of Driving Results are crucial to high-performance leadership; they are often what distinguishes the teams that go the extra mile from the other teams that merely meet their targets. No team executes their work flawlessly; to the extent that leaders know what to look for and when to intervene, they will address problems earlier on, achieving higher levels of success down the road.

## WHEN HIGHLY EFFECTIVE LEADERS DRIVE RESULTS

When it comes to Driving Results, exceptional leaders can be distinguished by the following characteristics.

## Looking for Process Improvement Opportunities

The strongest leaders tend to recognize process improvement opportunities that their peers do not see. This may stem in part from greater experience with process improvement; however, it also seems to reflect a greater tendency to *look* for these opportunities. Process improvement is more a general orientation for this group than a tool to be brought out for use on identified problems.

## Staying Focused

In addition to their ability to spot process improvement opportunities, exceptional leaders also tend to keep themselves and others continuously focused on process improvement. They can readily bring any conversation back to the ultimate goals (e.g., efficiency, quality, bottom line).

## Keeping Organized

These leaders also have a knack for keeping track of agendas and milestones that their peers may allow to fall through the cracks. Some leaders accomplish this by keeping excellent notes or using project management tools; others methodically delegate record-keeping. Both end up in the same place—with more reliable monitoring.

## Having Boundless Energy

Being described as dependable and productive is one thing; being described as unstoppable is quite another. Exceptional leaders are often described in this way: Once they set their mind to something, it will either happen or it was not meant to be—period. On a day-to-day basis, these leaders tend to see every barrier as temporary, and they look to move around them as efficiently as possible. When the barriers are more indirect, these leaders will proactively surface them so they can be addressed head on. These leaders also tend to push themselves at least as hard as they push others. Their coworkers know they will be quick to step in and help when needed.

## WHEN DRIVING RESULTS IS NOT ALL IT COULD BE

Leaders' effectiveness in Driving Results can fall short for any of the following reasons.

## Lacking Energy or Drive

Some leaders do not have the energy and drive of their higher-performing peers. Less energetic leaders are more likely to procrastinate on pursuing initiatives or abandon efforts too early. In some cases, the difference between exceptional leaders and less effective leaders involves temperament, which is difficult to change. In other cases, however, a lower energy and drive involve internal conflicts that leaders may have about their initiatives or their roles.

## Underdeveloped Organizational Skills

Some leaders have energy and drive in spades, but their execution falls short because their organizational skills are not well honed. In some cases, leaders' energy levels can mask organizational problems; these leaders are outstanding at putting out fires but fail to recognize how many of these fires they themselves are setting. Common examples of where organizational skills undercut execution include failing to prepare meeting attendees ahead of time, forgetting to consistently monitor progress on goals that have been set with direct reports, and failing to make note of commitments to others and/or set specific times by which they will be completed.

## Developing Ineffective Working Relationships

Success in Driving Results depends on the development of effective working relationships. Some leaders find this part of their roles particularly challenging. A common barrier relates to leaders wanting to be liked. Leaders who are overly concerned about their coworkers liking them often have particular trouble holding people accountable. They may give in too readily to explanations for underperformance, or they may avoid addressing performance issues in the first place.

Even leaders with a more balanced orientation toward their coworkers will fall short if they have not mastered the art of clarifying priorities, setting clear and well-designed goals, and communicating about them on a consistent basis. All of these skills are learnable; leaders can master them most quickly by habitually seeking appropriate feedback (e.g., in times of confusion or underperformance, inquiring about how clear the goals were and how well the priorities and urgency were understood).

> **When Driving Results Is Not All It Could Be**
>
> - Lacking energy or drive
>   - Leaders procrastinate on some agendas and abandon other efforts too quickly.
>   - Leaders experience internal conflicts about their roles and initiatives.
> - Having poor organizational skills
>   - Leaders fail to track important goals and deadlines.
>   - Leaders come to meetings unprepared, fail to set clear agendas, or fail to prepare others.
> - Developing ineffective working relationships
>   - Effective goals are not consistent, clear, or measurable.
>   - Excuses for performance shortfalls are accepted too readily.
>   - Leaders are overly concerned with being liked by coworkers.

## MISUSE AND OVERUSE: HOW DRIVING RESULTS CAN WORK AGAINST YOU

Many of us have had first-hand experience pushing too hard for results at some point in our careers. We learn the lesson, and we adjust our style accordingly. Leaders who never learn this lesson may not see just how awful it can be to work with them. Here are the common patterns we see, and their underlying causes.

### Underemphasizing People

We have already mentioned the danger of letting a people-focus take precedence over a results-focus. There is ample danger in focusing too much on results as well. Some leaders neglect to celebrate successes and instead jump straight to raising the bar again. The consequence is that staff start to pace themselves because any improvements will only call for greater improvements later. Other leaders focus so strongly on individual accountabilities that they foster unhealthy competition among coworkers, undermining effectiveness when teamwork is called for.

Leaders who view their staff only in terms of their productivity tend to foster attitudes among their employees that their work is just a job. Organizational commitment will be lower, and people will be eager to find better arrangements elsewhere.

Leaders with this approach may also too quickly dismiss people who have good long-term potential but are underperforming in the near term. These leaders may undervalue coaching and other forms of skill development, and may have never mastered these skills.

## Overemphasizing Performance

Even when leaders do well with the people-related aspects of their jobs, they may still overemphasize performance. Some leaders have too much of their own self-concept tied up in achievement at work. This pattern shows up in leaders who consistently focus on the short-term win over the long-term success story. Some leaders will come full-steam into a new position, make a bunch of unsustainable changes, and then leave before that reality becomes apparent.

A related pattern is evident in leaders who focus on performance above all else and expect the same from their direct reports. Leaders who think the ends always justify the means can end up justifying what in hindsight can look overly self-serving or even ethically suspect. Leaders who view their job as the whole of their existence are also at risk for developing dangerous blind spots, not the least of which is a failure to recognize when they are no longer right for the job they have. Classic workaholism has been well described in popular books such as *Chained to the Desk* (Robinson 2014); if you have been told you exhibit these tendencies, they should get attention as part of your professional development.

## Lacking Flexibility

Leaders often find themselves in situations where an initial course of action seems no longer tenable—perhaps the external market has changed, or the leader was working from some misinformation in the first place. Some leaders can effectively admit they were wrong and change course. For other leaders, the very idea of failure is so aversive that they may instead push even harder on their original course of action. The problem becomes framed not in terms of faulty assumptions but as not working hard enough. Patterns like this can end badly, with everyone but the leader recognizing the futility of a given plan, eventually abandoning support and becoming suspicious of the leader's judgment.

> **Misuse and Overuse: How Driving Results Can Work Against You**
>
> - Underemphasizing people
>   - Staff pace themselves to avoid having their leader raise the bar too often or too high.
>   - An overemphasis on individual accountabilities undermines teamwork.
>
> *(continued)*

*(continued from previous page)*

- Overemphasizing performance
  - Leaders focus on short-term wins rather than long-term successes.
  - Performance is pursued at all costs, and ethical issues are not adequately considered.
- Lacking flexibility
  - Leaders may push for results beyond what is best for their organizations.
  - Changing course when necessary becomes difficult.

## HOW TO IMPROVE ON DRIVING RESULTS

### Finding Role Models

Unlike with some of the other competencies in this book, role models in Driving Results are often relatively easy to identify because their accomplishments tend to speak for themselves. Within any organization, strong role models will distinguish themselves as the people whom senior leaders always want to turn to first to take on large, messy projects. They are also constantly at risk of being overcommitted to task forces and special projects because they tend to be nominated more often than others.

If you work as a leader within a specific type of department or profession, you might seek out role models who are your counterparts in similar organizations. Meetings and conferences sponsored by professional associations are good hunting grounds. Look for presenters describing particularly complex turnaround efforts or program expansions. Find opportunities to meet these individuals to learn more about the secrets of their successes.

### Additional Opportunities for Personal Development

If you notice yourself having lower energy or drive around a specific project or process, take some time to think about the ambivalences you may have. The same advice goes for your job: If you feel you are not pursuing it with your fullest commitment of energy, give some thought to the reasons why. Surfacing these internal conflicts can help you work through them, or you may reconsider whether your current role is a good fit for you if these conflicts are more serious.

If your overall energy level is simply sapped, assess your track record of physical activity and outside interests. Gaining balance in life by expanding time spent pursuing family matters or personal hobbies may pay healthy dividends in the workplace. Alternatively, if you have considerable difficulty periodically unplugging from work, or have been described multiple times by coworkers and loved ones as a workaholic, consider reading a book such as Robinson's (2014) *Chained to the Desk* to reflect on the hidden costs this pattern may be having on the people you work and live with.

If you find yourself challenged by tracking and monitoring, consider attending a workshop or course on project management. Most business schools and many graduate healthcare management programs, as well as a number of professional associations, offer these. If you are not using productivity tools (e.g., software-based collaboration tools, such as shared calendars and project sites), look to your more organized peers for advice on technologies that may be useful for you to adopt. If you have an administrative assistant, look for ways he can help you better track and organize your work.

If holding people accountable is a challenge for you, you may need to work on improving your skills and/or your comfort with delivering constructive feedback. Working with an internal or external coach can be very helpful in developing and practicing these skills. Also, be sure to review Chapter 7 of this book, "Giving Great Feedback."

A good general book we suggest is *Getting Results the Agile Way: A Personal Results System for Work and Life* by J. D. Meier (2010).

Several books provide excellent first-person accounts of leaders who are masters at Driving Results. *Who Says Elephants Can't Dance?* describes Lou Gerstner's (2002) dramatic turnaround success story with IBM. Although not about a hospital or healthcare system, the challenges Gerstner faced in many ways parallel ones familiar to health administrators. In *Execution,* Honeywell's Larry Bossidy teamed up with academician Ram Charan (2002) to provide a highly readable, first-person account of his philosophy and successful approach to Driving Results at large, diverse organizations.

## SUMMARY

People have a natural tendency to set performance goals at a level they feel comfortable achieving. Selling staff on higher levels of performance can involve instilling in them a confidence that they are capable of more than they think. Exceptional leaders are able to instill this confidence, while not overdriving to the point where people give up.

## Consider This

Consider change management. (If you are unfamiliar with the concept, review John Kotter's [2012] book *Leading Change*, or review Kotter's eight-step change management process at his website, www.kotterinternational.com/our-principles/changesteps/changesteps.)

- Is the competency Driving Results part of change management, or is change management part of Driving Results?

## Consider This

The best organizations have a central culture of Driving Results. Small things—such as starting and ending meetings on time, hitting deadlines, respecting budgets, having clear performance standards, giving meaningful evaluations, and using dashboards and scorecards—all add to this type of culture.

- Think of a specific organization that lacks a results-driven culture. Describe how you would begin to develop one.

## REFERENCES

Bossidy, L., and R. Charan. 2002. *Execution: The Discipline of Getting Things Done.* New York: Crown Business.

Gerstner, L. V., Jr. 2002. *Who Says Elephants Can't Dance? Inside IBM's Historic Turnaround.* New York: Harper Business.

Kotter, J. 2012. *Leading Change.* Boston: Harvard Business Review Press.

Meier, J. D. 2010. *Getting Results the Agile Way: A Personal Results System for Work and Life.* Bellevue, WA: Innovation Playhouse.

Robinson, B. E. 2014. *Chained to the Desk: A Guidebook for Workaholics, Their Partners and Children, and the Clinicians Who Treat Them.* New York: NYU Press.

## CHAPTER FIFTEEN

# Competency 15: Stimulating Creativity

Staff and leaders of the operating room (OR) were clearly tense as they arrived at the conference center. They had little idea what to expect, other than they would be there for the whole morning and would be discussing ways to improve the OR climate. What they found when they got there was an enormous circle of chairs, with poster boards and markers on the walls.

They made small talk to break the tension, until Dr. Bernard Jacque, the chief quality officer, called for their attention. He introduced a facilitator, who laid out an agenda that was almost frightening in its simplicity. Staff would be asked to identify topics for OR improvement that they would like to discuss; other staff who were interested in their topic would then join them in a corner of the room. The convener would take notes, which would be posted on a central wall. The same process would be repeated several times; at the end of the session, individuals could volunteer to take on initiatives after they returned to work.

When it came time to suggest topics, the group was silent for what seemed like hours. Finally, someone suggested the first topic: "making sure we have supplies on time." Topics became successively more daring: "speaking up for patient safety," "making scheduling fair," and even "how about a little respect around here?" and "how do we make the changes we discuss actually happen?" When it came time for the discussions, there was a surprising amount of milling around, people leaving one discussion to join another, and some conveners with no discussants simply writing down their own thoughts.

*(continued)*

*(continued from previous page)*

At the end of the day, the group had a half-dozen topics with widespread interest and support. Dr. Jacque commended the group for their creative thinking and endorsed the plans to set up quality improvement teams around the six themes. He asked each of the conveners to have a progress report ready for presentation at the quarterly all-staff meeting.

THIS VIGNETTE DESCRIBES the use of "open space," a type of large group intervention that has been used to foster creative thinking and shared decision making. While the approach is more common in corporate settings than in healthcare, it typifies the kinds of innovative approaches that can be used to marshal people's creative energies around process improvement. We provide this vignette not as the right way to encourage creative thinking but rather as an illustration of the dynamics associated with an effective approach to the process.

## WHAT IS STIMULATING CREATIVITY, AND WHY IS IT IMPORTANT?

*Stimulating Creativity* involves two parts: the creativity and the stimulation. For our purposes, we can define *creativity* as the use of innovative approaches to problem solving and decision making. Stimulating Creativity, in turn, involves fostering a climate that is conducive to using these creative approaches.

**Stimulating Creativity** means you see broadly outside of the typical; are constantly open to new ideas; are effective with techniques for stimulating group creativity (e.g., brainstorming, design thinking, Nominal Group Technique, scenario building); see future trends and craft responses to them; are knowledgeable in business and societal trends; are aware of how strategies play out in the field; actively read within and outside of healthcare; and make connections between industries and other trends.

Leaders come to be viewed as exceptional in part for their ability to reach unprecedented levels of performance; as such, stimulating out-of-the-box creative thinking is a critical skill for exceptional leaders. Considering possibilities outside of the obvious requires creative thinking, and the expression of creative thinking requires license to do so. Organizations that embrace creative solutions are often the first to the market with new services and approaches to care, and they typically attract and retain the best clinicians and employees.

## WHEN HIGHLY EFFECTIVE LEADERS STIMULATE CREATIVITY

Before we define the high bar on Stimulating Creativity, we should comment on what Stimulating Creativity is *not*. Most important, it is not the same as being creative. Some leaders are exceptionally creative but not particularly good at fostering creativity in the people they work with. Other leaders are not creative, but they still may be exceptional leaders if they are outstanding at marshalling the creative thinking of others.

The process of Stimulating Creativity involves the following elements.

### Having a Positive Attitude Toward Challenges

Our natural response to many of the challenges we face at work is to think, "Oh no, what are we going to do?" The challenge becomes a problem that we must solve, a worry we must rid ourselves of. Highly effective leaders, in contrast, are skilled at fostering a positive perspective about these challenges. When faced with a new problem, they are quick to ask, "What are the opportunities that this challenge presents?" and can readily encourage this attitude in others.

### Fostering Perspective

Creative approaches require people to be able to view their work from a variety of perspectives—from near term to long term, from the very narrow to the very broad, and from multiple stakeholders' points of view. Highly effective leaders are adept at shifting between these perspectives and helping others to do so as well.

Consider the "getting respect" topic from our vignette. The solutions this group comes up with will likely reflect the biases of whoever chose that topic discussion: A group of nurses will define respect differently than a group of housekeepers or anesthesiologists will. An effective leader would help staff recognize the missing points of view and encourage people to see from those perspectives—or, better yet, to seek those perspectives out. For our case example, staff may be biased toward defining respect in terms of a specific recent incident in which someone was treated harshly. The effective leader will encourage people to view that incident not just as a case in point but also within the historical context of the department's culture: "What is the *first* example we can identify of this type of interaction? How far back do we think this goes?"

### Drawing Out Creative Ideas

The most skillful leaders are particularly effective at facilitating brainstorming. Many leaders do not have a highly sophisticated sense of brainstorming; they view it just as asking people for ideas and waiting a while before shooting them down. In reality, many creative discussions involve active debate about ideas *while* the ideas are being drawn out. The key is the climate: People should feel comfortable debating the merits of their ideas without feeling personally vulnerable. Highly effective leaders are skilled at drawing out creative ideas during brainstorming and keeping the dialogue focused on building rather than debating during this step.

### Building Up to Creative Solutions

A final quality distinguishing these leaders is their capacity to synthesize people's ideas into a coherent whole. They are able to recognize common themes and trends, and they can effectively articulate them for a group's consideration. They create cycles of divergence (adding new ideas and perspectives) to convergence (summarizing into a new whole) and back again, until new perspectives have been largely exhausted or accounted for.

## WHEN STIMULATING CREATIVITY IS NOT ALL IT COULD BE

Leaders who are not highly effective at stimulating creativity will miss some of the opportunities for innovation that their peers may spot first. This can happen for a number of reasons, but the following three tend to be the most common.

### Focusing Only on the Presenting Problem

When faced with a problem of almost any type, the natural response of most leaders is to attempt to solve it quickly and efficiently. The more pressing the problem, the faster they will rush to a solution. The approach can be and often is overdone, causing some leaders to "solve" the same problem over and over again and never identify the root cause.

For example, one of us knows a leader who has outstanding service-recovery skills. He can readily mend just about any client relationship through a combination of owning up to shortfalls, showing willingness to do whatever it takes to make things right, and possessing incredible interpersonal charm. So skillful is he in these areas that the root causes of his client-relations challenges (e.g., under-specified proposals, disorganization, failure to anticipate communication needs) have not prevented his success. But with additional creative thought, he would probably find much better ways of working with his clients to his own benefit as well as theirs.

## Approaching Problems Too Conservatively

Some leaders demonstrate a clear bias toward what has worked for them in the past. These leaders may be particularly skillful at developing reliable processes but can be extremely reluctant to change them. The surest sign of this bias is when a leader dismisses a suggestion with little rationale other than the fact that it has not been tried before, or she describes unusually dire outcomes that are likely to come from such a move.

## Underemphasizing Integrative Approaches

The vignette that begins this chapter describes a group of people in a context in which their ideas are allowed to build on each other. The techniques used recognize the power of group construction and creativity. Some leaders would never use such techniques because of their need to keep a tight control on group discussion outcomes. For example, some leaders feel threatened if group discussion is not flowing through them (sometimes called the hub-and-spoke communication model). Other leaders view creative thinking as part of their job and will feel threatened if *any* creative ideas come from their staff. In these cases, staff will learn to self-censor their ideas, creating a collusive pattern in which leaders solicit input but do not receive any.

In milder cases, the barriers stem from failing to fully capitalize on creative ideas through effective facilitation and synthesis. For example, opinions may be solicited but then turned into a laundry list rather than an integrated set of themes, or ideas may not be fed back to their sources for further refinement.

> **When Stimulating Creativity Is Not All It Could Be**
>
> - Focusing only on the presenting problem
>   - The same problem gets "solved" over and over again.
>   - The patterns and root causes underlying the problems are not identified.
> - Approaching problems too conservatively
>   - The bias toward what has worked in the past is too strong.
>   - The leader is overly cautious about new approaches.
> - Underemphasizing integrative approaches
>   - Creative ideas from others are discouraged.
>   - The leader fails to synthesize others' input and ideas.

## MISUSE AND OVERUSE: HOW STIMULATING CREATIVITY CAN WORK AGAINST YOU

Leaders can also undermine performance through an overuse or misuse of creativity. The following are the common patterns we have seen.

### Being Creative Rather Than Encouraging Creativity

This pattern is particularly common with leaders who are creative people themselves—those who might be considered role models if they did not get the process wrong. Some of these leaders are outstanding creative thinkers who fail to take their staff along with them—in other words, they may arrive quickly at solutions and innovations, but no one can figure out how they got there. They may have little patience for explaining themselves and may not recognize the importance of getting buy-in.

Other highly creative leaders have too little respect for real-world considerations. They may enjoy the creative thinking process for its own sake and get annoyed and frustrated when people dampen their enthusiasm by reminding them of reality. While occasionally these leaders may reach brilliant, inventive solutions they would not have otherwise been able to put together, the more frequent result is taking too much time to arrive at unworkable solutions.

### Focusing Too Much on Innovation

The pattern of overfocusing on innovation can come from several places, but in each case the process is the same: Innovations are pursued for reasons other than organizational performance. One of these patterns is that of the excitement junkie—leaders who push for innovations to keep themselves from being bored. Such leaders may be used to high levels of chaos in their environments and will seek to create this excitement whether it serves the department's goals or not.

A variant on this theme is the overzealous career-ladder climber. Such leaders may push innovation as a way to get themselves noticed. The result can be a focus on dreaming rather than planning, or a habit of perpetually overextending themselves and their staff to the point of underperformance on everything.

## Overemphasizing New Ideas

The final dangerous pattern is an overemphasis on the idea-development process itself. While speculation about the future can be helpful in generating potential courses of action, some leaders are never happier than when they are in a creative brainstorming session, and they are too quick to block out time for these activities. They may find themselves and their staff recreating their vision of the future far more often than is really needed or even thinking through change initiatives for departments and domains over which they have no control.

Having an overemphasis on ideas is another way that excitement-junkie leaders can misuse the creative thinking process. For many such leaders, this pattern coexists with a tendency to view the necessary day-to-day "administrivia" as so dull that it is not enough to keep them meaningfully engaged in their work. The creative thinking process becomes an escape for them, but one that is used beyond the point of meaningful gains. At the senior levels, this pattern can be seen in how leadership teams are structured; a CEO may pay far more attention to the creative thinking departments (e.g., strategy and marketing), giving short shrift to other departments that are vital for effective stewardship of the organization (e.g., environmental or information services).

---

**Misuse and Overuse: How Stimulating Creativity Can Work Against You**

- Overfocusing on one's own creativity rather than fostering creativity in others
    - The thinking processes of creative leaders are not well explained.
    - Ideas are not tempered by real-world considerations.
- Focusing too much on innovation
    - Leaders push change for change's sake.
    - Creativity is used as a tool for personal recognition.
    - Leaders and staff become overextended and thus underperform.

*(continued)*

---

*(continued from previous page)*

- Overemphasizing new ideas
  - New ideas and approaches are encouraged, while the mundane day-to-day is given short shrift.
  - Creativity in staff is overvalued, and operations are undervalued.

## HOW TO BETTER STIMULATE CREATIVITY

### Finding Role Models

Some of the best role models for creative thinking in leadership will be found in areas where creativity is central to the role: marketing management, communications, and philanthropy departments are good choices. Outside of the hospital, creative organizations, such as advertising agencies and design firms, will tend to attract the leaders most skilled at fostering creativity.

If you can, find opportunities to sit in on meetings in which creative thinking or problem-solving discussions are on the agenda. Focus specifically on process: How does the leader ensure participation? How are good ideas received? What about off-the-mark ideas? How does the leader synthesize ideas and move people forward? If the leaders are open to it, review the meeting with them afterward. Tell them what you noticed, and ask for additional commentary.

### Additional Opportunities for Personal Development

Most leaders can improve their skills in stimulating creativity simply by making a conscious effort to attend to the creative process and by improving the feedback they receive on how they are doing.

A good exercise to get started is to focus on regular meetings in which creative thinking or decision making is particularly helpful to outcomes, such as a meeting in which members are present based on their unique background or experience. Make a point at the end of each meeting to ask the group for feedback. Useful questions include the following:

- How well did we do in getting each of your ideas out on the table?
- At what point in the process was it most difficult to get ideas out?

For group members who had their ideas shot down, you could circle back after the meeting to check in on the effects of that process. If they are feeling particularly discouraged, give them some positive feedback about having a "tough hide" about it and encourage more of the same in the future.

Sometimes groups develop a habit of undercontributing over time, and the habit can be especially hard to break. In these cases, bringing an outsider—a process consultant— into a group meeting can be helpful. This person is charged with tracking the process of the group: who is talking, who is keeping quiet, who is supporting whom. His or her goal is to bring these patterns to the group's attention so that they can be discussed and evolved.

Several excellent books focus specifically on enhancing understanding of the creative process. Our favorites include *When Sparks Fly: Harnessing the Power of Group Creativity* by Dorothy Leonard and Walter Swap (2005), *Creativity, Inc.: Building an Inventive Organization* by Jeff Mauzy and Richard A. Harriman (2003), and *The Art of Engagement* by Jim Haudan (2008). Several other highly accessible books focus on the design process, and the critical role creativity plays, including Tim Brown's (2009) *Change by Design* and Tom and David Kelly's (2013) *Creative Confidence*.

## SUMMARY

At a time when healthcare is undergoing unprecedented change, stimulating creativity becomes particularly important. When incremental change will clearly not take us where we need to go, exceptional leaders communicate that innovative thinking is not only tolerated, but will be essential to our success.

### Consider This

Assuming that having great perspective and being open to new ideas and approaches are some of the hallmarks of Stimulating Creativity, is it possible that having too much experience may actually inhibit creativity? Consider: Typically, one of the most important requirements when hiring a leader is experience—the more, the better.

- Is this necessarily true?
- What is the possibility that the more experience one has, the less likely one is to have truer perspective?
- Can too much experience cause leaders to fail to examine all the possibilities when confronting a problem?

## Consider This

Senior VP of business development Dave Damron, VP of marketing and PR Nancy Groves, and VP of planning Susan Edwards were talking one day about how executives could become more creative. Groves suggested that the most creative people she knew were ones who had broad liberal arts–type educational backgrounds. Damron replied, "So, you feel that creativity can be developed? I think that for the most part, it is inborn and hereditary." Edwards joined in, "Well, I think both can be true. But I do think that it is crucial that executives have a strong skill of creativity."

- Detail specific ways in which a leader can become more creative.

## REFERENCES

Brown, T. 2009. *Change by Design: How Design Thinking Transforms Organizations and Inspires Innovation.* New York: Harper Business.

Haudan, J. 2008. *The Art of Engagement: Bridging the Gap Between People and Possibilities.* New York: McGraw-Hill.

Kelly, T., and D. Kelly. 2013. *Creative Confidence: Unleashing the Creative Potential Within Us All.* New York: Crown Business.

Leonard, D., and W. Swap. 2005. *When Sparks Fly: Harnessing the Power of Group Creativity.* New York: Harvard Business School Press.

Mauzy, J., and R. Harriman. 2003. *Creativity, Inc.: Building an Inventive Organization.* Boston: Harvard Business School Press.

## CHAPTER SIXTEEN

# Competency 16: Cultivating Adaptability

A morning in the life of John Vardez, the COO for the flagship hospital of the St. Nicholas system.

*7:00–8:00 a.m.:* Vardez meets with a group of 15 physicians from cardiology, radiology, and cardiothoracic surgery to talk about the development of a new service line that will exist across several of the St. Nicholas Health System's hospitals. During the hour, he rarely makes a definitive statement; he instead spends the time asking probing questions, carefully drawing out the physicians' thoughts to further discuss the potential barriers to cooperation.

*8:00–9:00 a.m.:* Vardez calls in his key operational vice presidents for a budget meeting. He starts the meeting by noting the loss of four key surgeons. He then informs the group that because of the anticipated reduction in admissions, he will need to mandate an 8 percent across-the-board budget cut on expenses. "I don't care how you do it, only that it gets done," he says. The vice presidents walk out of the room with the understanding that the next time they get together, their budgets had better reflect the cuts.

*9:00–10:00 a.m.:* Vardez meets with Josiah Branson, the administrative director of the labs. They discuss his career with the medical center as well as his future plans. Vardez tells Branson he sees potential for him to eventually rise into the executive ranks and recommends he consider enrolling in a master's program in health systems management. He also suggests that Branson join one of the hospital-wide strategic planning task forces Vardez is putting together, to broaden his exposure to other departments in the hospital.

*10:00 a.m.–12:00 p.m.:* Vardez meets with the directors of business development and community affairs. They spend two hours together, brainstorming

*(continued)*

*(continued from previous page)*

ways they can develop new programs that will involve community physicians and bring additional admissions into their medical center. He provides whatever ideas he can come up with and suggests additional people they might contact, always in the spirit of broadening the list of options rather than mandating the next step.

*11:15 a.m.:* Vardez's meeting is interrupted by his administrative assistant. Dr. Rodriquez is on the phone, and he is very upset to learn that the lot he tells patients to park in is being torn up and no one bothered to tell him. Vardez steps out of the meeting for ten minutes, listens patiently to the doctor's concerns, apologizes for the lack of communication, and offers to have one of his assistants prepare a map with parking alternatives. The call ends with Vardez thanking him for the feedback, giving the follow-up request to his assistant, and returning to his meeting.

---

THIS VIGNETTE ILLUSTRATES many of the situations healthcare leaders find themselves in throughout a typical day. While a single, general leadership approach might get an executive through these meetings, leaders who move into each exchange with a specific approach in mind, given their sense of the meeting's purpose and audience, will often find themselves much better able to navigate toward the ends they are pursuing.

## WHAT IS CULTIVATING ADAPTABILITY, AND WHY IS IT IMPORTANT?

*Cultivating Adaptability* in leadership involves the mastery of three fundamental skills:

1. reading the environment,
2. assessing the ideal course of action among a number of choices, and
3. responding with an appropriate leadership style.

**Cultivating Adaptability** means you quickly see the essence of issues and problems, effectively bring clarity to situations of ambiguity, approach work using a variety of leadership styles and techniques, track changing priorities and readily interpret their implications, balance consistency of focus against the ability to adjust course as needed, balance multiple tasks and priorities such that each gets appropriate attention, and work effectively with a broad range of people.

Let us look more closely at the three parts of this definition. The first—reading the environment—suggests an ability to attend to the most important aspects of a given leadership situation. For example, a leader must determine who is involved in a situation, what kinds of challenges are being faced, what history may be on people's minds, and how much real and perceived urgency exists. The second part of the definition—weighing appropriate courses of action—involves a leader's judgment about which approach will work best given her read on the environment. The third part of the definition—responding with an appropriate leadership style—involves the quality of a leader's toolbox, her mastery of a breadth of leadership styles.

## WHEN HIGHLY EFFECTIVE LEADERS CULTIVATE ADAPTABILITY

Exceptionally adaptable leaders have mastered each of the three skills previously described. They are good at reading situations, have a firm handle on the implications of different leadership styles, and have a well-stocked toolbox of practiced leadership styles to choose from.

### Reading Environments

An important first step in reading environments is investing the time to do so. Exceptional leaders will think through their meetings ahead of time to pull out the most salient elements related to their role. Examples of useful diagnostic questions include the following:

- *Situation.* What must happen as a result of this exchange? What would I like to have happen? What would others like to have happen? What kinds of time pressures are we facing?
- *People.* How many people will I be meeting with? Are all of the decision makers in the room? Who will be missing, and why? What is each person's function in this meeting? How does each person seem to be reacting?
- *Relationships.* How do these individuals get along with each other? How are they feeling about me right now? How much leeway will they want, and how much will be appropriate for me to give them?
- *History.* What has been the track record for this group? Have they been getting what they want, or are they being turned down left and right?

Have their departments been stable, growing, or recently downsized? What approaches have worked well or poorly with this group in the past? Do new members need a better understanding of the long-term history? Do older members need to get better at overcoming their histories?

◆ *Outcomes.* How will the various potential outcomes affect the people involved? Who should be recognized as the decision maker or decision makers? How should these outcomes be communicated, and by whom? How might the outcomes be used to inform our approach in the future?

## Understanding Different Leadership Styles

Exceptional leaders will take their read of the environment and use it to select the approach they think will be most successful. Although this process involves more art and experience than science, some general guidelines are emerging from research. The following are a few styles that appear to be particularly robust.

### Autocratic or Coercive

An autocratic or coercive style is a top-down approach in which leaders make unilateral decisions and hold their direct reports accountable to them. "Driving Results" (Chapter 14) is an example of a competency that can inform this leadership style. This approach seems to be most useful in times when decisive action is imperative—for example, when facing a natural disaster or a threat of impending bankruptcy. However, the approach is counterproductive in almost all other cases.

### Authoritative or Inspirational

An authoritative or inspirational style involves reaching out to people in a way that gets them charged up about a particular vision or agenda. "Energizing Staff" (Chapter 10) and "Communicating Vision" (Chapter 4) are examples of competencies that are closely aligned with this style. This approach is particularly useful when employees in a department or organization lack a compelling sense of purpose in their efforts or roles.

### Democratic or Consultative

A democratic or consultative style involves engaging staff in an action or decision-making process as a peer or consultant. With this approach, decisions may be fully delegated to the group, and the leader may simply serve as a facilitator or as an additional source of creative ideas. This approach can be particularly useful when the staff involved are highly experienced and skilled, when the best actions or decisions are unclear to the leader, or when an employee is being given a project as a developmental assignment.

### Encouraging or Supportive

When leaders adopt an encouraging or supportive style, their focus is on attending to the individual needs of their staff or peers. "Earning Trust And Loyalty" (Chapter 5) and "Developing High-Performing Teams" (Chapter 9) are examples of competencies closely associated with this style. The approach is particularly useful when employees have suffered a hit to their morale (e.g., losing a highly regarded colleague, facing the closing of a program they are emotionally invested in), or when there has been a violation of employee trust.

### Standards Setting

When leaders adopt a standards-setting style, they are focusing primarily on process: how it is measured, how it can be improved, who is accountable, and so on. Used sparingly, this approach can be helpful in clarifying roles and goals as well as in improving systems that are in need of immediate attention. Used too often, however, the style will be experienced as fatiguing and micromanaging.

### Coaching

When leaders use a coaching style, they are focusing on the nexus between an employee's development needs and the goals of the organization. Some evidence suggests the style is used less often than other approaches, which is unfortunate given the high value that direct reports see in the practice as well as its demonstrated relationship to supporting a positive organizational culture. The approach is particularly useful for ensuring that staff forge a long-term relationship with the organization and remain mindful of their development needs as related to their career goals. The "Mentoring" competency (Chapter 8) is closely aligned with this leadership style.

## Perfecting Multiple Leadership Styles

Leaders who have a sense of the environment and a planned approach to leadership are two-thirds of the way to exceptional adaptability. The last leg involves mastering a variety of leadership styles and getting comfortable enough with each to employ them effectively when needed. For most leaders, this learning process is ongoing; most of us naturally gravitate toward a single leadership style, or, at most, a couple. Gaining comfort with a broader variety of styles requires practice, feedback, and more practice.

## WHEN CULTIVATING ADAPTABILITY IS NOT ALL IT COULD BE

Many leaders are less adaptable than they could be because they fall into one or more of the following traps.

### Giving In to Time Pressures

Perhaps the most common trap is time pressure. The dominant theme in health administration roles often seems to be "get it done, get it done!" Leaders can fall into the habit of rushing from meeting to meeting; in the process, they fail to step back and consider the nuances of each setting they are walking into. The same problem can happen on the back end: Leaders fail to do even a brief self-assessment of how their meetings or conversations went and lose these opportunities to gain a greater reflective awareness of the interpersonal aspects of these exchanges.

### Lacking Sensitivity to Environmental Cues

Reading the environment is a skill that comes more naturally to some than to others. The tendency for some leaders is to be more internally focused; these leaders may need to be more deliberate in attending to environmental cues.

### Having a Dominant Leadership Style

A common problem many leaders face is being too aligned with a single leadership style (or two). For example, some leaders are people oriented; they may foster wonderfully supportive environments but may also fail when it comes to holding people accountable. Others may be very process focused; they are great at ensuring things get done on deadline but may not develop their people effectively and may also have trouble holding on to good people.

### Failing to "Hear" When an Approach Is Not Working

A more serious problem some leaders face is in not recognizing when an approach is not working, because either they are insensitive to the environmental cues or not appropriately concerned about them. These leaders may not seek out feedback on how well their approaches are working, and they may fail to accurately read others' reactions—for example, these leaders cannot see when things are boiling over or when they are crossing the line. Chapter 6, "Listening Like You Mean It," provides more information about overcoming this barrier.

---

**When Cultivating Adaptability Is Not All It Could Be**

- Giving in to time pressures
  - Leaders fail to take the time to consider audience, situation, history, urgency, and relevant challenges in planning their approach.
  - Self-assessments to increase one's awareness of interpersonal exchanges are not done after meetings or conversations.
- Lacking sensitivity to environmental cues
  - Leaders have difficulty reading environmental cues.
  - Important facets of situations may blindside leaders.
- Having a dominant leadership style
  - One or two leadership styles tend to dominate; these styles work well in some situations but not as well (or not at all) in others.
- Failing to "hear" when an approach is not working
  - Feedback that a given approach is not working well is not heard.
  - Leaders fail to read others' reactions, so they cannot see when things are boiling over or crossing the line.

---

## MISUSE AND OVERUSE: HOW CULTIVATING ADAPTABILITY CAN WORK AGAINST YOU

Occasionally, a leader may be described as too adaptable. If a leader is thought of in this way, usually at least one of the following associated problems is present.

### Being Too Quick to Change Course

Some leaders have trouble sticking to their guns in the face of challenges to their approach. For example, leaders using an inspirational style may allow themselves to be fatigued by naysayers; an appropriately autocratic style may be abandoned in the face of push-back. These leaders have difficulty living by their personal convictions, which is discussed in Chapter 1.

### Changing Leadership Styles Erratically

Some leaders fail to keep a consistent style within a particular context. Often this lack of consistency reflects a leader's difficulty in accurately reading how the people in that context are feeling or reacting. Such leaders should work on reading cues and planning for these interactions, using the methods described in earlier sections of this chapter. Other leaders have trouble keeping a consistent style going because it feels monotonous to them. These leaders may find the innovative and creative aspects of their job to be the most interesting, and they may actively change things up to keep themselves more fully engaged. These leaders fail to ask themselves why they are changing styles and to evaluate their reasons before switching to a different approach.

---

**Misuse and Overuse: How Cultivating Adaptability Can Work Against You**

- Being too quick to change course
  - Leaders abandon leadership styles and waver in their approaches to challenges.
- Changing leadership styles erratically
  - Leaders change their leadership style midstream, which creates confusion.
  - Leaders are too enamored with doing things differently and find a consistent style to be too monotonous.

---

## HOW TO BETTER CULTIVATE ADAPTABILITY

### Finding Role Models

You will typically find the best role models in positions where aspects of adaptability are most regularly required. Leaders who spend significant time working with physicians tend to be quite adept at adaptability. Operations executives are also good role models because their day-to-day working world often presents many unexpected twists and turns.

In healthcare, another group that is particularly strong in this area is the medical service corps officers in the military branches. These individuals, most of whom are active within the American College of Healthcare Executives and other professional organizations, are excellent role models to get to know to learn how they adapt and modify their leadership approaches to frequently changing circumstances.

Leaders who have great sensitivity to differences in audiences can also be found in marketing and communications departments. These professionals can be helpful in thinking through the unique aspects of different stakeholder groups. Leaders working in offices of philanthropy are often required to have a keen awareness of history as well as an acute sense of individual interests and needs.

### Additional Opportunities for Personal Development

The best way to hone your adaptability is to find opportunities to practice a variety of leadership styles and to receive feedback on how they are working. The resources listed in this section describe a number of robust leadership styles that can be learned and practiced. Chapter 20 provides additional guidance on developing a feedback-rich environment. We recommend using this chapter and these suggested readings in tandem.

A great resource to start with is Daniel Goleman's (2000) article, "Leadership That Gets Results." This classic article provides a brief, readable summary of research about six leadership styles from the consulting group Hay/McBer. A terrific book on leadership styles related to the organizational lifecycle is *Risk Taker, Caretaker, Surgeon, Undertaker: The Four Faces of Strategic Leadership* by W. E. Rothschild (1993). Each style is treated in some depth, with a focus on how it relates to developing and executing strategy. Yukl and Lepsinger's (2004) book, *Flexible Leadership: Creating Value by Balancing Multiple Challenges and Choices*, provides an in-depth treatment of three leadership styles: efficiency-oriented, people-oriented, and change-oriented. Each style is described in a detailed, behavioral way, and the book includes a separate chapter on organizational processes that can further support and enhance the effectiveness of the styles. Lastly, Bob Kaplan and Robert Kaiser's (2013) book, *Fear Your Strengths,* provides an engaging analysis of the imbalances in leadership style that can grow out of overreliance on a particular approach.

## SUMMARY

Fostering an adaptive approach requires leaders to take a more active role in planning for their interactions, and reflecting on how they went, and doing so on a consistent basis. Most leaders do not consistently invest in developing their adaptability in this way, and it shows over time in a less flexible or imbalanced approach to their roles. Exceptional leadership requires the discipline to continuously challenge oneself to improve in adaptability, through a more rigorous and systematic approach.

## Consider This

Chapter 2 presented emotional intelligence as one of the 16 competencies in the competency model. The commonly accepted facets of emotional intelligence are (a) self-awareness; (b) self-management; (c) social awareness; and (d) relationship management.

- Detail how each of these four facets might relate to the ability of leaders to enhance their adaptability.

## Consider This

The theory of contingency leadership suggests that there is no one best style of leadership. Goleman's (2000) article suggests further that leaders need to be adaptable.

- Research the history of contingency leadership and describe how this approach might be more critical in today's organizations than it perhaps was in years past.

## REFERENCES

Goleman, D. 2000. "Leadership That Gets Results." *Harvard Business Review* (March/April): 78–90.

Kaplan, R., and R. Kaiser. 2013. *Fear Your Strengths: What You Are Best at Could Be Your Biggest Problem.* New York: Berrett-Koehler.

Rothschild, W. E. 1993. *Risk Taker, Caretaker, Surgeon, Undertaker: The Four Faces of Strategic Leadership.* New York: John Wiley & Sons.

Yukl, G., and R. Lepsinger. 2004. *Flexible Leadership: Creating Value by Balancing Multiple Challenges and Choices.* New York: John Wiley & Sons.

# Part V

# PUTTING THE
# COMPETENCIES TO WORK

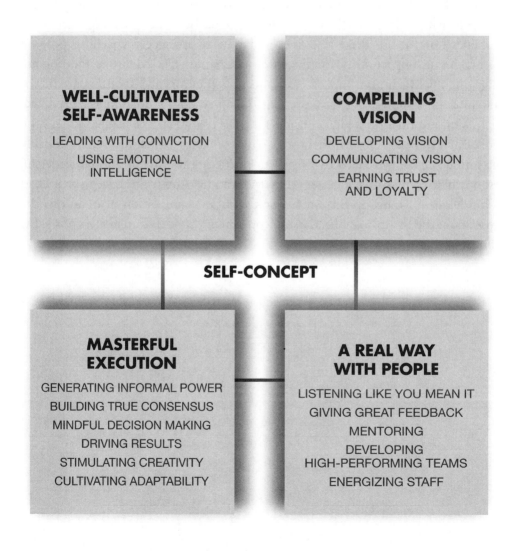

**WELL-CULTIVATED
SELF-AWARENESS**

LEADING WITH CONVICTION

USING EMOTIONAL
INTELLIGENCE

**COMPELLING
VISION**

DEVELOPING VISION

COMMUNICATING VISION

EARNING TRUST
AND LOYALTY

**SELF-CONCEPT**

**MASTERFUL
EXECUTION**

GENERATING INFORMAL POWER

BUILDING TRUE CONSENSUS

MINDFUL DECISION MAKING

DRIVING RESULTS

STIMULATING CREATIVITY

CULTIVATING ADAPTABILITY

**A REAL WAY
WITH PEOPLE**

LISTENING LIKE YOU MEAN IT

GIVING GREAT FEEDBACK

MENTORING

DEVELOPING
HIGH-PERFORMING TEAMS

ENERGIZING STAFF

THE FIRST FOUR parts of this book focus on building your understanding of the Dye–Garman Exceptional Leadership competency model—the *what* of exceptional leadership. Beyond the specific suggestions in each of the first 16 chapters about how to build your own leadership competencies, organizations can do many things to ensure leadership strength across their operations. The chapters in this part provide you with more information about how to put leadership competencies to work in your organization, both for yourself and for all leaders, so that your entire leadership team is continuously strengthening.

Chapter 17, "Systems Approaches to Leadership Development," provides a system-level overview of how to maximize investments in strengthening healthcare leadership. Chapter 18, on "Leadership Coaches and Coaching Programs," describes how to use these resources and how to manage a coaching program for maximum impact at most efficient cost. Chapter 19, "Mentors: Finding and Engaging for Maximum Impact," explains how mentors and sponsors are important internal resources for development. Chapter 20, "Developing a Feedback-Rich Working Environment," considers the use of 360-degree feedback and other tools. In "Physician Development and Competencies," Chapter 21, we consider the unique challenges faced by physicians in taking on organizational leadership responsibilities. The final chapter, "Final Questions About the Exceptional Leadership Model," wraps up the entire book with an examination of questions that arose about the Exceptional Leadership competency model from readers of the first edition of this book.

## CHAPTER SEVENTEEN

# Systems Approaches to Leadership Development

Although leaders must take responsibility for their own learning and development, organizations have important roles to play in supporting these activities. Taking leadership development seriously as an organizational capability requires thinking beyond the development needs of individual leaders and toward the leadership needs of the entire organization. It also means developing a discipline around leadership practices, to temper enthusiasm about what's new and flashy so that the focus over time is on maximizing proven returns on the time and resources expended.

In this chapter we take an evidence-driven approach to describing the components of a high-performance leadership development system.

## COMPONENTS OF A HIGH-PERFORMANCE LEADERSHIP DEVELOPMENT SYSTEM

In this chapter we consider the most important components of organizational leadership development systems within the context of healthcare.

### Strategic Alignment

For a leadership development system to fully accomplish what it can for a health system, it must be aligned with the strategic goals of the organization. Many health systems have attempted to implement leadership development from the middle, giving full responsibility to the human resources or organizational development department or, worse, to an external vendor.

Fully aligned leadership development means, at a minimum, senior leadership has ownership of the process, even if implementation is a department-specific responsibility. Ideally, however, the ongoing agenda for leadership development should flow from the organization's strategic planning process. Too often, strategic planning overemphasizes the *what* and the *how* and underemphasizes the *who* of future plans. Gaps in leaders as well as leadership competencies form the priorities for identifying new talent and developing those individuals to pursue emerging leadership roles.

Additionally, leadership development should be something senior leadership actively participates in, not just as agenda setters but also as mentors and learning facilitators. A study by the Economist Intelligence Unit (2006) found that senior executives at organizations that have a stellar reputation for developing their staff devote as much as 20 percent of their time to development activities. This same study suggests that at least 5 percent (or several hours per week) of a senior manager's time should be invested in developing staff.

## Attracting and Selecting Leaders

Leadership potential is the critical raw material for successful leadership development systems. As such, giving attention to positioning their organization as an attractive place for high-potential leaders to work is crucial. The strongest leadership development systems tend to be associated with organizations that invest the effort to develop a communicable concept of how the organization approaches leadership, sometimes referred to as a leadership brand (Ulrich and Smallwood 2007). Communicating this brand through channels such as conference presentations, internships, and administrative residencies can also expand the reach of the organization to high-potential applicants. Dye (2002) discusses how organizations can become magnets for highly talented leaders, stating that the organizations that attract and retain strong leaders "have a vigorous commitment to continuing education and make provision for leaders to gain new skills and exposure."

In addition to strengthening the applicant pool, health systems must develop a rigorous discipline around selecting the best candidates for leadership roles. Although hiring managers often prefer autonomy and discretion in their selection decisions, a substantial body of research has consistently shown that using more systematic approaches leads to much better hires (Posthuma, Morgeson, and Campion 2002; Schmidt and Hunter 1998). As a general rule, the best predictor of future performance is past performance under similar circumstances; as such, methods that allow work to be sampled (e.g., experience-based interviews, simulations) tend to provide the greatest accuracy. Competency models, such as the one described throughout this book, can be useful tools for systematizing the selection process, as long as they are appropriately validated for the specific contexts in which they are being used.

## Preparing New Leaders for Success

Organizations differ widely in how they onboard new leaders. Those that provide a more thoughtful and systematic approach tend to find greater success rates with their newly hired leaders, both in job performance and retention (Bauer 2010). Practices that support effective onboarding include scheduled check-ins at 30, 60, and 90 days; planned approaches to organizational socialization; and provision of coaching (see Chapter 18).

## Identifying and Developing High-Potentials

Preparation for leadership roles takes time and experience. Senior leadership roles, in particular, can take many years to prepare for successfully. A strategically aligned approach to leadership development allows a health system to identify the leadership capacity needs it is likely to experience over time, and prepare future leaders in advance of taking these positions. An important part of this preparation process involves the proactive identification of "high-potentials," individuals with the aptitude and interest in preparing for progressively more responsible leadership roles. Competency models such as the one described in this book, once appropriately validated within a given organization, can be useful aids in identifying potential, as they can help articulate the qualities an organization is seeking to cultivate in its future leaders. Once identified, high-potentials can be developed through a combination of cohort learning programs (or leadership academies) as well as other types of developmental experiences.

As noted previously in relation to selection, a more structured approach to this process will outperform one that is driven by individual agendas, and adding a structured assessment component can help ensure investments in development are getting maximized. Assessment data is also highly useful for tailoring leadership development to a specific individual's needs.

## Providing Developmental Experiences

Although leadership academies and other formal learning programs can provide essential foundations for higher levels of performance, most leadership learning takes place through experience. More comprehensive approaches to leadership development incorporate this reality as part of the planning process by identifying good experience-based learning opportunities and assigning them strategically. Such assignments could include leadership of cross-departmental or systemwide performance-improvement initiatives; participation in special projects, such as building projects or fundraising campaigns; or even full-time rotation into other positions to provide exposure to different parts of the organization and/or system.

## Providing Performance Feedback

Performance feedback is another area where the research is clear: Leaders who receive higher-quality feedback on an ongoing basis develop faster than those who do not. Research also shows that more feedback is not necessarily better feedback, and poor-quality feedback will do more harm than good (Kluger and DeNisi 1996).

Chapter 7 of this book describes the importance of effective feedback for continuous skill development. Leadership development systems should help ensure leaders are getting the feedback they need and are using it to maximum effect. Chapter 20 describes approaches to cultivating a feedback-rich environment in more depth.

## Succession Planning

A high-performance approach to leadership development includes directing ongoing attention to the need for future leaders, as well as the need to replace current leaders who may retire or move on. The broader approach to proactively planning for future needs is called *talent management*; the narrower activity of planning for specific roles is called *succession planning*. Having leaders who are prepared to step in as needed to positions of greater responsibility is critically important for ensuring smooth transitions and maintaining organizational momentum (Garman and Glawe 2004). However, preparing for senior-level roles, in particular, can require years of development (Garman and Tyler 2007).

## Monitoring Results

Investments in leadership development must be monitored on an ongoing basis against a specific set of objectives. In our experience, the ideal monitoring platform involves a manageable set of outcome metrics that are straightforward to explain to senior leadership and other stakeholders. Commonly used metrics include percentage of leadership academy graduates retained over time, percentage promoted within a specified period of time, and perceptions of changes to the competencies of program participants. For organizations using leadership development as part of a diversity and inclusion strategy, additional metrics can include the percentage of leaders from under-represented backgrounds at various levels of the organization.

## REFERENCES

Bauer, T. N. 2010. *Onboarding New Employees: Maximizing Success.* Society for Human Resource Management. www.shrm.org/about/foundation/products/Pages/OnboardingEPG.aspx.

Dye, C. F. 2002. *Winning the Talent War: Ensuring Effective Leadership in Healthcare.* Chicago: Health Administration Press.

Economist Intelligence Unit. 2006. "The CEO's Role in Talent Management: How Top Executives from Ten Countries Are Nurturing the Leaders of Tomorrow." www.ddiworld.com/pdf/eiu_ddi_talentmanagement_fullreport.pdf.

Garman, A. N., and J. Glawe. 2004. "Research Update: Succession Planning." *Consulting Psychology Journal: Practice & Research* 56 (2): 119–28.

Garman, A. N., and J. L. Tyler. 2007. "Succession Planning Practices and Outcomes in US Hospital Systems: Final Report." Report prepared for the American College of Healthcare Executives. www.ache.org/pubs/research/succession_planning.pdf.

Kluger, A. N., and A. DeNisi. 1996. "The Effects of Feedback Interventions on Performance: A Historical Review, a Meta-Analysis, and a Preliminary Feedback Intervention Theory." *Psychological Bulletin* 119 (2): 254–84.

Posthuma, R. A., F. P. Morgeson, and M. A. Campion. 2002. "Beyond Employment Interview Validity: A Comprehensive Narrative Review of Recent Research and Trends over Time." *Personnel Psychology* 55: 1–81.

Schmidt, F. L., and J. E. Hunter. 1998. "The Validity and Utility of Selection Methods in Personnel Psychology: Practical and Theoretical Implications of 85 Years of Research Findings." *Psychological Bulletin* 124 (2): 262–74.

Ulrich, D., and N. Smallwood. 2007. *Leadership Brand: Developing Customer-Focused Leaders to Drive Performance and Build Lasting Value.* Cambridge, MA: Harvard Business School Press.

## CHAPTER EIGHTEEN

# Leadership Coaches and Coaching Programs

ELSEWHERE IN THIS book we describe the critical role of practice and sage feedback in the development of exceptional leadership. We also note how difficult it can be to access high-quality feedback on a consistent basis. Many factors contribute to this lack of feedback, including the more harried nature of executive jobs as well as the constriction within senior leadership ranks over time. Given this trend, many leaders and the healthcare systems they work within have begun using leadership coaching as an adjunct to other leadership development activities they provide.

*Leadership coaching* can be defined as "a formal engagement in which a qualified coach works with an organizational leader in a series of dynamic, private sessions designed to establish and achieve clear goals that will result in improved business effectiveness for the individual, as well as his or her team and organization" (Riddle 2008). With this definition in mind, leadership coaching is most clearly distinct from mentoring (as described in Chapter 20) in two ways. First, leadership coaching involves a formal engagement, which typically is a paid (usually by the employer) relationship with a contract. Under this contract, the coach agrees to consult with the leader over a specified period of time, to work on enhancing a specified set of competencies or skills, to provide guidance to the leader in individual and/or team interactions, and/or to oversee a broader program of overall leadership development. (Sometimes this work involves addressing an identified performance deficit, but increasingly coaching is being used to prepare high-performing leaders for role expansions or promotions.) Second, a leadership coach is expected to be qualified through specialized training in the coaching process itself, above and beyond any contextual experience she brings to the relationship.

In this chapter we provide guidelines for working with a coach as well as setting up a coaching program within your organization.

# WORKING WITH A LEADERSHIP COACH

Can a leadership coach help you in your quest to become an exceptional leader? While the short answer may be yes, you must first determine whether this step is right for you, given your goals, readiness, and time within your career. Hiring a coach involves a substantial investment in time and money; thus, investing time in making the decision to pursue and use a coach makes sense. Asking your organization to cover the expenses of a coach when it has never done so can also be a challenge.

Using a leadership coach can be particularly helpful in these four circumstances:

1. You are preparing for a specific position that requires substantively different leadership skills than you currently possess.
2. You are taking a new position within your organization.
3. You are transitioning to a different organization.
4. Someone has expressed concern about a deficit in your leadership skills that may be negatively affecting your performance.

Each of these circumstances involves a distinct leadership challenge, requiring different approaches depending on the organizational context as well as the competencies (and blind spots) you bring to them. A coach can help you prioritize your development work, identify specific goals, and keep focused on these goals.

## Identifying Competencies You Want to Develop

Once you have specific development goals in mind, the next step is to determine the competencies you need to master to achieve your goals. A performance evaluation, a 360-degree feedback program (see Chapter 21), or other developmental programs can be good sources for identifying the areas in which you need to improve.

Coaching is most useful when coupled with other developmental options; however, coaching can also be powerful for developing competencies when other development options are not readily available—either the role models just are not there or they cannot take the time to work with you. Additionally, the more opportunities you have to practice a given competency on the job, the more effective coaching is in helping you develop your skills rapidly. The converse is also true, however: Coaching will do little good if you are not gaining the work experience at the same time.

## Determining Your Personal Readiness

A good coach is supportive but is also able to challenge you, in the no-pain, no-gain sense of the word. Not everyone does well with this type of feedback. Some people find it too disconcerting and thus have trouble hearing it (the Listening Like You Mean It competency is particularly relevant here). Kilburg (2001) provides some diagnostic questions that, with a little adaptation, can work well in assessing your own readiness to be coached:

1. How *personally* motivated are you to develop these competencies? Is this something you want for yourself, or are you doing it mostly to appease someone else (e.g., a superior, spouse)?
2. Have you tried to work on these competencies before? If so, what have you tried, and how long were you able to stick with the approach?
3. What concerns do you have about being coached? How optimistic/pessimistic are you about its potential results?
4. Have you ever had problems following through on developmental assignments in the past?
5. How easy/difficult do you find it to accept constructive feedback?
6. How often have you given up on things because they became too personally challenging?

If you have trouble with constructive feedback, give up on efforts that become too personally challenging, have trouble with follow-through, or are pursuing coaching for reasons outside of yourself, then you are much less likely to see positive outcomes from a coaching engagement. Conversely, if you tend to be tenacious in following goals, are able to wince your way through constructive feedback, and are doing this for yourself, you are much more likely to see successful results.

## Finding and Selecting a Coach

When it comes to determining a coach's qualifications, some words of caution: Despite what some organizations may tell you, no universally accepted preparatory background or certification exists for professional coaching. Several different organizations represent and/or certify coaches, including the International Coaching Federation (www.coachfederation.org) and the International Association of Coaching (www.certifiedcoach.org). However, certification from these or other organizations does not ensure a given coach will be right for your needs, and conversely, there are outstanding coaches in the field with no such certification. For example, we know several retired hospital and health system CEOs and senior executives who provide coaching services and have been quite successful in doing so—and they are not certified by any organization. In short, screen coaches cautiously, and do not mistake a coaching-branded credential for effectiveness.

In general, the best source for coaches is a referral from someone you know well and trust. You may ask colleagues who have worked with coaches to recommend someone; you may also ask them specific questions such as the coach's experience, style, and availability. Another good source of referral may be the chief human resources officer or head of employee development in your organization. If your organization is currently contracting with coaches, they are the most likely to know about the arrangements and be able to provide appropriate referrals.

If you want to broaden your search, the American College of Healthcare Executives (ACHE) maintains the Executive Coaches Directory Guide (www.ache.org/newclub/career/execcoach/intro.cfm). The guide lists coaches who are affiliated with ACHE and provides an in-depth description of the nature of their practice, approach, and fee structure. Although it is a directory and not a screening tool, the guide can be a starting point for identifying potential coaching resources. It is searchable by several fields, including practice location. The nonprofit National Center for Healthcare Leadership (www.nchl.org) also maintains a referral list of certified coaches, who are all experienced in healthcare, and several consulting firms also specialize in executive coaching.

The question of whether someone is qualified to provide effective coaching will vary according to the reasons the coaching is used. For example, if one of your greatest needs is to learn how to better interact with peer members of your senior team, your best coach might be someone who has actually served as an executive and interacted with senior teams before. Having visited senior team meetings is vastly different from having been an actual member of a senior team. As another example, many new physician leaders have commented to us that they sometimes feel a stronger identity with other more seasoned physician leaders when it comes to coaching. In short, having a coach who has actually experienced life in your shoes may be one of the best factors to use in the evaluation process.

In addition to considerations of experience and expertise, the quality of the working relationship between a coach and a client is critical to the effectiveness of the engagement (de Haan et al. 2013). With this in mind, we strongly recommend that you interview at least two, but preferably three or more, coaches before making a decision. You should feel free to ask any questions about the coach's experience, approach, and fee structure before you get started on the process. You should find that the coach's answers to these questions make sense to you and are building trust in the relationship at a comfortable pace. If a coach tries to dodge your questions or hard-sell you, look for someone else.

### Questions for Screening a Coach

*How did you come to be a coach? How did you prepare for this role?* Given the wide variation in backgrounds and experience among coaches, it is important to find out how a coach has prepared for his role, and some types of training certainly are more desirable than others. For example, if a coach has an advanced degree in adult education or psychology, he may have a much deeper font of process skills to draw from than someone whose sole credentials involve experience. If a coach states that he attended a training program, ask for details about it (e.g., how long, what was involved).

*How long have you been working as a coach? How much coaching do you do?* Many coaches do not practice coaching full time. In general, however, more experience as a coach means better skills and a stronger pool of experience from which to draw.

*What kinds of positions have you coached?* Give preference to coaches who have experience working at *and* above your current level in the organization.

*How much of your work is focused in healthcare? What kinds of healthcare organizations?* Experience in the field may be more or less important, depending on the specific competencies you wish to develop. In general, however, a coach with relevant experience may better understand the complex environment healthcare leaders face. If a coach claims she has healthcare experience, be sure to ask about the specific types of healthcare organizations she has worked with. We have heard some coaches describe working within the pharmaceutical or health insurance industries as "having healthcare experience."

*What kinds of work did you do before you became a coach (e.g., amount of time on the job, organization type, position level/span of control)?* Although a coach need not have been a healthcare leader himself to be an effective coach, all else equal, coaches who have worked as leaders themselves will have a better-developed mental model of the challenges leaders face.

*How would you describe your approach to coaching? Do you have a particular area of focus or expertise?* As a coach responds to these two questions, ask yourself whether the approach sounds clear, reasonable, and effective and like something you will be comfortable with. However, be cautious of coaches who seem overly enamored with their models or who seem to love to talk.

*What types of engagements/arrangements will you work with?* Determine whether the coach and/or her employer has worked with your organization in the past, and if so, whether they have a formal contract with your organization. If they do, chances are you will be able to receive more favorable rates than if you contract individually. No standard contracting fees currently exist in coaching, and coach arrangements can be all over the map. The most typical arrangements are flat-fee retainer (often for a specific number of months), day rate (usually an hourly rate billed in eight-hour blocks), hourly, and per session.

*Can you provide client references?* While references can be very helpful, some coaches (especially psychologists and other behavioral health professionals) do not provide client references because of confidentiality concerns. Sometimes in these cases, a coach will, if asked, provide the name of a general contact from a client's organization (e.g., a vice president of HR) who can comment more generally about the coach's services.

### Other Considerations

1. Coaching is a relationship, and you get what you give. A coach cannot do the work for you; if you do not take the work seriously, you will not get the maximum value out of the consultation.
2. Coaching takes time (sometimes a lot of time) to yield results. If you are working on changing fundamental aspects of the way you work with others, you should plan on being involved with the coach for at least 12 months before you can observe significant results.

## IMPLEMENTING AND MANAGING ORGANIZATIONAL COACHING PROGRAMS

In many health systems, the process for using and contracting with executive coaches is decentralized, pursued at the discretion of individual leaders out of departmental budgets. This approach supports leaders' autonomy and responsibility for their own development. However, it also means the organization is missing valuable opportunities for quality control, leveraged contracting for more favorable rates, and opportunities to use coaching resources more strategically in engagements where they might be particularly helpful. For these and other reasons, an increasing number of health systems have developed centralized approaches to identify, contract with, and deploy leadership coaching, particularly in recent years as the pace of organizational change has escalated.

The National Center for Healthcare Leadership has an ongoing council supporting organizations in sharing best practices for efficient and effective use of external coaching resources. The following recommendations are based on the experiences of council members.[1]

## Step 1: Clarify the Program Goals

Before investing any resources in a centralized coaching program, you should first be clear about what you are hoping to accomplish with your program and how these accomplishments will support the strategic objectives of the organization. For example, do you want to make coaching available for developmental purposes (e.g., preparing leaders who are new to your organization to hit the ground running? Preparing current leaders for expanded future roles)? Do you want it to be available for remedial purposes (e.g., addressing performance gaps)? A coaching program can support more than one goal, but it's important to be clear in advance on how it is positioned.

In addition to the goals of the program, you will need to determine how broadly you want to make coaching resources available. Starting with a smaller scale and more focused effort to gain experience with the program and its management is typically the best route.

## Step 2: Develop Your Coaching Resources and Policies for Accessing Them

Once you are clear on the goals of the program, you will need to develop a means for determining appropriate qualifications for coaches to participate in the program. Professional coaches can come into these roles from a wide variety of backgrounds, which can make credentialing efforts difficult, particularly if a large number of coaches participate in the program. Some third-party certification programs are beginning to appear (the International Coach Federation is one of the more widely recognized); however, some experienced and highly effective coaches have no such certification, so some flexibility is often required.

Some of the most useful elements to consider in credentialing of coaches include the following:

◆ **Specialized training.** How has the coach formally prepared for this work? Does he have an advanced degree in a specialization relevant to coaching (e.g., adult education/adult learning, industrial psychology, performance) and/or certification from a coach training program you consider reputable?

◆ **Coaching experience.** How many clients has the coach seen in his coaching career? Approximately how many total hours of coaching does this represent? At what levels within the organization has the coach worked? What has been his experience, if any, with leaders in clinical or other specialized roles (e.g., physician chairs, nurse leaders)?

- **Coaching philosophy.** How does she describe her approach to her work? Does this description seem compatible with the goals you have for the coaching program?
- **Industry expertise.** How much work has the coach done previously within the context of health systems? Within organizations structured similarly to yours? While it is possible for a coach who works primarily in other industries to be effective in healthcare settings as well, a sparse background should be weighed carefully against the goals of a specific engagement.
- **Organizational experience.** How much work has the coach done for your organization specifically? For how many years? Knowledge of the history and relational topography of the organization can be very helpful to coaching, particularly at higher levels.
- **References.** Can the coach provide third-party references who will speak to the quality of her work?

With coaching resources identified, a contracting process must be put in place. Contracts should typically be arranged for individual engagements and should specify (a) the goals of the engagement, including how progress will be measured; (b) the length of the engagement; and (c) how progress will be reported, and to whom.

### Step 3: Continuously Measure and Improve

Coaching programs must evolve along with the strategic needs of the organization. With this in mind, planning ahead for the compilation and reporting of the outcomes of the coaching program is important. On at least an annual basis, the program should be reviewed against questions such as the following:

- *Focus.* Looking across coaching engagements, does the program focus on the right areas?
- *Outcomes.* What have been the results of the coaching engagements over the past year? Do these results clearly justify the investment in the program? Although putting a specific dollar value on individual leader performance improvements can be difficult, at minimum a gut check should address whether the improvements are more than covering the costs.
- *Scope.* Is the program reaching the leaders it needs to? Does the size and accessibility of the program seem appropriate (limited enough to ensure that each engagement has a high potential impact, but not so limited that high-value opportunities are getting passed over)? How effectively is the program

integrated with the broader continuum of leadership development supports your organization offers (e.g., high-potentials programs, job rotations)?

◆ *Resource development.* Are the current coaches the right ones for the organization's emerging needs? How effectively are we ensuring the coaches we use are well prepared to be effective with our leaders?

## SUMMARY

Approached wisely, coaching can help leaders quickly upgrade their skills in their current work as well as ensure they are maximizing the learning value from the work experience they are receiving. Well-designed and carefully monitored coaching programs can provide similar benefits across an entire organization. Given the high relative cost of coaching, managing these resources carefully is important; conversely, the development of leaders is an area in which organizations can scarcely afford to underinvest.

## NOTE

1. The authors wish to thank members of the National Center for Healthcare Leadership's Coaching Council, chaired by Joan Evans, chief learning officer, vice president, organizational performance and effectiveness at Cone Health, upon whose work this summary is based.

## REFERENCES

de Haan, E., A. Duckworth, D. Birch, and C. Jones. 2013. "Executive Coaching Outcome Research: The Contribution of Common Factors Such as Relationship, Personality Match, and Self-Efficacy." *Consulting Psychology Journal: Practice & Research* 65 (1): 40–57.

Kilburg, R. R. 2001. "Facilitating Intervention Adherence in Executive Coaching: A Model and Methods." *Consulting Psychology Journal* 53 (4): 251–67.

Riddle, D. 2008. *Leadership Coaching: When It's Right and When You're Ready.* Greensboro, NC: Center for Creative Leadership.

## CHAPTER NINETEEN

# Mentors: Finding and Engaging for Maximum Impact

THE TERM *MENTOR* has a breadth of definitions (Haggard et al. 2011). For our purposes we define a mentor as a person you do not report to who is willing to provide you with support, guidance, and advice for your development. The definition contrasts most clearly with leadership coaching, as described in Chapter 19, in that the relationship is not formally contracted, and the mentor does not necessarily have any specialized training in mentoring or coaching.

Mentoring is widely recognized as an important resource for leadership development generally and healthcare leadership specifically (Allen et al. 2004; Eby et al. 2008). Mentors, in turn, tend to find greater job satisfaction, organizational commitment, and career success than their nonmentoring counterparts (Ghosh and Reio 2013). Used strategically, organization-wide mentoring programs can enhance recruiting and retention (Craig et al. 2013; Payne and Huffman 2005), and may be particularly helpful to women and other historically underrepresented groups seeking progression into senior executive leadership roles (Sexton et al. 2013).

This chapter's recommendations follow this research-based approach and are designed to help you take these steps for yourself.

## WORKING WITH A MENTOR

Identifying a good mentor starts with getting a clear understanding of what you want out of the relationship—guidance on the career track you are pursuing, help with skills you are trying to learn—as well as what you are willing to put into the relationship to get what you want.

If you are interested in a specific career path, identify individuals like yourself who are further along the path than you are. If you work in a large organization, you may be able to find potential mentors by reaching out through cross-departmental projects. If you are already at or near the top of your organization, then your alumni group or professional associations—such as local chapters of the American College of Healthcare Executives, Healthcare Information and Management Systems Society, Healthcare Financial Management Association, or Medical Group Management Association—are excellent places to start your search. If you are interested in developing more specific skills, identify individuals who are not only particularly strong in these areas but also have spent time and attention on improving these skills. Each chapter in this book provides some guidelines about where these individuals are most likely to be found.

## APPROACHING A MENTOR

Mentoring relationships can take many different forms, and sometimes an informal arrangement works best. However, if you want to get a longer-term commitment from someone, requesting a more formal arrangement may make sense. A good approach is to simply say, "I am really interested in learning more about _____. I was given your name by _____ as someone who is particularly skilled in this area. Would you be willing to meet with me so I could pick your brain a bit about this?" Most people are flattered by the opportunity to share their experiences and will gladly meet with you, but if your invitation happens to be declined, be sure to accept it gracefully before moving on to another potential mentor.

Once a potential mentor has agreed to meet with you, be sure to make the meeting as easy as possible for this person. Offer to come to his office at a time that is convenient for him; having the meeting over lunch at a restaurant he likes can also be helpful.

When you meet with a mentor for the first time, take full responsibility for the meeting. Come in with an agenda, a point of view, and a good set of questions. Toward the conclusion of this first meeting, ask yourself how well the two of you meshed. Is this someone who could be helpful to meet with on occasion in the future? If you think so, at the end of the meeting and after you have thanked the person for his time, ask if he would be willing to meet again, perhaps on a quarterly (or bimonthly, monthly) basis over the year. If he is amenable, then you have found yourself a mentor.

## USING A MENTOR

Always approach your mentor with the mind-set that she is a valuable resource in finite supply. In each meeting with your mentor, always convey two messages: (1)

you are grateful for her help and (2) you want to be as helpful to her as she is being to you, if not now, then in the future. The following tips ensure you both get the most out of this relationship.

## TIPS FOR AN EFFECTIVE MENTORING RELATIONSHIP

### Prepare Well for Your Meetings

Come to any meeting with your mentor as well prepared as possible, and do whatever you can to honor the meetings you arrange. Before the meeting, review the goals you set out for the mentoring relationship. Consider the successes, as well as the challenges, you have experienced since the last time you met. Write these down so you remember to discuss them. Make particular note of any advice you took from the last meeting and the impact it had on your work.

In considering the challenges, write down enough detail so that you can give your mentor a clear sense of the situation. Also, try to formulate specific questions you can pose to your mentor. These questions should be open-ended enough that they allow for dialogue, but they should not be so open-ended that they leave the burden of work to the mentor.

Here's an example. Say you are working with your mentor to develop your skills in physician relations. Over the past month, an incident occurred that you find troubling: You were discussing renovations with a medical department director when suddenly he became angry with you and stormed out of the meeting. Asking your mentor, "Can you believe that?" is probably too open-ended. It is better to ask, "What do you think might have caused him to react that way?" Even better, however, is asking something even more specific, like the following: "In trying to make sense of this situation, I came up with three possible reasons why he became so upset. Given what I've told you, would you come to the same conclusions? How might you handle each of these?"

### Use Time Between Meetings Effectively

Before you end a meeting with your mentor, identify at least one specific "homework assignment" to complete before your next meeting. The assignment may be as simple as following up on a situation the two of you discussed or using an approach the mentor suggested, or as complex as finding and pursuing opportunities to practice a skill you are working on. On top of keeping you focused on the skills you are developing, assignments can add continuity to the mentoring relationship: You are giving your mentor a compelling reason to see you again. In turn, she will want to know about your progress or the outcome of your most recent success or challenge.

## Look for Ways to Make It a Two-Way Relationship

Although the express purpose of a mentoring relationship is to help you develop professionally, you will both get less out of the relationship if you limit it to a one-way arrangement. Look for ways to maintain a two-way dialogue with your mentor. Find out what your mentor is doing in his own role, what dilemmas he may be facing, and what issues are keeping him up at night. For you, this exchange is a learning opportunity: You get to hear your mentor's own thinking process. For your mentor, it allows her to sound out her challenges and concerns and clarify her stance on those issues. Occasionally, you may find that you are able to offer useful contacts, articles, or other resources that could be of help to your mentor. This type of sharing ensures that your mentor is getting something from the relationship.

## Build in Periodic Reviews

Although many people pursue open-ended mentoring relationships, adding the element of time can ensure that the relationship is productive and progressing toward its goals. Scheduled check-ins are helpful. For example, if your goal is to improve your influencing skills over the coming year, looking at your progress after a year makes sense. Periodic reviews are also helpful when considering whether to continue the relationship and, if so, what that continuation should ideally look like. For example, if you selected your mentor because of her strengths in a particular area, the two of you may evaluate your competency and then decide if you have sufficiently mastered or developed it. You may then make an intentional decision to either wrap up or continue the relationship at that point.

## End the Engagement Well

Too often mentoring relationships meet a vague and less satisfying end, where meetings get canceled and not rescheduled, then eventually both parties lose touch. A periodic review can be particularly helpful for ensuring that the mentoring relationship comes to a definitive and satisfying conclusion. We recommend a final meeting to discuss the future or the end of the relationship and to review your progress toward your goals. This is also a good time for you to express gratitude to your mentor.

Even after the mentoring relationship has formally ended, we recommend you periodically check in as a way of keeping in touch. For example, you might send an e-mail or a card to your mentor a year after your final meeting, and occasionally thereafter. In the communication, you can give an update on your career and mention ways that you have used skills you learned. As always, end your note by thanking your mentor for the help he provided.

Historically, the healthcare field has taken a top-down approach to mentoring—that is, encouraging seasoned leaders to become mentors, then finding less tenured individuals to become their mentees. However, research suggests that mentoring has greater impact when the mentee takes greater personal responsibility for the entire process—that is, finding a mentor to work with, taking the initiative to work with the mentor, and often finding other mentors at other points in her career (Underhill 2006).

## ESTABLISHING AN ORGANIZATIONAL MENTORING PROGRAM

Just as distinguishing between mentoring and leadership coaching is important, so too is distinguishing organizational coaching programs from mentoring programs. While both can be useful components to an organization's broader leadership development and talent management strategy, each involves unique opportunities and challenges. Running effective mentoring programs creates substantial additional complexity. For one, unlike with a leadership coaching program, visible senior leadership participation is critical and must be established as part of the initial design. Second, the paraprofessional nature of the mentoring role means greater attention to mentor and protégé preparation is needed. Lastly, the mentors' dual roles as organizational employees can require a different sort of management as well.

If you are interested in establishing a formal mentoring program within your own organization, we encourage you to review Tammy Allen and colleagues' (2009) book, *Designing Workplace Mentoring Programs: An Evidence-Based Approach*. The authors provide a readable approach to defining mentoring while still keeping true to what is empirically known about mentoring.

As mentioned in Chapter 8, the American College of Healthcare Executives (ACHE) website (www.ache.org) supports a virtual mentorship program, called the Leadership Mentoring Network. Their website also provides extensive information on mentoring, including a compilation of articles from *Healthcare Executive* magazine's (2014) "Leadership in Mentoring" column.

## SUMMARY

Exceptional leaders can be distinguished in part by the level of personal responsibility they take for their own development, as well as the energy they put into cultivating the kinds of mentoring relationships that can help them develop over time. In working with mentors, keep in mind that many people have three key reasons for agreeing to be a mentor: (1) being viewed as an expert is flattering, (2) helping others develop is rewarding, and (3) the relationship is a useful learning opportunity. Ensure that your meetings with your mentor remind him of these three reasons, and you will be guaranteed that your mentor will remain fully engaged in the process. Be sure also to recognize the opportunities to make these relationships a win-win, both for the mentors you find as well as the mentoring requests that you will be receiving as your career progresses.

## REFERENCES

Allen, T., L. Eby, T. Lillian, and M. Poteet. 2004. "Career Benefits Associated with Mentoring for Proteges: A Meta-Analysis." *Journal of Applied Psychology* 89 (1): 127–36.

Allen, T., L. Finkelstein, and M. Poteet. 2009. *Designing Workplace Mentoring Programs: An Evidence-Based Approach.* Malden, MA: Wiley-Blackwell.

Craig, C. A., M. Allen, M. Reid, C. Riemendschneider, and D. Armstrong. 2013. "The Impact of Career Mentoring and Psychosocial Mentoring on Affective Organizational Commitment, Job Involvement, and Turnover Intention." *Administration & Society* 45 (8): 949–73.

Eby, L., T. Allen, S. Evans, T. Ng, and D. DuBois. 2008. "Does Mentoring Matter? A Multidisciplinary Meta-Analysis Comparing Mentored and Non-Mentored Individuals." *Journal of Vocational Behavior* 72 (2): 254–67.

Ghosh, R., and R. Reio Jr. 2013. "Career Benefits Associated with Mentoring for Mentors: A Meta-Analysis." *Journal of Vocational Behavior* 83 (1): 106–16.

Haggard, D., T. Dougherty, D. Turban, and J. Wilbanks. 2011. "Who Is a Mentor? A Review of Evolving Definitions and Implications for Research." *Journal of Management* 37 (1): 280–304.

*Healthcare Executive.* 2014. "Leadership in Mentoring." *American College of Healthcare Executives.* www.ache.org/newclub/career/MentorArticles/Mentoring.cfm.

Payne, S., and A. Huffman. 2005. "A Longitudinal Examination of the Influence of Mentoring on Organizational Commitment and Turnover." *Academy of Management Journal* 48 (1): 158–68.

Sexton, D., C. Lemak, J. Gahlon, J. Wainio, and A. Garman. 2013. "Critical Career Inflection Points for Women Healthcare Executives." March 13. Presentation at the Congress on Healthcare Leadership, Chicago.

Underhill, C. M. 2006. "The Effectiveness of Mentoring Programs in Corporate Settings: A Meta-Analytical Review of the Literature." *Journal of Vocational Behavior* 68 (2): 292–307.

# Developing a Feedback-Rich Working Environment

THROUGHOUT THE BOOK we highlight the value of cultivating a feedback-rich working environment, which you may think is easier said than done. Indeed, changing the quality of feedback in your working environment sometimes requires the transformation of organizational or departmental culture (Edmonson 2011). However, it can be done, and the rewards for doing so can be substantial.

The techniques that follow are proven to improve feedback within a healthcare environment. They are listed roughly in order of the depth of feedback they can yield; the first techniques are the easiest and most straightforward to implement. The best approach for each technique is to lead by example—that is, first implement the technique yourself, then encourage your staff to adopt it. Continue this process until it becomes the habit within your team.

## INSTANT FEEDBACK SESSIONS

Instant feedback is feedback provided on a routine basis immediately after a given performance. If you or your team do not routinely stop to reflect on your work, a simple technique for getting started is to commit to providing instant feedback at least once a week related to an important area of performance. Good subjects for this type of feedback include a presentation to an important group, a negotiation session with a vendor, or a joint meeting with a patient's family. To use this technique, a leader (or coworker) first asks the principal performer (e.g., the person managing the presentation or facilitating the meeting) to comment on her own performance in two steps: (1) what she thought went particularly well, and (2) what she would do differently if given a chance to do the performance over again. Once the person is done with her self-assessment, the leader (or coworker) provides his own assessment, building on what the performer already described (what went well, what could be done differently).

The structure of this instant feedback approach serves several goals. By starting with the performer's perceptions, the feedback providers are in the best position to tailor their comments to the performer's understanding of her own performance. Also, the feedback is more likely to be viewed as value-added knowledge rather than redundant information (or what the performer already knows).

## AFTER-EVENT REVIEWS

A more structured and formal approach to feedback sessions is the after-event review (AER). Originally used in the military, AER and similar approaches have been gaining use in healthcare and other settings, and research suggests the approach can be particularly beneficial for leadership development (DeRue et al. 2012). The approach involves a structured team discussion that takes place after a given activity to identify and label successful approaches that should be repeated as well as problematic approaches that should be avoided in the future. Many different approaches to AERs exist, but most involve addressing the following four key questions:

1. What was our expected outcome?
2. What actual outcome did we experience?
3. What caused the differences between what we expected and what actually happened?
4. Based on our experiences this time, what should we do and not do next time?

## DEVELOPING A SHARED COMPETENCY LANGUAGE

In environments where performance-related discussions do not take place frequently, staff may not have a good font of performance language to work with. The meanings of words such as *respect*, *feedback*, or *vision*, for example, may vary greatly among staff depending on their history or level of experience. Additionally, staff skills for delivering performance feedback can vary. By meeting as a group to develop shared competencies, you can help staff develop their own language and reach a comfort level with it. If these meetings are developed in a climate of sufficient psychological safety, they can evolve into process improvement meetings in which performance-related dialogue is present.

## SHARING INDIVIDUAL GOALS

Too often, individual developmental goals are perceived to be blemishes: We recognize the need to work on them, but we also do our best to hide them from the rest of the world. Sharing individual goals, while uncomfortable at first, is often a more robust approach to making meaningful strides in improvement. For example, a director who has been told that he occasionally delivers critiques in a harsh and demoralizing way may be able to improve by simply being mindful of his emotions. However, he will improve much faster if he articulates his developmental goal to his direct reports. In doing so, he gives himself an opportunity to get feedback from those who are most familiar with his performance. For example, he may say to a staff member after giving her feedback, "As you know I am working on delivering constructive feedback in a more even fashion. How did you think that went?"

## PERFORMANCE CALIBRATION MEETINGS

Even leaders who are highly experienced in providing feedback can start to drift into their own unique interpretations of performance. For example, taking two weeks to resolve a payroll issue may seem acceptable to one leader but may be incredibly insensitive to another.

Leaders can help each other refine their internal yardsticks through a process of performance calibration. The process involves leaders within a particular department or service line having a dialogue about how staff are being rated on performance appraisals. The idea is to show one another how they rate employees and to get each other's opinions on whether the ratings and rationales are about right, too generous, or too harsh. Through this process, leaders have an opportunity to refine their own thinking by hearing from their peers and to view and discuss performance in new ways. For more information about performance calibrations, see Garman and Dye (2008).

## TALENT REVIEWS

A talent review is a periodic meeting of leaders to discuss employee performance levels vis-à-vis current and emerging organizational needs. Many different approaches to the talent review process exist, but all of them typically involve discussing questions about the fit of a certain employee for a specific current or future role. Like calibration meetings, talent reviews can afford leaders the opportunity to check their own thinking about performance against that of their peers. Additionally, the process provides a forum for discussing performance-related needs at the broader organizational and strategic levels. Talent reviews also help to promote the perspective that leaders are not expected to occupy a role forever; instead, they should be preparing for transition and succession.

Implementing a talent review process should not be taken lightly. Because talent reviews involve active discussions about whether a person is right for a role, they can be threatening. Talent reviews usually require top-level support, and occasionally a major culture change, to implement.

## 360-DEGREE FEEDBACK

A 360-degree feedback program involves soliciting feedback from a variety of actors surrounding a role—such as peers, direct reports, superiors, and clients, to name a few—and then providing that feedback to the person being reviewed in a way that masks the source of the feedback. Following are the eight major steps in a 360-degree feedback process, including the associated decisions that must be made and current thoughts on best practices in each step.

### Step 1: Define the Participants and the Goals

A 360-degree feedback process can be implemented for a single leader, a team of leaders, or the leadership of a whole organization. If broad participation is sought, starting at the top of the organization and moving down is often best; this allows senior-level executives to gain familiarity with the process first and to lead by example.

In terms of goals, the main decision that must be made is whether the process is used for development or for appraisal (i.e., will the feedback have an impact on the participant's formal performance evaluation?). In general, 360-degree feedback programs are most useful when used strictly for developmental purposes; this means that the only people allowed to view the results are the leader and the feedback facilitator. If used for appraisal purposes, these programs tend to fall prey to the same biases that cloud regular performance appraisals (Eichenger and Lombardo 2003).

### Step 2: Develop (or Identify) the Survey Instrument

The survey instrument used should serve the needs of the people who will participate in the feedback process. While many off-the-shelf surveys are available, many of these surveys are an awkward fit when it comes to a specific application for certain leadership roles. Some competencies may be relevant and on target, while others may be irrelevant or not as important. For this reason, many organizations elect to either develop their own survey or modify an existing one. Organizations such as the American College of Healthcare Executives, the Healthcare Leadership Alliance, the National Center for Healthcare Leadership, and the National Health Service all have competency models that can be adapted for organizational purposes.

When developing a survey, avoid the temptation to throw in everything but the kitchen sink—in reality, less is often more. Surveys that go on for 40 items or more risk causing survey fatigue, where responders adopt a fixed mind-set about the person being reviewed and respond to all items accordingly. Conversely, we have seen surveys that asked only for a dozen or so ratings work very well; they placed heavy emphasis on open-ended feedback to clarify ratings. In any case, space for open-ended comments should be provided, and their use should be encouraged (or mandated). The open-ended feedback often contains the most useful data a person receives in this process.

## Step 3: Decide How to Manage the Process

Internet-hosted surveys are the preferred choice from an efficiency perspective. Systems from online survey vendors (e.g., SurveyMonkey.com) can provide low and even no-cost options, particularly for small-scale projects. Specialty vendors provide options for larger-scale projects; prices vary widely so comparison shopping is useful.

We strongly encourage you to use an outside party to handle the data-management portion of any 360-degree project. Given the potentially highly sensitive nature of the feedback, being able to ensure confidentiality in both fact and appearance is crucial. The outside party does not necessarily have to be outside of your organization. For example, if you have a highly regarded employee/organization development group in-house, the group may have the capabilities to manage such a project.

If you do go outside the organization for assistance, consider contacting the industrial psychology department of your local university. The school may have an academic consulting group that can provide high-quality oversight at a fraction of what private-sector consultants charge.

## Step 4: Identify Feedback Sources

All participants in a 360-degree feedback process must reach out to the individuals they work with to solicit feedback. Setting the parameters ahead of time for the process—who to ask to participate (e.g., peers, superiors, direct reports), how many participants to solicit, and/or whether to allow anyone who wishes to participate—is helpful.

General guidelines for setting participant parameters include the following:

- If people choose their own raters, encourage them to include people (colleagues, direct reports, supervisors) they do not work well with or even have a conflict with. From these individuals, they often learn the most about themselves and their limitations.
- More feedback providers tend to be better than a smaller number of participants. With more respondents, the key themes across working relationships are often easier to identify.

## Step 5: Distribute and Collect the Survey

Set a deadline for feedback, but anticipate that you will need to extend it at least once and likely twice. Depending on how the distribution and collection process is being managed, the survey can be wrapped up in as little as two weeks or as long as four.

## Step 6: Develop the Reports

With online systems, the development of feedback reports can be an automatic or semiautomatic process. However, distributing print copies is still helpful as they are more likely to be kept for later review or reference.

## Step 7: Provide Feedback and Formulate Development Plans

Feedback can be delivered in a number of ways. At one extreme is the desk drop, in which a person receives his report without being given a chance for discussion or any expectation for follow-up. At the other extreme is a facilitated meeting between the person, a feedback coach, and the person's superior to discuss the results, brainstorm developmental plans, and set specific improvement goals and a timeline for follow-up.

In our experience, the approach that works best is to have a feedback facilitator (again, usually someone outside the person's immediate chain of command) meet with the individual to go over the feedback results and think through the implications for development. These meetings typically take at least 60 minutes on average, but this investment is worth the time as it improves the person's feedback receptivity and clarifies his developmental plans.

## Step 8: Follow Up

People participating in a non-self-initiated 360-degree process should be given clear expectations for how they should use their results. At a minimum, the participant should discuss with her superior the development plan they created together. Additionally, the participant should follow up with people who provided feedback. For example, a participant may address her staff during a staff meeting not only to express gratitude for their participation but also to note the areas of strength and the developmental needs the report revealed. The participant may also share her plans to address the areas identified and ask the staff to continue giving feedback on her progress. Taking this extra step serves three goals: (1) it demonstrates the leader's receptivity to her direct reports' feedback, (2) it models good feedback-receiving behavior, and (3) it holds the leader publicly accountable for making progress.

In terms of tracking progress, leaders are often interested in conducting additional 360-degree feedback sessions to look at change over time. Although this step can sometimes be helpful, it is often equally effective (and less labor intensive) to simply ask colleagues and staff whether they have noticed change in the areas of interest. This approach also serves to encourage a feedback-rich work environment. If you do decide to conduct additional 360-degree feedback, realize that change can be difficult to measure directly. There is a tendency to "raise the bar" over time, and even if a leader's skill levels go up, his average ratings may remain stable or even decline (Martineau and Hannum 2004). For this reason, asking survey participants to comment on change over time (better, worse, the same) is often better than using the same survey structure to attempt to measure change.

## SUMMARY

The best way to ensure continuous skill development is taking place is to ensure that all staff are receiving high-quality feedback on their work on an ongoing basis. The techniques discussed in this chapter are strategies that have worked well in healthcare and other settings. In environments where feedback is the exception rather than the rule, implementing any of these techniques on a consistent basis can take some effort; like exercise, the temptation early on will be to skip the process "just this once, in the interest of time." Developing a culture in which staff feel safe openly discussing failures as well as successes also takes time. Overcome these challenges, and you will be well on your way to developing a stronger feedback culture.

## REFERENCES

DeRue, D. S., J. D. Nahrgang, J. R. Hollenbeck, and K. Workman. 2012. "A Quasi-Experimental Study of After-Event Reviews and Leadership Development." *Journal of Applied Psychology* 97 (5): 997–1015.

Edmonson, E. 2011. "Strategies for Learning from Failure." *Harvard Business Review* (April): 48–55.

Eichenger, R. W., and M. M. Lombardo. 2003. "Knowledge Summary Series: 360-Degree Assessment." *Human Resource Planning* 26: 34–44.

Garman, A. N., and C. Dye. 2008. *The Healthcare C-Suite: Leadership Development at the Top.* Chicago: Health Administration Press.

Martineau, J., and K. Hannum. 2004. *Evaluating Leadership Development Programs: A Professional Guide.* Greensboro, NC: Center for Creative Leadership.

## CHAPTER TWENTY-ONE

# Physician Leadership Development and Competencies

The two most senior physician executives of St. Nicholas Health System—Dr. Howard James, senior vice president of medical affairs, and Dr. Bob Borman, president of the St. Nicholas Medical Group—were discussing the critical need for their organization to develop a physician leadership development program. "With our system growth the past two years and the anticipated expansion we are seeing in our western suburbs, we really need to get more physicians into leadership roles," said Dr. James.

Dr. Borman replied, "Of course. And with healthcare reform, we have to get more physicians involved at the helm. We both need a lot of additional physician leaders to help us do the heavy lifting. But it seems like we have been getting nowhere with the leadership development programs we have been offering from the two outside companies we have used. Their programs are really just outside speakers teaching seminars, and that seems to be falling short. I think we need a novel approach to the younger physicians that we have identified as our key up-and-comers."

Dr. James responded, "I think that the new programs using the leadership competencies that Jim Batten, our HR guy, has introduced, could be the answer for us." Dr. Borman asked, "How so?" Dr. James replied, "First of all, if you look at the competencies, they are all about what we need to be able to do. Second, when Jim teaches to them, he does it in a realistic and practical way. He's not a 'death by PowerPoint' instructor. He will provide at most a ten-minute introduction, and the participants spend the rest of the time actively discussing or solving problems. What's more, Jim uses cases based on the real problems we are actually facing. The way I see it, we could build

*(continued)*

*(continued from previous page)*

a large part of our physician development program around applying each of these competencies. Each one could be a course by itself. Let's get with Jim and see what he can do for us."

Two weeks later as the three executives met to discuss the program, Batten explained, "I have heard from several of the physician leaders that they have not really liked the seminar approach the outside firms are using. They want something that is more applicable to us. Also, I know that physicians are not that patient with learning the softer side of management. As scientists, they work mostly with data and view leadership education as subjective and something that is just not that useful. I know they find the theory part not applicable to day-to-day matters. However, I think they will find that using specific leadership competencies will provide a more objective way to define and describe leadership skills and actions. I also think they will be quick to get the idea of needing to practice these behaviors and get feedback on them. Working together, I believe we can come up with some practical examples for them to work on that will illustrate each of the competencies nicely, and give them the initial practice they need to be more effective using them."

The two physicians looked at each other and smiled. Then James responded, "This sounds like exactly what we were looking for. Let's get started!"

## WHY A SEPARATE CHAPTER ON PHYSICIAN LEADERSHIP?

At the time of this writing, the healthcare world is being upended. The passage of the Affordable Care Act (ACA), the movement of public and private payers into value-based reimbursement, clinical integration, population health management, and provider shortages have all coalesced to create a climate of volatile change. Most of the changes in the industry the next few years will require significant increases in physician leadership. Physician impact on quality and cost is indisputable. Moreover, consumer interest in quality outcomes has risen. Improving clinical quality as well as the patient experience has taken a much higher level of emphasis than it has in the past. As Dr. Frank Byrne comments, "There is no way forward without integration and collaboration with physicians, and coordination of quality care and improvement efforts across the continuum of care." Expert and system-oriented physician leadership will be essential for addressing all of these issues.

While a significant uptick has occurred in the focus on physician leadership and developing physician leaders, many organizations are still struggling with it.

Dr. Carl Couch of the Baylor Quality Alliance recently remarked, "Doctors are a highly educated group of people. But their education and career is mostly technical and clinical. The whole subject of physician leadership training has only received attention in the last ten to 15 years" (Jacob 2013).

The first edition of this book has gotten considerable response from the physician executive community. Many physicians have expressed appreciation for the articulation of leadership competencies, which have helped many of them see how leadership could be more definable and understandable. The concept of leadership competencies also fits well with the scientific nature of physicians. As scientists, physicians are quantitative and prefer to deal with objective data. While leadership does not fully lend itself to quantitative measure (for example, it is misleading to believe that an assessment can declare that Leader A is an 83.4 leader while Leader B is a 96.5 leader), the use of competencies does move the understanding of leadership toward a more objective view.

Another factor that makes the development of physician leaders unique is the age that physicians typically move into leadership positions. Many nurses take their first lead roles at age 24 or 25; business-track executives in healthcare have typically had 15 to 20 years of leadership experience by their early 40s. In contrast, most physicians are often 45 to 50 years old before they move into their first leadership roles. As a result, management and leadership can be confounding. The understanding of leadership competencies can help physician leaders up to speed quicker.

Are physician leaders different in terms of what they do as leaders? In a word, no. Certainly they bring a different perspective to management and leadership than their counterparts without clinical training do. But the functions and practices of leadership are the same. And it should be noted that just because they are physicians does not mean that they are qualified to be leaders. Physicians must receive management and leadership training just as nonphysician leaders do. Regarding this, Dr. Frank Byrne commented, "The breakthrough moment for many physician leaders is attending their first leadership course, wherever it may be, and realizing that, similar to our clinical domain, there is a science to leadership and specific skills that can be acquired to increase the probability of achievement of desired outcomes. That was our motivation for sending a cohort of 30 key physician leaders through a ten-month custom leadership curriculum developed with a local business school. In addition to the faculty, we had health system leaders attend each session, to ensure relevance and to provide examples of deployment in our system of the skills being taught."

What does differentiate physician leaders is their clinical background. The fact that they have the perspective of knowing what is done in the care process can give physician leaders a significant edge as they move to shape strategy and implement change in healthcare organizations. Dr. John Byrnes comments, "The depth of understanding what is done in the clinical setting often lets physician leaders see and comprehend things that nonclinicians will miss."

Most would agree that having a greater number of physicians engaged in leadership activities, both part-time and full-time, will enhance the outcome of both patient care and wellness initiatives. A *McKinsey Quarterly* article reported that "hospitals with the greatest clinician participation in management scored about 50 percent higher on important drivers of performance than hospitals with low levels of clinical leadership did" (Mountford and Webb 2009, 2).

Finally, it must be said that for too long the management and leadership of healthcare organizations has been the domain of professional managers without clinical backgrounds; physicians and other clinicians have often been viewed as separate and distinct—us versus them. If management and leadership become too separated from those who are working with the patients, the ability to work collaboratively and sustain an agenda of change will be impaired.

## CONTRASTING PHYSICIANS WITH EXECUTIVE LEADERS

"Physicians as leaders are often like fish out of water," write Saunders and Hagemann (2009). To be certain, significant differences exist between physicians and professional managers. When considering leadership competencies, keeping in mind the background and nature of physicians is important. Dye and Sokolov (2013) present a contrast between physician and administrators, as shown in Exhibit 21.1.

Although much has been written about these differences, several points have a direct bearing on leadership competencies and bear a closer look.

**Exhibit 21.1 Characteristics of Physicians Versus Administrators**

| Physicians | Administrators |
|---|---|
| Science-oriented | Business-oriented |
| One-on-one interactions | Group interactions |
| Value autonomy | Value collaboration |
| Focus on patients | Focus on organization |
| Identify with profession | Identify with organization |
| Independent | Collaborative |
| Solo thinkers | Group thinkers |

*SOURCE:* Dye and Sokolov (2013).

## Science Orientation

To begin with, physicians are scientists. They are quantitative by nature; they seek to solve problems through clearly definable and measurable factors, and avoid basing decisions on hunch or intuition. In contrast, while executives typically use some science and quantitative skills in their work, their decisions are often driven by "good enough" analysis. Deciding on a strategic course for an organization has as much subjective feeling involved as it does objective analysis. As much as strategic planners wish to bring analytics into their work, some degree of intuition is always involved in setting strategy. And when dealing with people issues, the complexity of humans makes it impossible to make this type of leadership entirely scientific.

The competencies Developing Vision, Communicating Vision, Mindful Decision Making, Driving Results, and Stimulating Creativity are all rooted in science; physician leaders can often be exemplary in them. These competencies will also be critical ones as enormous changes occur over the next several years in how medicine is practiced.

## Time Perspective

In their clinical work, physicians have encounters in which they interact with patients, usually in as little as 5 to 15 minutes. During this brief time, the physician moves through a process of assessment, diagnosis, outcome identification, planning, and follow up. One physician was heard at a board strategic planning retreat stating, "Look, I do all of my work in 10- to 15-minute increments all day long. Trying to determine strategy for this organization for the next three years does not fit on my radar screen." Administrative activity rarely is achievable in such a short time. Because much of the work of leaders is done through collaborative efforts and coordinating the work of many people, the time span often bridges days, weeks, and months. It is easy to see how physicians can be frustrated by this. Also of note is the emphasis on productivity within many health systems as they work with their employed cadre of physicians (see more patients; generate more productivity).

Dr. John Byrnes notes that physicians have been trained with a reactive mind-set. "We see one patient at a time, respond to their needs, and move on to the next patient visit. We react to whatever situation or patient need presents itself. We weren't trained to be proactive, to plan, to proactively manage large-scale projects, or to project strategy over several years. This proactive mind-set is very foreign to the average physician and must be deliberately learned for physicians to be successful in administrative roles."

The competencies Developing High-Performing Teams, Energizing Staff, Generating Informal Power, Building True Consensus, and Driving Results have significant time elements to them. For many hopeful physician leaders, these competencies are among the most difficult to develop and use effectively.

## Personal Versus Organizational Accountability

Another major difference between physicians and administrators is that physicians are held more *personally* accountable for their actions. With the issuance of an individual license to practice medicine, the physician is held to specific personal standards *as an individual*. While administrators also have personal accountability for their actions, their accountability and authority are more organizationally assigned. Moreover, physicians are accountable to the medical standards practiced within a community, and those standards are based on clinical practice within that community. Conversely, administrators are accountable to either a higher administrator, or in the case of the CEO, to a board of trustees, and the standards are applied differently.

When considering accountability, the competencies Leading With Conviction, Using Emotional Intelligence, and Earning Trust And Loyalty most closely support this principle within organizational life.

## Time Urgency of Decision Making

Physician decision making is typically immediate, while administrators often deliberate for long periods and require input from many sources, which adds to the time needed to take action. Particularly true of surgeons, emergency medicine physicians, or physicians faced with critical life-saving judgments, physicians have to be able to make quick decisions. One physician remarked, "One thing that drives me crazy is the amount of time it takes for these administrators to make decisions. If I took that kind of time, my patients would die."

Because of the way physicians make decisions in clinical settings, the competencies Listening Like You Mean It, Giving Great Feedback, Developing High-Performing Teams, Building True Consensus, and Mindful Decision Making are often challenging for physicians as they enter leadership roles.

However, a final point should be made. Physicians are often criticized inappropriately and maligned by business leaders when they fail to follow administrative procedures. Readers are warned to be mindful that this unfair criticism can be dangerously divisive. Dr. Ginger Williams comments, "Administrators and others far too often make the mistake of thinking that maladaptive behaviors like not completing your budget on time, not keeping people in the loop, et cetera, are intentional and something you just have to put up with because 'that's the price we have to pay to have physician leaders.' While that's sometimes true, I think it's more often the case that these things simply are not axiomatic to the physician leader like they are to the nonphysician executive."

We sum up this point by saying, "Don't always blame the physicians." Some organizations tend to point the finger at the physicians and say as one CEO did, "They just are not capable of learning this." Dr. Kathleen Forbes sums this up quite effectively:

> It is great to have physician leaders at the table. With the appropriate training they can have quite an impact on strategy development and execution of organizational strategies. But the misstep that can happen is when physicians are brought to the table as key leaders and then not held accountable for the performance of their areas of responsibility. While they attend the necessary meetings, they may not be fully contributing to the effort since they feel they hold a figurehead role only. Digging deeper into this, you will find this to be multifactorial: Physician leaders may feel that their input doesn't matter since the strategy was developed without their input; the physician leaders are not held accountable to actively participate in key discussions regarding the strategy; the physician leaders may not be invited to the key meetings in which the true planning or execution is accomplished; organizations often assume a lack of business skills by physician leaders and hire a number of support leaders who work around the physician executives to keep efforts moving forward. Bottom line—bring physicians to the table and engage them. Strong physician alignment is critical in the post-ACA healthcare delivery system, but it is not enough. You must have true physician engagement. This is a big investment and one that needs to be maximized by the organization. Do not underestimate what a well-trained physician leader brings to the table.

## WHERE PHYSICIANS TYPICALLY MISS THE MARK WITH LEADERSHIP COMPETENCIES

In their chapter on managerial derailment, Dye and Sokolov (2013) suggested that the cost involved when physician leaders have to be terminated is very high. *Derailment* is the common term used in management and leadership literature to describe situations in which individuals who have had great success suddenly find themselves failing. Dye and Sokolov (2013, 182) write that many of these failures are caused by the "inability of physician executives to detect common derailment factors." Many of the reasons for derailment are the results of failures in the 16 competencies. Ready (2005) suggested several causes for derailment, including the inability to manage teams and others, flawed execution of strategy, failure to engage and inspire employees, poor listening skills, and failing to fit with the company's values. Clearly, mastering several of the 16 competencies would help avoid these career stoppers.

We suggest an in-depth reading of some of the derailment literature. Two of our favorites are Sydney Finkelstein's (2004) *Why Smart Executives Fail: And What You Can Learn from Their Mistakes* and Jeffrey Sonnenfeld and Andrew Ward's (2007) *Firing Back: How Great Leaders Rebound After Career Disasters.* We also suggest Benjamin James Inyang's (2013) article, "Exploring the Concept of Leadership Derailment: Defining New Research Agenda" in the *International Journal of Business and Management.*

On the basis of the derailment research and anecdotal observation, we have found physicians have considerable problems with the 16 leadership competencies in several specific areas. A note to the reader is important here: Although this next section presents suggestions of shortcomings among physicians aspiring to work in leadership positions, it is not intended to suggest that physicians cannot make highly effective leaders. In fact, the opposite is true—physicians skilled in the 16 competencies can be extraordinarily successful leaders. However, examining leadership from a competency perspective and considering the challenges physicians in particular often face in developing fully as leaders can be helpful.

## Applying the Competencies in Practice Begins with Deep Self-Reflection

Because of the nature of their work and the way they are trained, physicians often are less self-reflective. During the time of life (late teens and through the 20s) when most business-oriented leaders are gaining insights from early mentors and learning how to navigate the difficult politics of organizational life, physicians are focused almost exclusively on the rigorous academic study of medicine. Saunders and Hagemann (2009) describe the problems that physicians often have in socialization, stating, "An issue that is not often discussed is that many physicians have personality or character issues due to a prolonged period as a student. Many do not start their careers until their early 30s. They work long hours and study in their off-hours. They have little time to develop social skills. Their social skills often stop developing when they enter medical school. By the time they are asked by the healthcare organization to take a leadership role, they will have bridged some of the social skill gap, but it is very likely that there are still some socialization skills that are significantly lagging." It should be no surprise that physicians focus almost exclusively on growth in clinical knowledge and skills in the first years of their careers. They don't have the time to learn or explore business and leadership concepts.

Drummond (2012) also notes, "What we do pick up automatically in our clinical training is a dysfunctional leadership style based on 'giving orders.' The clinical actions of diagnosis and treatment are simply adopted as our default leadership style. When faced with any practice challenge, we assume we must be the one who comes up with the answers (diagnose) and then tell everyone on the team what to do (treat)."

Dr. Akram Boutros commented, "Physicians are used to being trusted by virtue of the job. Patients either go through a discernment process in choosing a physician and therefore have committed to trust their physician, or they are in dire need of emergency treatment and instinctually give their trust to those caring for them. Being trusted by others, therefore, has become an expectation for physicians. To ignite trust by team members in nonclinical situations, physicians have to exhibit vulnerability. For physicians, showing vulnerability is antithetical to how they were trained—that is, to project strength and confidence in every situation."

Exhibit 21.2 lists the 16 competencies, showing those in which physicians often lack expertise. Note that many of the ones listed in the far right column, "Often a challenge to master," pertain directly to interpersonal leadership competencies. Deficiencies in these competencies are often derailing factors in leadership jobs.

The reasoning behind Exhibit 21.2 follows.

**Cornerstone 1: Well-Cultivated Self-Awareness**. If one meaning of *conviction* is "a firmly held belief," physicians certainly possess this characteristic. We see this competency as requiring strong drive and being confident in actions. It is the rare physician who does not possess this. However, when it pertains to emotional intelligence, many physicians fall short in this competency—often as the result of the relative inattention to socialization described earlier. Moreover, as they begin clinical practice, physicians rarely receive direct feedback on their interpersonal practices.

**Cornerstone 2: Compelling Vision**. Because of the shorter-term nature of their work, physicians often have difficulty developing longer-term vision. Strategic planning can be frustrating. Beckham (2010) writes, "For physicians, strategic planning is a bureaucratic and amorphous undertaking run out of a hospital administrator's office. There is usually a flurry of interviews, some retreats and then lofty commitments. Physicians rightly ask, 'What has that got to do with me?' And, too often, the answer may be, 'Very little.'" The experience of many physicians is that they are invited to strategic planning retreats (which may be held every three years or

# Exhibit 21.2 Physicians and the 16 Competencies

| Cornerstone | Competency | Often a strength among physicians | Usually not well developed among physicians | Often a challenge to master |
|---|---|---|---|---|
| Well-Cultivated Self-Awareness | Leading With Conviction | X | | |
| | Using Emotional Intelligence | | | X |
| Compelling Vision | Developing Vision | | | X |
| | Communicating Vision | | | X |
| | Earning Trust And Loyalty | | X | |
| A Real Way With People | Listening Like You Mean It | X (pediatricians, family medicine, psychiatrists) | | X (most other physician specialties) |
| | Giving Great Feedback | | X | |
| | Mentoring | | | X |
| | Developing High-Performing Teams | | | X |
| | Energizing Staff | | | X |
| Masterful Execution | Generating Informal Power | | | X |
| | Building True Consensus | | | X |
| | Mindful Decision Making | X | | |
| | Driving Results | X | | |
| | Stimulating Creativity | | | X |
| | Cultivating Adaptability | | | X |

so), asked for their input, and then sent "back to the clinical factory" while over the next several years, the executives of the organization make changes to that strategy or in many cases, reverse course—all without any further consultation or touching base with those same physicians who participated in the original planning retreat. A better understanding of this factor is expressed by Dr. Frank Byrne: "In our clinical careers, we generally work linearly, from one patient to the next, attempting to solve problems on the spot, alone, or in small groups. Administratively, we balance a number of projects, goals, and priorities, some of which need to be addressed by noon today, and others are multiyear, complex endeavors involving scores of people and multiple disciplines to achieve the desired outcome."

**Cornerstone 3: A Real Way With People**. Gartland (2009) states it well: "A frequent criticism of physicians expressed by patients is that the rigorous scientific training required for their medical educations depersonalizes some of them to the extent that effective medical technicians are produced who, upon entering the clinical practice of medicine, have fewer communication and interpersonal skills than they had upon entering medical school." Although this observation was made regarding interactions with patients, the same deficiencies often present themselves in other workplace interactions as well.

One differentiation in the competency Listening Like You Mean It is made here between specialties. Specialties that require intensive listening to patients—such as pediatrics, family medicine, and psychiatry—often transfer those effective skills into leadership positions. Dr. Frank Byrne drives this point further: "Virtually every problem that I've either caused or had to adjudicate, in both my clinical and administrative careers, has had a communication component to its root cause. It concerns and mystifies me that we don't provide specific communication training every step of the way in physicians' clinical and administrative training."

Increasingly the medical education and practicing clinician communities are recognizing that teaching team skills is critical for medical students, residents, and new physicians. In his commencement address to the Harvard Medical School, Atul Gawande (2011) described a "skill that you must have but haven't been taught—the ability to implement at scale, the ability to get colleagues along the entire chain of care functioning like pit crews for patients." Although Gawande addresses the need to have this skill for those who are working directly with patients, the same holds true for those physician leaders who work with leadership teams running today's healthcare organizations. An interesting observation along these lines was made by Dr. Frank Byrne: "I had the benefit of practicing in a clinical setting where the ICU nurses I worked with made it clear that our shared work was a team sport. I carried that into my executive leadership roles, and also had the benefit of working with nonphysician executives and board members who both valued my unique perspective and helped me develop my leadership skills."

**Cornerstone 4: Masterful Execution.** Similar to their stance on strategic planning, physicians are not accustomed to practices such as generating informal power, creativity, adaptability, and consensus building. They come from a more controlled environment where they are the expert and their orders are final. *Execution* for physicians means following the orders of the clinician in charge. Orders are to be carried out—and usually not questioned. However, this "command and control" culture does not lend itself to contemporary approaches to decision making.

Despite their shortcomings in many of the 16 leadership competencies, physicians are often quick to see their gaps when it comes to themselves personally. In an unpublished paper written for his doctoral thesis in management, Deegan (2002) writes, "As a consequence of the way American physicians have been selected, educated, and socialized during their training, many are highly competitive, relatively independent practitioners. They often eschew teamwork and collaboration and other affiliative behaviors. Their education and socialization fosters pacesetting or commanding leadership styles that may be appropriate in certain clinical circumstances, e.g., a busy emergency department or a critical care unit, but could be counter-productive when used in other care settings."

Finally, Kirch (2011), CEO of the Association of American Medical Colleges, discussed the importance of teamwork and being able to relate to patients: "When I entered medical school, it was all about being an individual expert. Now it's all about applying that expertise to team-based patient care."

## HOW CAN PHYSICIANS DEVELOP FURTHER IN EACH COMPETENCY?

Physicians are typically quick learners. Using the 16 competencies as a guide, they can learn and practice leadership quite effectively. This section includes suggestions for physicians to develop their leadership skills as they contemplate moving into either part-time or full-time leadership and management positions. Dr. Frank Byrne reflected, "During a previous wave of disruptive, transformational change in healthcare in the mid-1990s, it became fashionable to place physicians in executive roles. I was one of them. Unlike many physicians at that time, I had support and a development plan to assist my transition. It was tragic that we burned through a significant percentage of that generation of physician leaders by placing them in complex leadership roles without providing the support and training they needed to be successful."

Organizations need to lay some groundwork to ensure that physicians successfully grow as leaders. Some of this involves structure, while some of it involves the willingness of other senior leaders to personally take a stand in helping physician leaders develop. Dr. David James summarizes this quite effectively: "I think there are two compelling organizational circumstances that substantially enhance the successful integration of physician leadership into the organizational matrix: The first is a servant leadership style on the part of those to whom the physician leaders report. Physicians often initially find that the maze of bureaucracy built into large-scale corporate systems is extraordinarily difficult to navigate, and the servant leader can help ensure success by helping remove obstacles, facilitating and navigating heavily matrixed environments until the physician executive has assimilated the corporate acumen. The second lies in implementing a dyad leadership model pairing strong clinical leaders with strong business leaders into one functional leadership unit. This can serve as a quick way to fill competency gaps in either while speeding the skill acquisition for competencies in both."

## Gain Adequate Assessment and Feedback

Physician leaders often have great difficulty in getting effective feedback. We believe this happens for several reasons. First, because most physician leaders are older when they enter leadership positions, others may hesitate to provide input on their leadership or interpersonal behaviors. Second, physician leaders often move into high-level positions as their first roles. In these settings, which could be board rooms or senior management conference rooms, discussion focuses more often on organizational matters and rarely on specific personal styles and approaches to leadership. Third, physicians typically hold the "captain of the ship" position and are not challenged as much as a result. The Dye–Garman 16 Competency Model is adaptable for 360-degree feedback (see Chapter 20), which can be an effective approach to overcoming these feedback barriers. However, to reach the level of exceptional leadership, it is essential that physician leaders listen, understand, internalize, and appropriately act on the feedback they receive.

Dr John Byrnes adds, "It's critical that physicians actively reflect, internalize, and study the results of feedback and link this information directly to a formal plan of study to gain needed competencies. I remember my training on the surgical side of the house—it was a very combative and aggressive environment, and I quickly learned the behaviors needed to succeed. However, in my first management role, I quickly found that the behaviors that served me well in the OR were the exact opposite of what I needed as an administrator. The bottom line: I needed to unlearn most of my surgical behaviors and consciously replace them with the 16 Competencies. Yearly feedback has become an invaluable tool in this journey."

## Learn by Doing

Leadership is best learned by doing—and doing while something is riding on the outcome. Dye and Sokolov (2013) discuss the importance of crucible experiences in learning leadership, where the learning takes place when real-world situations or problems are encountered, not classroom examples or case studies. While classroom time is important, it is most powerful when used as a supplement to applied work, rather than the other way around. Dr. Greg Taylor considers this when he thinks about the impact of experience on physicians: "Those missed diagnoses, whether it's a heart attack, or cancer, are the cases physicians carry to their graves. But those are mistakes physicians rarely repeat, and in fact, they frequently become laser-focused experts in those areas. Likewise, leadership mistakes, such as failure to communicate, provide the opportunity to dissect and analyze, setting the stage for future competency and strength."

As Dr. Ginger Williams stated, "The most productive and effective educational experience of my life was getting my master's in medical management. When I started the program, I had been in my first administrative position (chief medical officer) for six months; I understood by that point that I knew nothing about executive leadership. During my master's program I was learning in class what I was expected to do at work, and doing at work what I was learning in class. It was ideal!"

## Use an Executive Coach

Physician leaders are using leadership coaching, as described in more detail in Chapter 18, with increasing frequency. One reason an outside coach can be so effective is that by the time physicians come into leadership positions, they are often old enough that feedback and input on matters such as leadership competencies are not common. Use caution, however, to ensure that the coaches selected have prior first-hand experience in relevant settings and, ideally, with physician clients. Dr. Frank Byrne commented, "When I hire a physician for a complex leadership role, I include mandatory provision of a coach in their job offer, and we work together to find a coach with appropriate background and experience to help them succeed." Dr. Greg Taylor added, "After 11 years of practicing medicine, and 17 years in a chief medical officer role, when I took over the chief operating officer position, I found it invaluable to secure an executive coach, who was experienced with physician executives. We focused on communicating vision (Compelling Vision) and energizing staff (A Real Way With People). Assistance in articulating and communicating my vision and creating energy with our staff was the key to a successful start in the new role."

## Avoid Overconfidence

Physicians train and work in a culture where confidence is paramount. Not knowing something or to being unable to do something are often viewed as signs of weakness. Highly effective leaders, in contrast, recognize that they can only know and do so much themselves, so they surround themselves with strong and capable individuals, and much of their work is to coordinate the work of those individuals. Physicians in leadership positions must recognize that they do not have to have all the answers to every problem and that allowing others to take the lead is acceptable. For a deeper understanding of the risks of overconfidence as well as other derailment risks, we recommend *Why CEOs Fail: The 11 Behaviors That Can Derail Your Climb to the Top and How to Manage Them* by David Dotlich and Peter Cairo (2003). The website of Hogan Assessment Systems (www.hoganassessments.com), a leading provider of personality-based leadership assessments, also provides excellent insights into behaviors that can harm the ability of any leader to enhance and improve leadership skills.

## SUMMARY

Dyche (2007) captured it well when he wrote, "An understanding physician must be able to tolerate ambiguity because science's clear solutions often do not match people's lives." Leadership is exceedingly complex, but a good competency model can provide a helpful roadmap to the terrain. As more physicians move into the leadership ranks of healthcare organizations, they will be doing well by themselves and their organizations to learn and adopt a competency-based approach to leadership.

The essence of this chapter is summarized well by Dr. Lee Hammerling: "The challenges healthcare faces today are best addressed by physicians who have not only mastered the clinical aspects of patient care but also have a deep understanding and training in management. These physician executives will be the industry's best opportunity to implement the changes necessary to achieve a sustainable high-quality, cost-effective healthcare model for the United States."

## NOTE

The authors are deeply indebted to the many physicians liberally quoted in this chapter. As nonphysicians, we felt it important to garner the input from these practitioners. We humbly thank each of them for their special review and contributions to this chapter.

Akram Boutros, MD, president, MetroHealth, Cleveland, Ohio

Frank Byrne, MD, president, St. Mary's Hospital, Madison, Wisconsin

John Byrnes, MD, Byrnes and Anderson, Ada, Michigan

Kathleen Forbes, MD, chief clinical officer, OSF Health System, Peoria, Illinois

Lee Hammerling, MD, chief medical officer and president, PMG, ProMedica, Toledo, Ohio

David James, MD, CEO, Memorial Hermann Medical Group, Houston, Texas

Greg Taylor, MD, COO, High Point Regional Medical Center, High Point, North Carolina

Ginger Williams, MD, president and CEO, Oaklawn Hospital, Marshall, Michigan

## REFERENCES

Beckham, D. 2010. "Physician Involvement in Hospital Strategic Planning." *Trustee* 63 (6): 6–7.

Deegan, M. J. 2002. "Emotional Intelligence Competencies in Physician Leaders: An Exploratory Study." Presented at Academy of Management Annual Meeting, Denver, CO. http://digitalcase.case.edu:9000/fedora/get/ksl:weaedm139/weaedm139.pdf.

Dotlich, D., and P. Cairo. 2003. *Why CEOs Fail: The 11 Behaviors That Can Derail Your Climb to the Top and How to Manage Them.* San Francisco: Jossey-Bass.

Drummond, D. 2012. "The Frustrating Gap of Physician Leadership Skills." *KevinMD.com.* Published June 18. http://www.kevinmd.com/blog/2012/06/frustrating-gap-physician-leadership-skills.html.

Dye, C., and J. Sokolov. 2013. *Developing Physician Leaders for Successful Clinical Integration.* Chicago: Health Administration Press.

Finkelstein, S. 2004. *Why Smart Executives Fail: And What You Can Learn from Their Mistakes*. New York: Portfolio Trade.

Gartland, J. 2007. *Better Physician Writing and Speaking Skills*. London: Radcliffe Publishing Ltd.

Gawande, A. 2011. "Cowboys and Pit Crews." *The New Yorker,* May 26.

Inyang, B. J. 2013. "Exploring the Concept of Leadership Derailment: Defining New Research Agenda." *International Journal of Business and Management* 8 (16): 78–85.

Jacob, S. 2013. "Physicians Gearing Up to Assume Leadership." *Dallas/Ft. Worth Healthcare Daily.* Published July 24. http://healthcare.dmagazine. com/2013/07/24/physicians-gearing-up-to-assume-leadership.

Kirch, D. 2011. "Doctors Must Now Pass Social Skills Tests to Attend Medical School." *EDU in Review.* Published July 21. www.eduinreview.com/blog/ 2011/07/doctors-must-now-pass-social-skills-tests-to-attend-medical-school.

Mountford, J., and C. Webb. 2009. "When Clinicians Lead." *McKinsey Quarterly.* www.mckinsey.com/insights/health_systems_and_services/ when_clinicians_lead.

Ready, D. A. 2005. "Is Your Company Failing Its Leaders?" *Business Strategy Review* 16 (4): 21–25.

Saunders, C., and B. Hagemann. 2009. "Physicians as Leaders: What's Missing?" *Health Leaders Media.* Published April 15. www.healthleadersmedia.com/ content/PHY-231588/Physicians-as-Leaders-Whats-Missing.htm.

Sonnenfeld, J., and A. Ward. 2007. *Firing Back: How Great Leaders Rebound After Career Disasters*. Cambridge, MA: Harvard Business Review Press.

## CHAPTER TWENTY-TWO

# Final Questions Regarding the Exceptional Leadership Model

IN OUR FINAL chapter, we consider several questions that frequently came up from the first edition about the Exceptional Leadership model within the broader context of healthcare management:

- "Is the Exceptional Leadership model comprehensive? Does it cover everything I need to be an exceptional healthcare leader?"
- "Where is _____ in the model?"
- "What's the best approach to adopting a leadership competency model in my organization?"
- "Can the Exceptional Leadership model help me with hiring?"
- "Are there any dangers to using a competency model?"

## IS THE EXCEPTIONAL LEADERSHIP MODEL COMPREHENSIVE?

The Exceptional Leadership model (or the Dye–Garman model, as some have described it) was designed with two broad goals in mind. The first was to capture the characteristics that most consistently distinguished exceptional healthcare leaders from their well-performing (just not exceptional) counterparts.

The second was to create a model that would be practical and useful to the field. At the time, many leadership models were appearing that were far longer, and we heard regularly about how cumbersome they were to work with. For example, Lombardo and Eichenger's (2004) model contained 67 competencies; other models from leading consulting firms and professional associations had many more than that. Models of this breadth can work fine in an educational setting, but they were not working well in applied settings. Can you imagine a CEO search committee trying to realistically assess candidates against 50 or 60 leadership competencies? Or a manager conducting a performance evaluation on each of her direct reports against 50 competencies?

The reality with competencies, as with other assessment tools, is that more is not always more: You hit a point of diminishing returns as people's attention starts to wane. We did not want our model to fall into that trap. Thus we purposely limited its length to just the top 16 and designed the scope of each competency accordingly.

So the model should not be considered all-encompassing. Indeed, other competencies clearly associated with the healthcare management profession do not appear within the model at all: process improvement, project management, financial management, information systems, and community orientation, to name just a few. Exposure to a broader array of management competencies would almost certainly strengthen any leader's toolkit and should be considered by anyone who is serious about rising in the leadership ranks.

With that caveat in mind, we can say, based on our experiences of the past seven years, a great many healthcare leaders have found the model helpful to their own development as well as the development of the people they work with. Many readers have described to us the ways they have been able to apply specific competencies to their work and the ways in which this has made them more effective in their leadership roles. We humbly accept these comments and hope that more leaders will receive help from this work in the future.

## WHERE IS _____ IN THE MODEL?

Readers who are familiar with other leadership models have occasionally asked us how particular components of the other models relate to the Exceptional Leadership model. Because many of these models are in constant evolution, the answer to this question is a moving target. We will address this in more detail in the section on Mapping Leadership Competency Models. Meanwhile, we will address four of the more frequent questions we have received.

1. Some have asked where the "drive to achieve" (from McClelland's Achievement Motivation Theory) fits most closely with the Exceptional Leadership model. We believe it relates most closely to the competencies Leading With Conviction, Driving Results, and Stimulating Creativity.
2. We have also been asked why the list does not contain oral and written communication, since surely this must be critically important to highly effective leadership. While we agree with the importance of communication, in

our experience, what differentiates exceptional leaders is not communication skills per se, but how they are applied. In particular, communication skills are essential to the competencies Developing Vision, Communicating Vision, Giving Great Feedback, and Mindful Decision Making.

3. We are frequently asked about problem solving. Like communication, problem solving is a broader construct relevant to a number of the competencies in the model, and mastery of those competencies will make a leader a more effective problem solver. For example, few complex problem-solving tasks do not draw upon the competencies Using Emotional Intelligence, Earning Trust And Loyalty, Building True Consensus, and Driving Results.

4. Many have asked where to find improving performance. We would argue that many of the 16 competencies help to drive this; for example, Developing High-Performing Teams, Energizing Staff, Mindful Decision Making, Driving Results, and Stimulating Creativity.

Also of note is the distinction between leadership competencies and functional/technical competencies. Functional/technical competencies match a specific job and indicate skills and abilities that are required for that particular job. For example, a chief financial officer needs to have competency in reading financial statements. Or a chief nursing officer must have certain clinical competencies in order to fully execute the job.

The intent of this brief discussion goes far past the exercise of being able to suggest that one or more of the 16 competencies will speak to every possible leadership competency imaginable. However, it does indicate that the 16 competencies cover practically all other competencies. But rather than engaging in a discussion of semantics, we hope that readers may find full application of the model and are able to apply it to their leadership needs.

## HOW DO I ADOPT A COMPETENCY MODEL IN MY ORGANIZATION?

As discussed in Chapter 17, adopting an organization-wide competency model can be particularly helpful for aligning talent investments with organizational strategy. In doing so, involving a breadth of people in developing the model you use will pay off down the road in easing implementation. Also, given how widespread the use of competencies has become, if your organization has not adopted an organization-wide leadership competency model, chances are that individual leaders, departments, or professional groups are already using a model of some kind. Be sensitive to the good work that may already be going on in your organization, and incorporate as much of this work as possible into the broader organizational effort.

One approach that can be particularly helpful in pursuing an organization-wide model is what is sometimes called cross-walking or cross-mapping of competency models. Cross-mapping involves comparing two or more models side by side to identify points of overlap, and then collapsing the models into a single one.

Exhibit 22.1 provides an example of a competency cross-map. In this example, the left column lists two specific leadership competencies from an unnamed health system that are not described with the same words or in the same manner as the competencies that are presented in this book. The second column shows those competencies from this book that map or match up with those from the health system.

**Exhibit 22.1 Competency Mapping**

| Competency from Organization A | Competencies from the Exceptional Leadership Competency Model |
|---|---|
| | **Leading With Conviction**<br>◆ Knows and is in touch with one's values and beliefs<br>◆ Is not afraid to take a lonely or unpopular stance if necessary<br>◆ Is comfortable in tough situations<br>◆ Can be relied on in tense circumstances<br>◆ Is clear about where he/she stands<br>◆ Faces difficult challenges with poise and self-assurance |
| Showing Trust and Respect, Practicing Collaborative Behaviors | **Building True Consensus**<br>◆ Frames issues in ways that facilitate clarity from multiple perspectives, keeps issues separated from personalities, and skillfully uses group decision techniques<br>◆ Ensures that quieter group members are drawn into discussions<br>◆ Finds shared values and common adversaries, and facilitates discussions rather than guides them |
| | **Generating Informal Power**<br>◆ Understands the roles of power and influence in organizations<br>◆ Develops compelling arguments or points of view based on a knowledge of others' priorities<br>◆ Develops and sustains useful networks up, down, and sideways in organizations<br>◆ Develops a reputation as a go-to person<br>◆ Effectively influences the thoughts and opinions of others, both directly and indirectly, through others |

*(continued)*

**Exhibit 22.1 Competency Mapping** *(continued from previous page)*

| Competency from Organization A | Competencies from the Exceptional Leadership Competency Model |
|---|---|
| Showing Trust and Respect, Practicing Collaborative Behaviors | **Listening Like You Mean It**<br>◆ Maintains a calm, easy-to-approach demeanor<br>◆ Is patient, open-minded, and willing to hear people out<br>◆ Understands others and picks up the meaning of their messages<br>◆ Is warm, gracious, and inviting<br>◆ Builds strong rapport<br>◆ Sees through the words to express the real meaning<br>◆ Maintains formal and informal channels of communication<br><br>**Using Emotional Intelligence**<br>◆ Recognizes personal strengths and weaknesses<br>◆ Sees the links between feelings and behaviors<br>◆ Manages impulsive feelings and distressing emotions<br>◆ Is attentive to emotional cues<br>◆ Shows sensitivity and respect for others<br>◆ Challenges bias and intolerance<br>◆ Collaborates and shares<br>◆ Handles conflict, difficult people, and tense situations effectively |

Other examples of mapping might include:

| Competency Not Listed in the Model | Corresponding Competencies from the Model |
|---|---|
| Critical thinking | Developing Vision, Stimulating Creativity |
| Resilience | Leading With Conviction, Driving Results |
| Influencing others | Listening Like You Mean It, Energizing Staff, Generating Informal Power |
| Persuasion | Developing Vision, Communicating Vision, Earning Trust And Loyalty, Driving Results |
| Judgment | Using Emotional Intelligence, Earning Trust And Loyalty, Mindful Decision Making |
| Showing passion | Leading With Conviction, Energizing Staff, Driving Results |

## HOW THE EXCEPTIONAL LEADERSHIP MODEL HELPS IN HIRING DECISIONS

In addition to identifying areas for development, competency models can be particularly helpful for improving personnel selection processes. Dye and Sokolov (2013) present an approach for selection in which leadership competencies comprise one of nine criteria used for assessing candidates for leadership positions.

Many organizations fail to use leadership competencies in their assessment regimen. This happens often because of the superficial wording in the qualifications section of many job descriptions or in some cases because no well-developed leadership competency model exists. Consider the following list of qualifications lifted from an actual job description:

- Ability to manage and make independent decisions
- Strong interpersonal communication skills
- Ability to function as a leader
- Exhibits creative, positive problem-solving abilities
- Experience coaching and developing senior level leaders
- System thinker

The concern with this list is that the components do not easily lend themselves to adequate definition and comprehensive understanding—what is a system thinker, what are strong interpersonal skills, what does it mean to be able to function as a leader, what makes someone creative? They may mean different things to different interviewers. One interviewer may feel a candidate is a strong system thinker while another interviewer may feel this same candidate is deficient. Consider how the qualification "ability to function as a leader" carries so much ambiguity.

To improve the assessment process, each of the required competencies should be better defined, and as demonstrated throughout this book, linked to behavioral indicators. Each competency should have a number of observable actions or behaviors that show how the competency is practiced. Since the publication of the first edition of this book, many organizations have found the use of competencies helpful in their selection processes. But in each case of which we are aware, these organizations developed more detailed, drill-down descriptors that made the competencies more meaningful and understandable. Then when assessments were done of candidates, the competencies served as measuring rods in the judgment process that led to selection. Exhibit 22.2 shows how this process works.

**Exhibit 22.2 Making Competencies More Meaningful in Assessment**

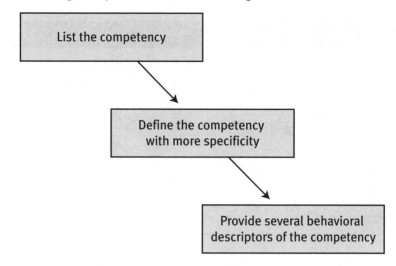

Additionally, the leadership competencies can be used to shape specific behavioral questions for interviews. Appendix C provides several specific examples of questions that match up with each of the 16 Competencies.

## Operations Focus Versus Strategic Focus

Finally, a more in-depth review of the 16 competencies shows that some are more operational while others are more strategic. For example, a system CEO would likely need far more strength in the areas of Developing Vision, Building True Consensus, Stimulating Creativity, and Cultivating Adaptability than would a chief operating officer of a smaller acute care hospital (who would likely need far more strength in areas such as Listening Like You Mean It, Developing High-Performing Teams, Energizing Staff, Mindful Decision Making, and Driving Results). Similarly, a leader tasked with the job of turning an organization around financially would require competencies that are more operationally focused. Exhibit 22.3 shows these distinctions. Readers may want to consider though the possibility that some of the competencies actually may fall into both categories.

We also tend to think of Leading With Conviction and Using Emotional Intelligence as "price of admission" or core competencies that are required in *all* exceptional leaders, no matter the title or place within the organization or the specific work objectives that are required in the job.

**Exhibit 22.3 Contrast of Operational and Strategic Competencies**

| More Operations-Oriented Competency | More Strategy-Oriented Competency |
| --- | --- |
| Listening Like You Mean It | Developing Vision |
| Giving Great Feedback | Communicating Vision |
| Mentoring | Stimulating Creativity |
| Developing High-Performing Teams | Mindful Decision Making |
| Energizing Staff | Cultivating Adaptability |
| Generating Informal Power | |
| Building True Consensus | |
| Driving Results | |

## POSSIBLE PROBLEMS WITH COMPETENCY MODELS

While competency models can be helpful, we have seen users run into trouble in at least three common ways. One relates to models that are too vague or ambiguous in their definitions. For example, listing "communications" as a competency is fine, but exactly what does this mean? The same confusion over meanings can come up for many different competencies, such as "leading teams," "respecting dignity," or "getting results." Taking the time to define competencies in detailed, clear, and observable terms is important.

Conversely, we have seen competency models become over-elaborated. Effron (2013) suggests that "today's typical competency model is an all-encompassing, multi-layered monstrosity whose complexity far outweighs its value. And, even with its verbosity and heft, it still doesn't tell managers exactly how to succeed." The length of the list can be problematic, as can typical human resources rules about how to use the competencies. As Roberto (2012) writes, "Senior executives have to boil down their expectations to a simple list of behaviors and capabilities that they value and wish to cultivate in aspiring leaders. Simplicity and brevity will breed behavioral change much more quickly and effectively than complexity and comprehensiveness."

A third challenge comes from leadership competency lists that are simply handed down from higher-level management without a commensurate emphasis on preparing people for their use and ensuring their implementation takes place. Refer to Chapter 17 for specific suggestions on how to successfully incorporate competencies into the organizational culture. In these cases, models tend not to live up to their full potential, or, worse, become ignored over time. Many competency lists such as these are viewed as the "management du jour" for the organization and are received with great skepticism.

## SUMMARY

This closing chapter provides a number of ways in which leadership competency models can support performance improvement. However, this review really only scratches the surface. For example, competencies can also be used to help in succession planning to better identify the competencies required for specific positions as well as to single out the gaps that high-potential possible successors may have. Competencies can also be helpful for onboarding by clarifying the expectations that are held for the new leader. Even strategic planning can be helped by defining the leadership competencies that will be needed to carry out the plan. We hope that this review has opened your eyes to the value of cultivating a common language of performance in your organization, and that you will be motivated to continue to learn more about competency-driven approaches to performance improvement—both for yourself and your organization.

## REFERENCES

Dye, C., and J. Sokolov. 2013. *Developing Physician Leaders for Successful Clinical Integration.* Chicago: Health Administration Press.

Effron, M. 2013. "Life After the Competency Model." *The Talent Strategy Group.* http://talentstrategygroup1.com/wp-content/uploads/2013/01/Life-After-the-Competency-Model.pdf.

Lombardo, M., and R. Eichinger. 2004. *FYI: For Your Improvement, A Guide for Development and Coaching,* 4th ed. Minneapolis, MN: Lominger Ltd Inc.

Roberto, M. 2012. "The Problem with Competency Models." Published January 25. http://michael-roberto.blogspot.com/2012/01/problem-with-competency-models.html.

# Appendix A: Self-Reflection Questions

THE FOLLOWING SELF-REFLECTION questions can help you determine what areas you need to work on to enhance a particular leadership competency. Read each question and reflect on a truthful answer, making notes as needed. After you have worked through the questions, review all question sets to determine which area you felt most strongly about. You may also want to share your answers with a trusted confidant.

## Chapter 1: Leading With Conviction

- To what extent are you driven by a clear set of values, principles, and goals?
- To what extent are your convictions based on ethical guidelines?
- How well do you understand how your values, principles, and goals developed?
- How broadly have your values been influenced? Were they developed by gaining perspective on a wide-ranging understanding of living and the issues of the world (as opposed to developing them from narrower experience)?
- How effective are you in recognizing when your fundamental belief systems are challenged? How methodical are you in reconciling these challenges?
- How reluctant are you to state your point of view?
- Are your convictions aimed at matters that count and are important to your organization (versus simply being selfish ones that serve to benefit only you)?

## Chapter 2: Using Emotional Intelligence

- To what extent are you aware of your emotions? To what extent do you understand rationally why you react the way you do?
- Do you see the link between your emotions and feelings and your behavior?

- To what extent can you manage your emotions? Can you control anger? Can you focus frustration? How effective are you at engaging others even when you are upset or irate?
- To what extent would you describe yourself as open, approachable, and sincere?
- Are you successful at developing rapport with others? With others who are different than you?
- Would others describe you as a respectful person?

## Chapter 3: Developing Vision

- Are you intellectually curious? Would you describe yourself as having broad interests?
- What do you read? Do you spend sufficient time reading professional journals and/or articles about trends and developments in business, science, and society? To what extent can you translate or apply those trends into your daily healthcare leadership roles?
- Are you able to analyze data and statistics and understand their broad implications?
- How often do you visit with people from other industries and walks of life to hear about their work and learn from their perspectives?
- How successful have you been at dealing with novel problems and challenges?

## Chapter 4: Communicating Vision

- How effectively do you balance working on day-to-day challenges with developing longer-term strategies?
- To what extent can you develop compelling arguments for change? How persuasive are you?
- How well can you distill and condense a strategic vision into something that can easily be communicated?
- Do you have proven techniques that get others engaged?

## Chapter 5: Earning Trust And Loyalty

- What is your do–say ratio—the number of times you actually do what you say you will do? Would others agree with your analysis of yourself?

- Would others say that you are concerned about their needs and affairs?
- Are you passionate about follow-through, particularly when it comes to getting back to others on their questions and concerns?
- Do you lead by example? Do you help out on routine jobs when you can? Are you a roll-up-the-sleeves person? How easily can others access you when they need you?
- To what extent would others say that you use your power and influence for the good of the organization and for others (versus selfish purposes)?

## Chapter 6: Listening Like You Mean It

- Are you approachable? (Ask yourself this question again.)
- Do you typically understand where others are coming from? To what extent do you care about their concerns?
- To what extent can you get to the heart of someone's verbal message to you?
- Do you frequently use questions to gain greater clarification?
- How open are your channels of communication? Do you have multiple informal and formal channels of communications and ways to discern what is happening in your organization?
- Do you occasionally (or even frequently) interrupt others or finish their sentences?
- Are you aware of the mechanical aspects of good listening (e.g., making eye contact, avoiding distractions such as smart phones, keeping the right physical distance from the speaker) and, more important, do you practice them?

## Chapter 7: Giving Great Feedback

- How clear and direct is your communication style?
- How well do your direct reports understand their performance goals? Do they have a clear understanding of their performance appraisals, or do they feel blindsided after an evaluation?
- How disciplined are you in providing feedback regularly?
- How well balanced is your feedback (positive and negative)?
- Would others say that you occasionally give mixed messages?
- To what extent might your feedback be damaged by "tee-up" phrases (such as "Don't take this the wrong way, but . . ." or "I'm just saying" or "As far as I know'" or "To be perfectly honest" or "I'm not saying, but. . .")

## Chapter 8: Mentoring

◆ How firmly do you believe in career development? Do you have former staff who have gone on to higher-level positions?

◆ Would others describe you as a boss who regularly provides them with stretch assignments and opportunities to work outside their area of accountability or to gain exposure at higher levels of the organization?

◆ How supportive are you of others' needs to attend educational programs? Have you encouraged subordinates to earn advanced degrees?

◆ How often do you provide teaching moments—brief, informal, and unplanned explanations during the workday about a situation or event at hand?

◆ Can you point to others who have advanced their careers because of your support and guidance?


## Chapter 9: Developing High-Performing Teams

◆ How well do you support the concept of teaming (as opposed to dealing with people on a one-on-one basis)?

◆ Do you encourage cohesiveness by identifying common vision, goals, and threats among team members or by establishing team rules?

◆ What steps do you take to prevent small, subgroup cliques; team role ambiguity; and emotions from driving debate?

◆ Are your team members clear on their mutual accountability to one another?

◆ Would your team members indicate that they are closely connected in purpose and in esprit de corps?

◆ When your team meets, does it exhibit a passion about its purpose?

◆ To what extent can (does) your team function when you are gone?


## Chapter 10: Energizing Staff

◆ How often do you show personal energy and enthusiasm about your work and your achievements?

◆ Would others describe you as goal driven and passionate about achievements and accomplishments?

◆ Do you regularly use humor, wit, and levity in the workplace?

◆ To what extent do you inject spontaneity into the workday or workplace?

- How often do you make a point of recognizing the accomplishments of others and celebrating their achievements?
- Do you avoid bureaucratic rules and regulations that can create a disengaged workforce?
- Do you use daily huddles to instill purpose and focus into the workday?
- Do you have a practice of finding innovative ways to engage and enthuse staff?

## Chapter 11: Generating Informal Power

- Are you frequently sought out by people (besides direct reports) for your opinions?
- How strong are your informal networks? How well informed do you feel through these networks?
- How openly do you share information?
- If others do favors for you, how conscientious are you in reciprocating?
- To what extent do you understand power and sources of power in the organization?
- A wise CEO once said, "Informal power is directly related to the amount of care and concern you show for others multiplied by your visibility within the organization." To what extent do you practice this?
- Do you take the lead in informal settings?
- If you are the leader of a team that has just had a success, do you share the recognition with your team members?
- Do you make the time to congratulate others on their achievements, both inside and outside the workplace?

## Chapter 12: Building True Consensus

- How knowledgeable are you about group decision-making techniques (e.g., NGT, parking lot, brainstorming, affinity mapping, straw polls)? How comfortable are you with using them?
- How effectively do you make use of agendas, outlines, handouts, and the like when managing a meeting?
- How regularly do you provide opportunities for all group members to voice their thoughts and opinions during meetings? How effectively do you reach out to members who are visibly silent?
- To what extent are you able to keep a group focused on a solution to an issue or problem?

- Once a group decision is made, do you clearly summarize the conclusion so that everyone knows what was decided?
- During conflict situations, have you ever used silence or a brief break in the action to help the group decompress and get back to refocusing on the issue at hand?
- Do you have strong rules for engagement that define appropriate behavior during debate within the group?
- Have you mastered the ability to bring underlying causes of a conflict or problem to the surface so the conversations can have better focus?
- Do you have a record of honoring commitments once a group decision is reached?

## Chapter 13: Mindful Decision Making

- How well do you know what drives your decision making? Have you ever mapped your decision-making process in writing?
- To what extent are ethics, values, goals, facts, alternatives, and judgment incorporated into your decision-making processes?
- To what extent are you able to analyze and evaluate choices and choose the best one? Do you have a method for weighing various alternatives?
- How knowledgeable are you about decision-making tools (e.g., force field analysis, cost-benefit analysis, decision trees)? How comfortable are you with using them?
- When making decisions, do you hear out opposing viewpoints, or do you tend to focus on developing arguments in favor of your own viewpoint?
- When making important decisions, are you equipped to use mindfulness to focus with clarity on the issue at hand?
- To what extent are you able to focus on the real issue involved in a decision versus making a series of other decisions that do not relate to it?

## Chapter 14: Driving Results

- How effectively do you keep people focused and on task?
- If team members are derailing movement toward an objective, how comfortable are you with stepping in to take action?
- How regularly can you set a higher bar for your team's performance and help others to see it as an achievable goal?

- Do you fully understand the need to recognize that each team member likely has different motivations, and thus your leadership toward results must be customized for each one?
- Do you regularly use scorecards, scoreboards, or dashboards to show progress on major goals?
- Are the number of key goals and objectives reasonable (no more than nine or ten)?
- Are you adept at breaking key objectives into small achievable pieces so progress can be felt?
- Do you show the ability to demonstrate calmness and poise during extremely active times?

## Chapter 15: Stimulating Creativity

- How often do you pause before an important interchange (e.g., meeting, negotiation session) to think reflectively about the situation and people involved?
- Do you occasionally do something radically different? Read some book in an area in which you know very little? Explore new opportunities? Learn a new language?
- Have you gotten to know individuals who are very different from you?
- It is often said that fear of making mistakes is one of the greatest inhibitors of creativity. To what extent do you subscribe to this belief?
- How often do you create opportunities for your staff to mix and mingle with others outside of your team?
- When exploring new ideas to a problem, to what extent are criticism and debate encouraged?
- Do you create an equal playing field for your team when they debate an issue?

## Chapter 16: Cultivating Adaptability

- Do you have one primary style of leadership? If so, in what situations might this style be less useful?
- To what extent do you have the ability to read and assess the environment and to develop an appropriate leadership style of action?
- Do you understand the various styles of leadership?

- How comfortable are you with leading people to look at problems with fresh eyes?
- When the people you work with seem stuck in a rut, what kinds of approaches do you use to break them out of it?
- How often do you come up with new initiatives or solutions to problems that bring people together in new ways?
- To what extent are you comfortable with unpredictability or changing work settings?
- To what extent are you a person who prefers to live life by the book (typically a policy-driven individual)?
- Have you ever asked yourself, "If I were to leave my job today, what things would my successor change?"
- Do you frequently update your skills and knowledge?

# Appendix B:
## Sample Self-Development Plan

THINK OF A self-development plan as a business plan for your career development. Like a business plan, it should express your desired goals (both short-term and long-term), your objectives, and the resources you need. (Some development plans even include a calculation of return on investment, as anchored to market rates of salaries associated with promotions, although this is not necessary.) All elements of the plan should be specific enough to allow you to self-monitor your progress. The following is a sample outline for a development plan that you can adapt for your own use. A copy may be accessed on the Health Administration Press website: https://www.ache.org/PUBS/dye_garmenappb.pdf.

Name_____

Date_____

**Part 1: Career Goals.** In this section, define the direction you would like to see your career going. It is often most helpful to have at least three anchors—three, five, and ten years are used here, but you can select different anchors as you see fit for your circumstances. *Note:* If you are uncertain about your career goals, then identifying them should be your first step.

Answer the following questions for each of the numbered items below: What would you like to be doing, and where would you like to be? What would be your ideal work setting, position, lifestyle, etc.? If you are planning to remain in your current position, how would you improve the way you work or the way your position is structured?

1. Steps I will take to identify my career goals:

| What I need to learn | Whom I can learn this from | My action plan | Due date |
|---|---|---|---|
| _____ | _____ | _____ | _____ |
| _____ | _____ | _____ | _____ |
| _____ | _____ | _____ | _____ |
| _____ | _____ | _____ | _____ |
| _____ | _____ | _____ | _____ |

2. Three-year goals: _____

3. Five-year goals: _____

4. Ten-year goals: _____

**Part 2: Developmental Needs.** In this section, prioritize the developmental steps you will need to take in pursuit of your career goals. *Note:* If you do not have a clear sense of your developmental needs, then clarifying them should be your first step.

1. Steps I will take to clarify my developmental needs: _____
2. Competencies I need to develop: _____

| Competency | How I will develop | My action plan | Due date |
|---|---|---|---|
| _____ | _____ | _____ | _____ |
| _____ | _____ | _____ | _____ |
| _____ | _____ | _____ | _____ |
| _____ | _____ | _____ | _____ |

*Final Note:* If it is not written and developed in full detail, the Self-Development Plan will not have as much value.

# Appendix C: Sample Interview Questions Based on the 16 Competencies

| Exceptional Leadership Competencies | Interview Questions |
|---|---|
| **Competency 1: Leading With Conviction** | 1. Describe a specific situation in which you felt pressure to compromise your integrity.<br>2. What is the most courageous action you have ever taken?<br>3. Describe two situations in which you had to fight a specific battle with a key physician. How did the conflict start and escalate, and how did you manage through it?<br>4. Describe a specific situation in which you confronted unethical behavior and chose not to say anything in order to not rock the boat. |
| **Competency 2: Using Emotional Intelligence** | 1. In the most recent feedback you have received about yourself (e.g., annual evaluation, coaching, 360-degree), what did you learn?<br>2. How much feedback do you like to get from people you report to, and in what form (e.g., written, face to face)?<br>3. Describe some of the specific techniques you use to get feedback about how others perceive you.<br>4. What have you identified as your principal developmental needs, and what are your plans to deal with them?<br>5. What have been the most difficult criticisms for you to accept?<br>6. When were you so frustrated that you did not treat someone with respect?<br>7. How would you describe your sense of humor?<br>8. Tell me about a situation in which you were expected to work with a person you disliked.<br>9. What do you do to alleviate stress?<br>10. Describe a time in which you did not handle yourself well under stress and pressure.<br>11. Describe a time in which you lost your cool.<br>12. Describe a situation in which you were the angriest you have been in years. |

*(continued)*

| Exceptional Leadership Competencies | Interview Questions |
|---|---|
| **Competency 3: Developing Vision** | 1. What is your vision for your job? How did you develop this vision?<br>2. What professional development programs do you attend? What is the best program you have attended in the past year?<br>3. In the past year, what specifically have you done to remain knowledgeable about the competitive environment, market dynamics, technology trends, and clinical practices?<br>4. Are you more comfortable dealing with concrete, tangible, short-term issues or more abstract, conceptual, long-term issues? Please explain.<br>5. Provide an example of a time when you played a key leadership role in developing the vision for an organization.<br>6. Describe your experience in strategic planning.<br>7. What professional development programs do you attend? |
| **Competency 4: Communicating Vision** | 1. Give an example of when you had to present complex information in a simplified manner to explain it to others.<br>2. Give an example of when you built a business case or new program proposal and presented it to an audience. How did it turn out?<br>3. Give a specific example of when you had to reverse strategic direction and had to communicate the change.<br>4. Describe a situation in which you were most effective selling an idea.<br>5. Describe a situation in which your persuasion skills proved ineffective. |
| **Competency 5: Earning Trust And Loyalty** | 1. Give an example of when you have maintained good relations with a person even when you could not agree on certain issues.<br>2. Give an example of when others readily followed your lead and one when they did not.<br>3. If we were to ask others to comment about your personal leadership, what would they tell us? |
| **Competency 6: Listening Like You Mean It** | 1. Describe your specific methods and practices to ensure that another person feels you are listening to him/her.<br>2. How do you practice active listening?<br>3. What would coworkers say regarding how often and how effectively you use active listening?<br>4. How have you developed informal and formal channels of communication in the past? |

*(continued)*

| Exceptional Leadership Competencies | Interview Questions |
|---|---|
| **Competency 7: Giving Great Feedback** | 1. Describe the specific methods you use to evaluate the job performance of those who report to you.<br>2. Detail the specific methods and practices you use in conflict situations. Detail one situation where your approach failed.<br>3. What are the techniques you use to clarify obscure message meanings?<br>4. Describe a situation in which you had to terminate someone. What approaches were used? Would this person indicate that you had given them regular, honest feedback and sincere coaching efforts to help the situation? |
| **Competency 8: Mentoring** | 1. Describe a situation in which you acted as a mentor.<br>2. How would subordinates you have had in recent years describe your approaches to training and developing them?<br>3. (If adequate time in career has provided for this) How many individuals who have worked for you have moved on to higher positions? Describe some of those you are most proud of.<br>4. What processes have you put in place in the past to ensure that members of your team/organization have a development/career plan? |
| **Competency 9: Developing High-Performing Teams** | 1. Describe a situation in which you had to maintain peer relations with a team member when you could not agree on certain issues.<br>2. Describe your most recent teams and how you have led them.<br>3. What specific techniques have you tried to build teamwork? Which ones have worked well, and which have not?<br>4. Which of your teams has been the biggest disappointment in terms of cohesiveness or effectiveness?<br>5. Describe a situation in which you actively tore down walls or barriers to teamwork.<br>6. Describe situations in which you prevented or resolved conflicts.<br>7. Describe two to three situations in which subordinate team members were fighting, and describe what you did as the team leader.<br>8. Give examples of how you celebrate team and/or individual successes. |

*(continued)*

| Exceptional Leadership Competencies | Interview Questions |
|---|---|
| **Competency 10: Energizing Staff** | 1. Describe how you keep team members involved and motivated.<br>2. Give examples of steps you have taken to make team members feel important.<br>3. Describe a situation in which you were most effective selling an idea.<br>4. Describe a situation in which your persuasion skills proved ineffective.<br>5. Describe what hands-on management means to you. If contacted, what would your subordinates say about your degree of micromanagement? |
| **Competency 11: Generating Informal Power** | 1. Describe a situation where you had no organizational authority but had to be persuasive in getting a point of view accepted.<br>2. Give a specific example of a situation where you were able to convince independent physicians to change their minds about a situation (perhaps a joint venture proposal or a business deal).<br>3. Describe one or two political situations you have faced and detail how you worked through them.<br>4. I am curious about your style of interacting with others over whom you have no authority. Do you believe in collecting favors (for example, trading one action for another)? Give me some examples.<br>5. Can you describe a time when you actually had to pull strings via your influence with others to get something accomplished?<br>6. Is your ability to accomplish objectives in your current position tied a great deal to issues of favoritism? |
| **Competency 12: Building True Consensus** | 1. Describe a situation where you had to generate an agreement among parties who originally differed in opinion, approach, and objectives.<br>2. Describe a time when you had disagreement from another person or group but were able to persuade them to change their minds. How did you do it?<br>3. Give a couple of examples of how you facilitated discussions to guide a group that had people with different values to reach a common conclusion. |

*(continued)*

| Exceptional Leadership Competencies | Interview Questions |
|---|---|
| **Competency 13: Mindful Decision Making** | 1. Give two examples in which you had to make an immediate decision—one with a positive outcome and one with a negative outcome. What process did you follow?<br>2. Describe a time in which you reached a decision when additional information would have changed the action steps. Do you have a process to use when you have to make decisions without complete information?<br>3. Describe the decision-making approach you used when you faced an extremely difficult situation.<br>4. Describe a time in which you reached a decision when you were decisive and quick and the outcome was perfect. Now describe one in which the outcome was negative.<br>5. What is the most difficult decision you have made? |
| **Competency 14: Driving Results** | 1. Give an example of a successful change you helped implement.<br>2. Give an example of a change initiative that was less successful.<br>3. (For each job the person has held) Describe the three or four key challenges you faced in your new job and how you changed them to the positive.<br>4. Describe a situation where you raised the bar for others in getting things done. Explain your tactics, the problems you encountered, and the outcomes.<br>5. Describe your communication methods when you are announcing a critical decision for your organization. |
| **Competency 15: Stimulating Creativity** | 1. Give an example of a creative solution to an unexpected situation when your leadership skills were needed.<br>2. Give an example of an innovative solution you created to solve a problem.<br>3. Assuming you see yourself as a creative person, exactly what do you do to stimulate your creative thinking?<br>4. What processes or approaches do you use to drive creativity in your staff?<br>5. Discuss the differences you see in developing creative ideas versus implementing them. |

*(continued)*

| Exceptional Leadership Competencies | Interview Questions |
|---|---|
| **Competency 16:**<br>**Cultivating Adaptability** | 1. Describe a situation when you saw a problem no one else had identified. Detail the problem. Describe how you found out about it and what you did about it.<br>2. Describe one to two situations in which your negotiation skills proved effective or ineffective.<br>3. What would other leaders with whom you have worked in the past several years say about your ability to adjust and adapt to changing circumstances? |

Thanks to Richard Metheny for his work in helping to develop these questions.

# Additional Reading

**Chapter 1**
**Competency 1: Leading With Conviction**

Bennis, W. 2009. *On Becoming a Leader,* 4th ed. New York: Basic Books.

Christensen, C. M., and J. Allworth. 2012. *How Will You Measure Your Life?* New York: Harper Business.

Covey, S. 1992. *Principle-Centered Leadership: Strategies for Personal and Professional Effectiveness.* New York: Free Press.

George, B. 2007. *True North: Discover Your Authentic Leadership.* San Francisco: Jossey-Bass.

Kraemer, H. 2011. *From Values to Action: The Four Principles of Values-Based Leadership.* San Francisco: Jossey-Bass.

Maxwell, J. C. 2007. *The 21 Irrefutable Laws of Leadership: Follow Them and People Will Follow You.* Nashville, TN: Thomas Nelson.

Saar, S. S. 2013. *Leading with Conviction: Mastering the Nine Critical Pillars of Integrated Leadership.* San Francisco: Jossey-Bass.

Tichy, N. M., and W. G. Bennis. 2009. *Judgment: How Winning Leaders Make Great Calls.* New York: Portfolio Trade.


**Chapter 2**
**Competency 2: Using Emotional Intelligence**

Bradberry, T., and J. Greaves. 2009. *Emotional Intelligence 2.0.* San Diego, CA: TalentSmart.

Goldsmith, M., and M. Reiter. 2007. *What Got You Here Won't Get You There: How Successful People Become Even More Successful.* New York: Hyperion.

Goleman, D. 2006. *Emotional Intelligence: Why It Can Matter More Than IQ.* New York: Bantam.

Goleman, D. 2013. *Primal Leadership: Realizing the Power of Emotional Intelligence.* Boston, MA: Harvard Business Review Press.

## Chapter 3
## Competency 3: Developing Vision

Carroll, P. B., and C. Mui. 2009. *Billion Dollar Lessons: What You Can Learn from the Most Inexcusable Business Failures of the Last 25 Years.* New York: Portfolio.

Cowley, M., and E. Domb. 2011. *Beyond Strategic Vision.* New York: Routledge.

Lafley, A. G., and R. L. Martin. 2013. *Playing to Win: How Strategy Really Works.* Boston, MA: Harvard Business Review Press.

Magretta, J. 2011. *Understanding Michael Porter: The Essential Guide to Competition and Strategy.* Boston, MA: Harvard Business Review Press.

Mckeown, M. 2012. *The Strategy Book: How to Think and Act Strategically to Deliver Outstanding Results.* Upper Saddle River, NJ: FT Press.

Montgomery, C. 2012. *The Strategist: Be the Leader Your Business Needs.* New York: Harper Business.

Porter, M. 1998a. *Competitive Advantage: Creating and Sustaining Superior Performance.* New York: Free Press.

———. 1998b. *Competitive Strategy: Techniques for Analyzing Industries and Competitors.* New York: Free Press.

Raynor, M. E. 2007. *The Strategy Paradox: Why Committing to Success Leads to Failure (And What to Do About It).* New York: Crown Business.

## Chapter 4
## Competency 4: Communicating Vision

Becker, E. F., and J. Wortmann. 2009. *Mastering Communication at Work: How to Lead, Manage, and Influence.* New York: McGraw-Hill.

Berson, A. S., and R. G. Stieglitz. 2013. *Leadership Conversations: Challenging High Potential Managers to Become Great Leaders.* San Francisco: Jossey-Bass.

Bolton, R. 1986. *People Skills: How to Assert Yourself, Listen to Others, and Resolve Conflicts.* New York: Touchstone.

Fleming, C. 2013. *It's the Way You Say It: Becoming Articulate, Well-Spoken, and Clear,* 2nd ed. San Francisco: Berrett-Koehler Publishers.

Patterson, K., J. Grenny, and R. McMillan. 2011. *Crucial Conversations Tools for Talking When Stakes Are High,* 2nd ed. New York: McGraw-Hill.

## Chapter 5
## Competency 5: Earning Trust And Loyalty

Andersen, E. 2012. *Leading So People Will Follow.* San Francisco: Jossey-Bass.

Horsager, D. 2012. *The Trust Edge: How Top Leaders Gain Faster Results, Deeper Relationships, and a Stronger Bottom Line.* New York: Free Press.

Kohn, A. 1999. *Punished by Rewards: The Trouble with Gold Stars, Incentive Plans, A's, Praise, and Other Bribes.* Boston, MA: Houghton-Mifflin.

Pink, D. H. 2011. *Drive: The Surprising Truth About What Motivates Us.* New York: Riverhead Books.

Schein, E. H. 2013. *Humble Inquiry: The Gentle Art of Asking Instead of Telling.* San Francisco: Berrett-Koehler Publishers.

## Chapter 6
## Competency 6: Listening Like You Mean It

Ferrari, B. T. 2012. *Power Listening: Mastering the Most Critical Business Skill of All.* New York: Portfolio.

Garcia, H. F. 2012. *The Power of Communication: The Skills to Build Trust, Inspire Loyalty, and Lead Effectively.* Upper Saddle River, NJ: FT Press.

Goman, C. K. 2011. *The Silent Language of Leaders: How Body Language Can Help—or Hurt—How You Lead.* San Francisco: Jossey-Bass.

Goulson, M., and K. Ferrazzi. 2009. *Just Listen: Discover the Secret to Getting Through to Absolutely Anyone.* New York: AMACOM.

Hoppe, M. H. 2007. *Active Listening: Improve Your Ability to Listen and Lead. Center for Creative Leadership.* Hoboken, NJ: Pfeiffer.

Nichols, M. P. 2009. *The Lost Art of Listening: How Learning to Listen Can Improve Relationships,* 2nd ed. New York: The Guilford Press.


## Chapter 7
## Competency 7: Giving Great Feedback

Ford, J., and J. Ford. 2009. *The Four Conversations: Daily Communication That Gets Results.* San Francisco: Berrett-Koehler Publishers.

Maurer, R. 2011. *Feedback Toolkit: 16 Tools for Better Communication in the Workplace,* 2nd ed. New York: Productivity Press.

Stone, D., B. Patton, and S. Heen. 2010. *Difficult Conversations: How to Discuss What Matters Most.* New York: Penguin Books.


## Chapter 8
## Competency 8: Mentoring

Carriere, B. K., M. Muise, G. Cummings, and C. Newburn-Cook. 2009. "Healthcare Succession Planning: An Integrative Review." *Journal of Nursing Administration* 39 (12): 548–55.

Charan, R., S. Drotter, and J. Noel. 2011. *The Leadership Pipeline: How to Build the Leadership Powered Company.* San Francisco: Jossey-Bass.

Effron, M., and M. Ort. 2010. *One Page Talent Management: Eliminating Complexity, Adding Value.* Boston, MA: Harvard Business Review Press.

Garman, A. N., and J. L. Tyler. 2007. *Succession Planning Practices and Outcomes in US Hospital Systems: Final Report.* Prepared for the American College of Healthcare Executives. www.ache.org/pubs/research/succession_planning.pdf.

National Center for Healthcare Leadership. 2010. *Best Practices in Health Leadership Talent Management and Succession Planning: Case Studies.* http://nchl.org/Documents/Ctrl_Hyperlink/doccopy5306_uid72120111204372.pdf.

Rothwell, W. J. 2010. *Effective Succession Planning: Ensuring Leadership Continuity and Building Talent from Within,* 4th ed. New York: AMACOM.

## Chapter 9
## Competency 9: Developing High-Performing Teams

Dyer, W. G., Jr., J. H. Dyer, and W. G. Dyer. 2013. *Team Building: Proven Strategies for Improving Team Performance,* 5th ed. San Francisco: Jossey-Bass.

Kouzes, J. M., and B. Z. Posner. 2012. *The Leadership Challenge: How to Make Extraordinary Things Happen in Organizations,* 5th ed. San Francisco: Jossey-Bass.

Marquet, D. 2013. *Turn the Ship Around! A True Story of Turning Followers into Leaders.* New York: Portfolio.

Patterson, K., J. Grenny, and R. McMillan. 2013. *Crucial Accountability: Tools for Resolving Violated Expectations, Broken Commitments, and Bad Behavior,* 2nd ed. New York: McGraw-Hill.

Ramirez, C. M. 2013. *Teams: A Competency-Based Approach.* New York: Routledge.

Sinek, S. 2014. *Leaders Eat Last: Why Some Teams Pull Together and Others Don't.* New York: Portfolio.

## Chapter 10
## Competency 10: Energizing Staff

Blanchard, K., C. Olmstead, and M. Lawrence. 2013. *Trust Works!: Four Keys to Building Lasting Relationships.* New York: William Morrow.

Collins, J., and M. Cooley. 2013. *Creative Followership: In the Shadow of Greatness.* Decatur, GA: Looking Glass Books.

Lencioni, P. M. 2012. *The Advantage: Why Organizational Health Trumps Everything Else in Business.* San Francisco: Jossey-Bass.

Miller, M. 2013. *The Heart of Leadership: Becoming a Leader People Want to Follow.* San Francisco: Berrett-Koehler Publishers.

## Chapter 11
## Competency 11: Generating Informal Power

Cohen, A., and D. L. Bradford. 2005. *Influence Without Authority*. 2nd ed. New York: John Wiley & Sons.

Goulston, M., and J. Ullmen. 2013. *Real Influence: Persuade Without Pushing and Gain Without Giving In*. New York: AMACOM.

Kendrick, T. 2012. *Results Without Authority: Controlling a Project When the Team Doesn't Report to You*, 2nd ed. New York: AMACOM.

Schein, E. H. 2009. *The Corporate Culture Survival Guide*. San Francisco: Jossey-Bass.

## Chapter 12
## Competency 12: Building True Consensus

Baldwin, C., A. Linnea, and M. Wheatley. 2010. *The Circle Way: A Leader in Every Chair*. San Francisco: Berrett-Koehler Publishers.

Cialdini, R. B. 2006. *Influence: The Psychology of Persuasion*. New York: Harper Business.

Cooperrider, D. L., D. Whitney, and J. M. Stavros. 2008. *Appreciative Inquiry Handbook: For Leaders of Change*, 2nd ed. San Francisco, CA: Berrett-Koehler Publishers.

Fisher, R., W. L. Ury, and B. Patton. 2011. *Getting to Yes: Negotiating Agreement Without Giving In*. New York: Penguin Books.

Mayer, B. 2012. *The Dynamics of Conflict: A Guide to Engagement and Intervention*, 2nd ed. San Francisco: Jossey-Bass.

Neal, C., P. Neal, R. J. Leider, and C. Wold. 2011. *The Art of Convening: Authentic Engagement in Meetings, Gatherings, and Conversations*. San Francisco: Berrett-Koehler Publishers.

Tumlin, G. 2013. *Stop Talking, Start Communicating: Counterintuitive Secrets to Success in Business and in Life*. New York: McGraw-Hill.

## Chapter 13
## Competency 13: Mindful Decision Making

Giudice, M., and C. Ireland. 2013. *Rise of the DEO: Leadership by Design (Voices That Matter).* New York: New Riders.

Goleman, D. 2013. *Focus: The Hidden Driver of Excellence.* New York: Harper.

Rosenzweig, P. 2007. *The Halo Effect ... and the Eight Other Business Delusions That Deceive Managers.* New York: Free Press.

## Chapter 14
## Competency 14: Driving Results

Bossidy, L., R. Charan, and C. Burck. 2002. *Execution: The Discipline of Getting Things Done.* New York: Random House Business Books.

Govindarajan, V., and C. Trimble. 2013. *Beyond the Idea: How to Execute Innovation in Any Organization.* New York: St. Martin's Press.

Haudan, J. 2008. *The Art of Engagement: Bridging the Gap Between People and Possibilities.* New York: McGraw-Hill.

Keeley, L., H. Walters, and R. Pikkel. 2013. *Ten Types of Innovation: The Discipline of Building Breakthroughs.* New York: John Wiley & Sons.

Kotter, J. P. 2008. *A Sense of Urgency.* Boston: Harvard Business Publishing.

## Chapter 15
## Competency 15: Stimulating Creativity

Christensen, C. M. 2013. *The Innovator's Dilemma: When New Technologies Cause Great Firms to Fail.* Boston: Harvard Business Review Press.

Christensen, C. M., J. H. Grossman, and J. Hwang. 2008. *The Innovator's Prescription: A Disruptive Solution for Health Care.* New York: McGraw-Hill.

Christensen, C. M., and M. E. Raynor. 2013. *The Innovator's Solution: Creating and Sustaining Successful Growth.* Boston: Harvard Business Review Press.

Gawande, A. 2011. *The Checklist Manifesto: How to Get Things Right*. New York: Picador.

Gelb, M. J. 2000. *How to Think Like Leonardo da Vinci: Seven Steps to Genius Every Day*. New York: Dell.

Michalko, M. 2006. *Thinkertoys: A Handbook of Creative-Thinking Techniques*, 2nd ed. Berkeley, CA: Ten Speed Press.

Topol, E. 2013. *The Creative Destruction of Medicine: How the Digital Revolution Will Create Better Health Care*. New York: Basic Books.

## Chapter 16
## Competency 16: Cultivating Adaptability

Duncan, R. D. 2012. *Change-Friendly Leadership: How to Transform Good Intentions into Great Performance*. New York: Maxwell Stone Publishing.

Grenny J., K. Patterson, and D. Maxfield. 2013. *Influencer: The New Science of Leading Change*, 2nd ed. New York: McGraw-Hill.

Kotter, J. P. 2012. *Leading Change*. Boston, MA: Harvard Business Review Press.

## Chapter 17
## Systems Approaches to Leadership Development

Garman, A. N., and C. F. Dye. 2009. *The Healthcare C-Suite: Leadership Development at the Top*. Chicago: Health Administration Press.

Garman, A. N., A. S. McAlearney, M. I. Harrison, P. H. Song, and M. McHugh. 2011. "High-Performance Management Systems in Healthcare, Part 1: Development of an Evidence-Informed Model." *Health Care Management Review* 36 (3): 201–13.

Groves, K. 2011. "Talent Management Best Practices: How Exemplary Health Care Organizations Create Value in a Down Economy." *Health Care Management Review* 36 (3): 227–40.

Lombardo, M. M., and R. W. Eichenger. 2008. *The Leadership Machine*, 3rd ed. Minneapolis, MN: Lominger International.

McAlearney, A. S. 2006. "Leadership Development in Healthcare: A Qualitative Study." *Journal of Organizational Behavior* 27 (7): 967–82.

McCauley, C. D., and S. Brutus. 1998. *Management Through Job Experiences: An Annotated Bibliography.* Greensboro, NC: Center for Creative Leadership.

McCauley, C. D., D. S. Derue, P. R. Yost, and S. Taylor. 2013. *Experience-Driven Leader Development: Models, Tools, Best Practices, and Advice for On-the-Job Development,* 3rd ed. San Francisco: Jossey-Bass.

National Center for Healthcare Leadership. 2010. *Best Practices in Health Leadership Talent Management and Succession Planning.* http://nchl.org/Documents/Ctrl_Hyperlink/doccopy5306_uid72120111204372.pdf.

## Chapter 18
## Leadership Coaches and Coaching Programs

Crane, T. G. 2012. *The Heart of Coaching: Using Transformational Coaching to Create a High-Performance Coaching Culture.* San Diego, CA: FTA Press.

Kimsey-House, H., K. Kimsey-House, P. Sandahl, and L. Whitworth. 2011. *Co-Active Coaching: Changing Business, Transforming Lives,* 3rd ed. Boston: Nicholas Brealey Publishing.

Kotter, J. P. 1999. *What Leaders Really Do.* Boston: Harvard Business Review Press.

Morgan, H., P. Harkins, and M. Goldsmith. 2004. *The Art and Practice of Leadership Coaching: 50 Top Executive Coaches Reveal Their Secrets.* New York: John Wiley & Sons.

Passmore, J. 2010. *Leadership Coaching: Working with Leaders to Develop Elite Performance.* Philadelphia, PA: Kogan Page.

Passmore, J., and A. Fillery-Travis. 2011. "A Critical Review of Executive Coaching Research: A Decade of Progress and What's to Come." *Coaching: An International Journal of Theory, Practice & Research* 4 (2): 70–88.

Peltier, B. 2009. *The Psychology of Executive Coaching: Theory and Application,* 2nd ed. New York: Routledge.

Wahl, C., C. Scriber, and B. Bloomfield. 2008. *On Becoming a Leadership Coach: A Holistic Approach to Coaching Excellence.* New York: Palgrave Macmillan.

## Chapter 19
## Mentors: Finding and Engaging for Maximum Impact

Johnson, W. B., and C. R. Ridley. 2008. *The Elements of Mentoring.* New York: Palgrave Macmillan.

Pue, C. 2005. *Mentoring Leaders: Wisdom for Developing Character, Calling, and Competency.* Ada, MI: Baker Books.

## Chapter 20
## Developing a Feedback-Rich Working Environment

Edwards, M. R., and A. J. Ewen. 1996. *360-Degree Feedback: The Powerful New Model for Employee Assessment & Performance Improvement.* New York: AMACOM.

Fleenor, J. W., S. Taylor, and C. Chappelow. 2008. *Leveraging the Impact of 360-Degree Feedback.* Hoboken, NJ: Pfeiffer.

## Chapter 21
## Physician Development and Competencies

Beeson, S. C. 2006. *Practicing Excellence: A Physician's Manual to Exceptional Health Care.* Gulf Breeze, FL: Fire Starter.

Berry, L., and K. Seltman. 2008. *Management Lessons from Mayo Clinic: Inside One of the World's Most Admired Service Organizations.* New York: McGraw-Hill.

Cohn, K. H. 2006. *Collaborate for Success: Breakthrough Strategies for Engaging Physicians, Nurses, and Hospital Executives.* Chicago: Health Administration Press.

———. 2005. *Better Communication for Better Care: Mastering Physician-Administration Collaboration.* Chicago: Health Administration Press.

Cohn, K. H., and S. A. Fellows. 2011. *Getting It Done: Experienced Healthcare Leaders Reveal Field-Tested Strategies for Clinical and Financial Success.* Chicago: Health Administration Press.

Cosgrove, T. 2013. *The Cleveland Clinic Way: Lessons in Excellence from One of the World's Leading Health Care Organizations.* New York: McGraw-Hill.

Lee, F. 2004. *If Disney Ran Your Hospital: 9 1/2 Things You Would Do Differently.* Bozeman, MT: Second River Healthcare.

Martin, W. M., and P. Hemphill. 2013. *Taming Disruptive Behavior.* Tampa, FL: American College of Physician Executives.

Micherlli, J. 2011. *Prescription for Excellence: Leadership Lessons for Creating a World Class Customer Experience from UCLA Health System.* New York: McGraw-Hill.

National Center for Healthcare Leadership. 2014. *Physician Leadership Development Programs: Best Practices for Healthcare Organizations.* http://nchl.org/Documents/Ctrl_Hyperlink/NCHL_Physician_Leadership_Development_White_Paper_Final_05.14_uid6192014202392.pdf.

## Chapter 22
## Final Questions Regarding the Exceptional Leadership Model

Chaudhry, R. 2011. *Quest for Exceptional Leadership: Mirage to Reality.* Thousand Oaks, CA: Sage Publications.

# Index

Note: Italicized page locators refer to figures or tables in exhibits.

based on, 260; science orientation and, 225; self-reflection questions on, 250; St. Nicholas Health System vignettes, 29–30, 39–40; strategic focus and, *246*; understanding risks, rewards, and uncertainties, 32; when it is not all it could be, 33–35

Developmental decisions: miscommunicating, 96–97

Developmental experiences: providing for leaders, 191–92

Development plans, 257; feedback and formulation of, 217–18

Direct communication, untempered, 60, 61

Disruptive innovation theory, 38

Dissenting opinions: discouraging, 60, 61

Divergent perspectives: undervaluing, 34–35

Diversity: competencies and awareness of, xxiii; embracing, self-concept and, xxxiii–xxxiv

Diversity and inclusion strategies: leadership development and, 193

Dominant leadership style, 182, 183

"Do/say ratio," 56

Dotlich, David, 235

Drive: lack of, 160, 161

Driving Results (Competency 14), xxix, *xxx*, 157–65, 245; central culture of, 165; competency mapping for, *243*; definition and importance of, 158; highly effective leaders and, 158–59; misuse and overuse of, 161–63; operations focus and, *246*; performance improvement and, 241; personal development and, 163–64; physicians and, *230*; problem-solving tasks and, 241; role models and, 163; sample interview questions based on, 263; science orientation and, 225; self-reflection questions on, 254–55; St. Nicholas Health System vignette, 157; time perspective and, 226; when it is not all it could be, 159–61

Drucker, Peter, xxix

Due process, 128

Dyad leadership model: physician leaders and, 233

Dye, Carson F., xxiv, 11, 104, 190, 224, 227, 228, 234, 244

Dye–Garman model. *See* Exceptional Leadership Competency Model (Dye–Garman model)

Earning Trust And Loyalty (Competency 5), xxviii, *xxx*, 53–64; accountability and, 226; competency mapping for, *243*; definition and importance of, 54; encouraging or supportive leadership style and, 181; highly effective leaders and, 54–56; misuse and overuse of, 59–61; personal development and, 62–63; physicians and, *230*; problem-solving tasks and, 241; role models and, 61–62; sample interview questions based on, 260; self-reflection questions on, 250–51; St. Nicholas Health System vignettes, 53–54, 63–64; when it is not all it could be, 57–59

*Economist, The,* 32

Economist Intelligence Unit, 190

Edison, Thomas, 37

Effective leaders: competent leaders *vs.*, xxxvi. *See also* Exceptional leaders

Efficiency: consensus and, 137

Elation: listening derailed by, 76

Eli Lilly, xxvi

Emotional intelligence: acting with self-interest *versus* acting with selfless interest, 17; bright side/dark side leadership and, 25; definition and importance of, 16; engaging others *versus* maintaining distance, 17–18; enhancing, 22–23; facets of, 186; highly effective leaders and, 16; misuse and overuse of, 20–22; personal development and, 22–23; physician shortcomings with, 229; role models and, 22; trusting in self *versus* trusting in others, 18; using, 16; when it is not all it could be, 19

Emotional intelligence quotient, 16, 20

Emotional role, overextending, 21, 22

Emotional volatility, 71, 72

Emotions: listening and monitoring of, 75–76

Encouraging (or supportive) leadership style, 181

Energizing Staff (Competency 10), xxviii, *xxx*, 66, 113–20, 245; authoritative or inspirational leadership style and, 180; competency mapping for, *243*; definition and importance of, 114; highly effective leaders and, 115–116; mentors and, 119; misuse and overuse of, 117–19; operations focus and, *246*; performance improvement and, 241; personal development and, 119; physicians

High-EQ leaders, 20, 21, 22

High-performance leadership development system: attracting and selecting leaders, 190–91; components of, 189–93; identifying and developing high-potentials, 191; monitoring results, 192–93; preparing new leaders for success, 191; providing developmental experiences, 191–92; providing performance feedback, 192; strategic alignment in, 189–90; succession planning, 192

High-potential leaders: identifying and developing, 191

Hiring: Exceptional Leadership Model and decisions in, 244–45; minimizing mistakes in, xxiv; systematic approach to, 190

Hogan, R., xiv

Hogan Assessment Systems, 235

Horizons, broadening, 11–12

Hospitals: clinician participation in management and performance of, 224

Hub-and-spoke communication model, 171

*Humble Inquiry* (Schein), 77

Humor: having sense of, 115–16

IBM, xxvi, 164

Impatience, 71, 72

Implementation: underemphasizing, 37

Inattentive listening, 70, 72

Incentives: personal beliefs and, 7

Individual goals and practices: understanding, 115

Individual roles: overemphasizing, 105–106, 107

Ineffective working relationships: developing, 160, 161

Influence and People-Oriented (IP) style, xlvi

*Influence Without Authority* (Cohen and Bradford), 133

Informal networks: involving wrong people in, 129, 130

Informal power, 126; definition of, 126; stockpiling, 136; undervaluing, 128–29, 130

Information: lack of, in communicating vision, 46, 47

Ingham, Harry, 23

Innovation: focusing too much on, 172–73

*Innovator's Dilemma, The* (Christensen), 38

*Innovator's Prescription, The* (Christensen), 38

Insight, 2

Inspirational leadership style. *See* Authoritative (or inspirational) leadership style

Instant feedback sessions, 213–14

Integrative approaches: underemphasizing, 171–72

Integrity, xxiii; acting with, 148

International Association of Coaching, 197

International Coaching Federation, 197, 201

Internet-hosted surveys, 217

Interns, 98

Interpersonal conflicts: addressing, 60

Interpersonal economics, 128

Interpersonal feedback: within context of relationship, 83; definition of, 82

Interpersonal process: lacking sensitivity to, 139

Interpersonal relations: leader's roles and centrality of, xxviii

Interpersonal skills: competencies and, xxiii; emotional intelligence and, 16

Interview questions: sample, built on the 16 competencies, 259–64

Interviews: leadership competencies and shaping behavioral questions for, 245

Intrinsic motivation, 120

*Intuition at Work* (Klein), 153

Intuitive decision-making skills: developing, 153

Inyang, Benjamin James, 228

James, David, 233, 236

Job performance: self-concept and, xxxiv

Job satisfaction: self-concept and, xxxiv

Johari Window, *23,* 23–24

*Journal of Consumer Research, The,* 89

Judgment: quality of, 148

*Just Listen: Discover the Secret to Getting Through to Absolutely Anyone* (Goulston), 77

Kahneman, Daniel, 153

Kaiser, Robert, 185

Kaluzny, Arnold, 153

Kaplan, Bob, 185

Keeping the peace: overemphasis on, 108

Kelleher, Herb, 119

Kelly, David, 175

Kelly, Tom, 175

Klein, Gary, 153

Noninterpersonal work aspects, avoiding, 21, 22

Nurses: typical age leadership roles assumed by, 223

*Nuts!* (Freiberg and Freiberg), 119

Office politics, 134

Onboarding: leadership competencies and, 247

One-on-one conversations: finding opportunities for, 76–77

Online survey vendors, 217

Open door policy: listening and, 77

Open-mindedness, xxvii, 12

Openness: fostering, 55

Operations: balancing poorly between planning and, 36, 37

Organizational accountability: physicians *vs.* administrators and, 226

Organizational coaching programs: clarify program goals, 201; continuous measurement and improvement for, 202–203; develop coaching resources and policies, 201–202; implementing and managing, 200–203

Organizational mentoring programs, 205, 209–10

Organizational skills: underdeveloped, 160, 161

"Origin stories," 11

*Our Iceberg is Melting: Changing and Succeeding Under Any Conditions* (Kotter), 50

Outcomes: balancing process with, 120; coaching programs and, 202

Overconfidence: decision making and, 152; physician leaders and, 235

Overvaluing one's own perspective: strong convictions and, 8–9, 10

Owning one's own perspectives: failure in, 9, 10

Passive approach to listening, 72–73

Patterson, Kerry, 88, 99

People: underemphasizing, 161, 162

PepsiCo, xxvi

Performance: overemphasizing, 162, 163; underemphasizing, 118

Performance calibration meetings, 215

Performance feedback, providing for leaders, 192

Performance improvement, 247; Exceptional Leadership Model and, 241

Performance problems: failing to address, 97, 98

Pericles, 44

Periodic reviews: with your mentor, 208

Personal accountability: physicians *vs.* administrators and, 226

Personal agenda: focusing too much on, 131, 132

Personal convictions, xxviii; better living with, 10–12, 183; broadening your horizons and, 11–12; conflicted, 6–7, 8; demonstrating, 5; focusing less on personal goals and, 12; lack in, 7, 8; reconnecting with yourself and, 11; vision linked to, 5

Personal development: broadening your horizons, 11–12; Building True Consensus competency and, 141–42; Communicating Vision competency and, 49–50; Cultivating Adaptability competency and, 185; Developing High-Performing Teams competency and, 109; Developing Vision competency and, 38–39; Driving Results competency and, 163–164; Earning Trust And Loyalty competency and, 62–63; Energizing Staff competency and, 119; feedback skills and, 88–89; focusing less on your personal goals, 12; generating informal power and, 133; Leading With Conviction competency and, 11–12; Listening Like You Mean It competency and, 74–77; Mentoring competency and, 98–99; Mindful Decision Making competency and, 153; reconnecting with yourself, 11; Stimulating Creativity competency and, 174–75; Using Emotional Intelligence competency and, 22–24

Personal goals: focusing less on, 12; overfocusing on, 7–8

Personalized medicine, xv

Perspective, fostering, 169–70

Physical activity, energy level and, 163

Physician leaders: assessment and feedback for, 233; clinical background and pivotal roles of, 223–24; coaches for, 198; leadership coaching used by, 234; learning by doing and, 234; overconfidence and, 235; typical age leadership roles assumed by, 223

Physician leadership, 221–35; St. Nicholas Health Systems vignette, 221–22

Physicians: Compelling Vision (Cornerstone 2) and, 229, *230,* 231; further development in each competency for, 232–35; leadership competencies and, *230;* Masterful Execution (Cornerstone 4) and, *230,* 232; A Real Way With People (Cornerstone 3) and, *230,* 231; Well-Cultivated Self Awareness (Cornerstone 1) and, 229, *230*

Physicians *vs.* executive leaders, 224–27; characteristics of physicians *vs.* administrators, *224;* personal *vs.* organizational accountability of, 226; science orientation of, 225; time perspective of, 225–26; time urgency of decision making and, 226–27

Planning: balancing poorly between operations and, 36, 37; focusing too much on process of, 36–37

Plummer, Patrick, 39

Population health management, xv, 222

Porter, Michael, 38

Positive qualities in self-concept: building on, xxxv

Possessiveness, 95, 96

Power. *See also* Formal power; Informal power: six fundamental sources of, 127; strategic approach to, 127–28

Power imbalances, in teams, 106, 107

*Power In and Around Organizations* (Mintzberg), 133

Power politics: playing, 131, 132

Praise: hesitancy around, 85, 86

*Predictably Irrational* (Ariely), 153

Presenting problem: focusing only on, 170–71, 172

Probing questions: asking, 75

Problems: conservative approach to, 171, 172

Problem solving, xxiii; creativity and, 168; Exceptional Leadership Model and, 241

Process: balancing outcomes with, 120

Process improvement: focus on, 159; looking for opportunities in, 159

Procter & Gamble, xxvi

Productivity tools, 164

Professional organizations: locating mentor through, 206

Project management tools, 159

Public recognition, 115

Public speaking skills, fine-tuning, 50

*Punished by Rewards* (Kohn), 120

Reading the environment, 178, 179–80, 182

Real issues, defining, 83

Real Way With People, A (Cornerstone 3), xxvi, *xxvii,* xxviii–xxix; competencies related to, *xxx;* Developing High-Performing Teams competency and, 66, 101–11; Energizing Staff competency and, 66, 113–20; Giving Great Feedback competency and, 66, 81–89; Listening Like You Mean It competency and, 66, 67–79; Mentoring competency and, 66, 91–100; physicians and, *230,* 231

Reciprocity, 128, 130

Reconnecting with yourself, 11

Recruiting: mentoring programs and, 205

References, for coaches, 202

Referrals: for coaches, 198

Reflecting: on your work, 11

Relationship "bank accounts," 128

Relationship building: as fundamental element of leadership, 66; mentoring and, 93; overvaluing, 131, 132

Relationship management: emotional intelligence and, 186

Reliability, 149

Requesting specifics, 75

Research Thinker (RT) style, xlvi

Resource allocation: among team members, 105

Resource development: coaching programs, 203

Respect, xxiii, 169

Results: focusing too much on, 161

Retention: mentoring programs and, 205

Return on investment: development plans and, 257

*Revising Prose* (Lanham), 49–50

Rewards: understanding, 32

Rice, Tim, 119

Risks: understanding, 32

*Risk Taker, Caretaker, Surgeon, Undertaker: The Four Faces of Strategic Leadership* (Rothschild), 185

Risk taking, xxiii; unwillingness around, 149, 150

Role conflicts: listening and, 77

Role models. *See also* Mentoring competency; Mentors: Building True Consensus competency and, 141; Communicating Vision competency and, 49; Cultivating

Adaptability competency and, 184–85; Developing High-Performing Teams competency and, 109; Driving Results competency and, 163; Earning Trust And Loyalty competency and, 61–62; enhancing emotional intelligence and, 22; feedback skills and, 88; generating informal power and, 132–33; Listening Like You Mean It competency and, 73–74; Mentoring competency and, 98; Mindful Decision Making competency and, 152–53; personal conviction and looking for, 10–11; Stimulating Creativity competency and, 174; visioning improved with, 37–38

Roles and values: team building and, 110

"Rules of engagement": in group interaction, 155

Russo, J. Edward, 153

Scenario sketching, 141

Schein, Edgar, 77

Scope: of coaching programs, 202–203

Self-awareness, 2; cultivating, 17; developing, xxvii; emotional intelligence and, 186; Goleman's definition of, 24

Self-concept: critical importance of, xxxii–xxxiv; Exceptional Leadership Competency Model and, xxvi, *xxvii, xxx*; healthy, xxvi, xxxii; listening and, 79; low, building up, xxxiv–xxxv; positive, xxxiii; success and failures and, xxxiii; working with others and, xxxiii–xxxiv

Self-confidence, xxxii

Self-development plan, sample: career goals, 257–58; developmental needs, 258

Self-esteem, xxxii

Self-interest: balancing with selfless interest, 17

Self-knowledge, 2

Self-management: emotional intelligence and, 186

Self-reflection: physician application of leadership competencies and, 228–29, 231–232

Self-reflection questions: for leadership competencies, 249–56

Self-value, xxxii

Senior leadership teams: collective goals and, 104; dynamics commonly found in, 101–102

*Sense of Urgency, A* (Kotter), 50

Servant leadership style: physician leaders and, 233

Shared competency language, developing, 214

Shock: listening derailed by, 75

Shoemaker, Paul, 153

Six Sigma specialists, 141

Skill development: high-quality feedback and, 219–20

Smart phones and mobile devices: inattentive listening and, 70

Social awareness: emotional intelligence and, 186

Socialization skills: physicians and, 228–29

Socrates, 2

Sokolov, Jacque, 224, 227, 228, 234, 244

Sonnenfeld, Jeffrey, 228

Southwest Airlines, 119

St. Nicholas Health System Case Study, xviii, xxix; Building True Consensus competency and, 135–36, 142–43; business, xliii; Command and Control (CC) style, xlv; Communicating Vision competency and, 43, 51; Cultivating Adaptability competency and, 177–78; demographics and community, xlii; Developing High-Performing Teams competency and, 101–102; Developing Vision competency and, 29–30, 39–40; Driving Results competency and, 157; Earning Trust And Loyalty competency and, 53–54, 63; Energizing Staff competency and, 113; generating informal power and, 125–26; Giving Great Feedback competency and, 81–82, 89; individual styles and approaches in senior team, xlv–xlvi, *xlvii*; Influence and People-Oriented (IP) style, xlvi; introduction, xxxix; Leading with Conviction and hiring of new VP/COO, 3–4; Listening Like You Mean It competency and, 67–68, 78–79; Loyalty and Reliability (LR) style, xlvi; Mentoring competency and, 91, 100; Mindful Decision Making competency and, 145–46, 154; operations and staffing, xlii; organizational structure, xl, *xli,* xlii; physician leadership and, 221–22; Research Thinker (RT) style, xlvi; senior management group and work styles, *xlvii*; Stimulating Creativity competency and, 167–68, 176; strategic context, xlii–xliii; strategic plan, xliii–xliv;

team dynamics, xliv; Using Emotional Intelligence competency and, 15

Staff development: mentoring and participating in, 93–94; undervaluing, 95, 96

Standards-setting leadership style, 181

Star performers: overemphasizing, 97, 98

Stimulating Creativity (Competency 15), xxix, *xxx*, 167–76, 245; competency mapping for, *243*; definition and importance of, 168–69; highly effective leaders and, 169–70; misuse and overuse of, 172–74; performance improvement and, 241; personal development and, 174–75; physicians and, *230*; role models and, 174; sample interview questions based on, 263; science orientation and, 225; self-reflection questions on, 255; St. Nicholas Health System vignette, 167–68, 176; strategic focus and, *246*; when it is not all it could be, 170–72

*Straight A Leadership* (Studer), 119

Strategic alignment: in high-performance leadership development system, 189–90

Strategic planning, xxiii

Strategic vision, 33

Studer, Quint, 119

Successes: celebrating and sharing, 115; self-concept and, xxxiii

Succession planning: competencies and, 247; high-performance leadership development and, 192; mentoring and, 100

Summarizing: listening and, 75

Support, brokering of, 128

Supportive leadership style. *See* Encouraging (or supportive) leadership style

Survey instrument: 360-degree feedback and, 216–17

SurveyMonkey.com, 217

Surveys: feedback and, 217

Swap, Walter, 175

Tactical operations: too much focus on, 33–34, 35

Talent management, xxvi, 192

Talent reviews, 215–16

Taylor, Greg, 234, 236

Team-building exercises: issues related to, 110

*Team Decision-Making Techniques: A Practical Guide to Successful Team Outcomes* (Kelly and Kelly), 141

Team development: underemphasizing, 106, 107

Team roles: getting best people for, 103

Teams: definition of, 102; overemphasizing, 108; using for wrong reasons, 105, 106

Team skills: medical education and, 231

Technique: consensus and, 137–38

Thinking, xxiii

*Thinking, Fast and Slow* (Kahneman), 153

360-degree feedback, 196; decide how to manage the process, 217; define the participants and goals, 216; develop (or identify) the survey instrument, 216–17; develop the reports, 218; distribute and collect the survey, 218; follow-up to, 219; identify feedback sources, 217–18; physician leaders and, 233; provide feedback and formulate development plans, 218–19

Time-based probes, 75

Timelines: visions put on, 48

Time over attention, listening and, 71, 72

Time pressures: giving in to, 182, 183

Toastmasters International, 50

Tolerance, xxiii

Training: for coaches, 201

Trait theory of leadership, xxiv

Travel, broadening your horizons through, 11

Trends: maintaining awareness of, 31–32

Troubadour tradition, xiv

True consensus building: art *vs.* science of, 138

*True North: Discover Your Authentic Leadership* (George), 62

True urgency: gauging, 147

Trust/trustworthiness, 55, 66; building, 130; enhancing, 55; Mindful Decision Making and, 148; in self *versus* in others, 18; turning into loyalty, 56

Tufte, Edward, 50

Ulrich, D., xvi, 119

Unavailability, 57, 59

Uncertainties: understanding, 32

Underrepresented groups: mentoring programs and, 205

Universal agreement: being biased toward, 140

Using Emotional Intelligence (Competency 2), *xxx*, 15–25, 245. *See also* Emotional intelligence; accountability and, 226; competency mapping for, *243*; highly effective leaders and, 16–18; inward focus of, 2; mastery of, xxvii; misuse and overuse of, 20–22; personal development and, 22–24; physicians and, *230*; problem-solving tasks and, 241; role models and, 22; sample interview questions based on, 259; self-reflection questions on, 249–50; St. Nicholas Health System vignettes, 15, 25; when it is not all it could be, 19–20

Value-based reimbursement, xv, 222
Values: competencies and, xxiii
Veney, James, 153
Venture capitalists, 32
Vision. *See also* Communicating Vision; Developing Vision: communicating as an end rather than as a means, 48, 49; definition and importance of, 30–31; definition of, xxviii; overly specific communication about, 48, 49; personal conviction linked to, 5; viewing as the program du jour, 49, 48
Visionary leaders, 31, 32
*Visionary Leadership* (Nanus), 38
*Visual Display of Quantitative Information, The* (Tufte), 50
Vocal opposition: facing, 139
Volatility, 19, 20, 71

Walston, Stephen, 39

Ward, Andrew, 228
Well-Cultivated Self-Awareness (Cornerstone 1), xxvi, *xxvii*, xxvii–xxviii; competencies related to, *xxx*; as foundation of leadership competencies, 2; Leading With Conviction competency and, *xxx*, 3–13; physicians and, 229, *230*; Using Emotional Intelligence competency and, *xxx*, 15–25
*When Sparks Fly: Harnessing the Power of Group Creativity* (Leonard and Swap), 175
*Who Says Elephants Can't Dance* (Gerstner), 164
*Why CEOs Fail: The 11 Behaviors That Can Derail Your Climb to the Top and How to Manage Them* (Dotlich and Cairo), 235
*Why Smart Executives Fail: And What You Can Learn from Their Mistakes* (Finkelstein), 228
Williams, Ginger, 226, 234, 236
*Winning Decisions* (Russo and Shoemaker), 153
*Wired*, 32
Women: mentoring programs and, 205
Work: disconnection between conviction and, 7, 8; reflecting on, 11
Workaholism, 162, 164
Working with others: self-concept and, xxxiii–xxxiv
Wrong decisions: being overly fearful of, 149, 150

# About the Authors

**Carson F. Dye, MBA, FACHE,** is an executive search consultant with Witt/Kieffer. He conducts CEO, senior executive, and physician executive searches for a variety of organizations. His consulting experience includes leadership assessment, organizational design, and physician leadership development. He also conducts board retreats and provides counsel in executive employment contracts and evaluation matters for a variety of client organizations. He is certified to work with the Hogan Assessment Systems tools for selection, development, and executive coaching.

Prior to Witt/Kieffer, he worked in executive search with Lamalie and TMP Worldwide. His earlier consulting career was with Findley Davies where he was a partner and director of their Health Care Industry Consulting Division. Prior to his consulting career, he served 20 years in executive-level positions at St. Vincent Medical Center, Toledo, Ohio; The Ohio State University Medical Center; Children's Hospital Medical Center, Cincinnati, Ohio; and Clermont Mercy Hospital in Batavia, Ohio.

Dye serves as a faculty member for The Governance Institute, works as a special advisor to The Healthcare Roundtable, and has been named as a physician leadership consultant expert on the LaRoche National Consultant Panel. He served on the adjunct faculty of the graduate program in management and health services policy at Ohio State University from 1985 to 2008, and has also served as adjunct faculty at Xavier University and the University of Cincinnati. He currently teaches leadership for the University of Alabama at Birmingham (UAB) in their master of science in health administration program.

Since 1989, Dye has taught several programs for the American College of Healthcare Executives (ACHE) and is a frequent presenter at the ACHE Congress on Healthcare Leadership. He has won the James A. Hamilton Book of the Year twice—for *Developing Physician Leaders for Successful Clinical Integration* (Health Administration Press 2013) in 2014 and for *Leadership in Healthcare: Values at the*

*Top* (Health Administration Press 2000) in 2001. The latter book was revised and released as *Leadership in Healthcare: Essential Values and Skills* (Health Administration Press 2010) and is used by many graduate programs in health administration as a leadership test. With Andrew Garman, PsyD, he has also written *The Healthcare C-Suite: Leadership Development at the Top* (Health Administration Press 2009). Other publications include *Winning the Talent War: Ensuring Effective Leadership in Healthcare* (Health Administration Press 2002), *Executive Excellence* (Health Administration Press 2000), and *Protocols for Health Care Executive Behavior* (Health Administration Press 1993). Dye has also written several professional journal articles on leadership and human resources.

Dye earned his BA from Marietta College and his MBA from Xavier University.

**Andrew N. Garman, PsyD, MS,** is professor and associate chair, External Relations and Development in the Department of Health Systems Management at Rush University in Chicago. He teaches master's and PhD courses in topics including governance, leadership, organizational analysis and change, entrepreneurship, and healthcare industry studies, and leads or participates in a variety of executive education programs for partner organizations in the United States and abroad. In addition to his role with Rush, Garman also has a leadership role with the nonprofit National Center for Healthcare Leadership, helping health systems pursue high-efficiency, evidence-based approaches to leadership development and talent management. He also holds a leadership role with the United States Cooperative for International Patient Programs, a membership group of US health systems dedicated to providing world-class care to patients from other countries.

Dr. Garman is a recognized authority in evidence-based leadership assessment and development practice, as well as global market trends affecting the future of healthcare. His research and applied work have been published in dozens of peer-reviewed journals and books, including The Healthcare C-Suite: Leadership Development at the Top and The Future of Healthcare: Global Trends Worth Watching (both with Health Administration Press). For his work in leadership competency modeling and CEO succession planning, he has received three Health Management Research Awards from the American College of Healthcare Executives.

Dr. Garman's prior work experience includes a variety of practitioner and faculty roles with organizations, including the Federal Reserve Bank of Chicago, the